For my son, Nap, who was just getting started,
and my daughter, Lucy, who was there from the very beginning.

CONTENTS

ACKNOWLEDGMENTS

Many people helped in the crafting of this book, both by providing guidance along specific subject lines and by contributing to my education and experience over the years. First, there's the group I'll refer to as my Perennial Board of Advisors: Fal Allen, John Mallett, Will Meyers, Kevin Forhan, Bill Jenkins, Garrett Oliver, John Harris (who also provided extensive and valuable editing help), Vinnie Cilurzo, Tomme Arthur, Bill Metzger and the many others who have answered my calls and emails whenever I've needed the help we all provide each other. Then there are my Elysian co-workers, many of whom helped in discussing material and a few who were forced to listen to what I deemed particularly entertaining passages: Kevin Watson, Steve Luke, Corinne McNeilly, Matt Thompson, Keegan Kubisiak and my partners Joe Bisacca and David Buhler in particular.

As co-stewards of a shining example in our industry, New Belgium Brewing, I'd like to thank Peter Bouckaert, Grady Hull, Brandon Weaver, Alex Jesse, Kristin Coley, Christine Perich, Lauren Salazar, Jenny Briggs, Josh Holmstrom, Nate Turner, Dave Macon, Joe Menetre, Kelly Tretter, Jenn Vervier, the whole Northwest crew and the dozens of open-hearted others who have made our collaborations so fun, fascinating and rewarding. Greg Owsley too provided guidance for my sections on branding; Gary Nicholas of Bell's Beer helped substantially with safety issues; Peter Whalen offered and provided help on the subject of insurance; Chuck Skypeck of Bosco's and Ghost River Brewing executed an exemplary editing of the manuscript, as did Amahl Scheppach, who also did a masterful job of wrestling with my prose.

Many among the fine Brewers Association staff and Board of Directors helped along the way with points of information, suggestions for material and the opportunity to try some of it out in presentation to the National Homebrewers Conference: Bob Pease, Paul Gatza, Julia Herz, Kathryn Porter Drapeau and Erin and Gary Glass, as well as Chris P. Frey. Brewers Publications' Kristi Switzer deserves a spot of honor all to herself. She is certainly the Maxwell Perkins of the literature of our trade. Profound thanks to Sam Calagione for, in addition to everything else he does for our industry, writing the foreword to the book. Last and foremost I'd like to warmly, lovingly thank Kim Jordan, also of New Belgium, for the love and depth she has bestowed upon me for the past four years, on into the future of our life together.

FOREWORD

I remember when I first thought of starting Dogfish Head in 1995. I was a high-energy, inexperienced, anti-establishment, pro-trouble-making 24-year-old dreamer. I was also a home-brewer. I decided I'd found my life's calling the night I served my first batch of homebrew—a pale ale infused with a foolhardy quantity of so-ripe-they-were-on-sale cherries. The beer turned out awesome and I stood on the coffee table of my NYC apartment and announced to my roommates and the world, "This is what I am going to do with my life; I am going to be a professional brewer!" My next two batches of homebrew both sucked but I had made up my mind that I would open a brewery. I spent my evenings waiting tables and my days researching small breweries and artisanal food companies, and reading small business startup articles in the main branch of the New York Public Library. No single publication as broad and yet as detailed as this one existed.

So I mined what I could about the craft beer industry and related industries in those articles. I learned from what Ken Grossman of Sierra Nevada Brewing Company and Fritz Maytag of Anchor Brewing were doing in California but I also gathered inspiration from James Beard on the east coast and Alice Waters on the west coast—they believed that regional, local American agricultural ingredients when simply and honestly combined could yield beautiful indigenous dishes true to their local terroir. I recognized that the burgeoning craft brewing niche was really a niche within a niche of first-wave localvore restaurants and artisanal food, bread, and coffee companies. I read about the first generation of successful craft brewers who had the unenviable task of convincing beer drinkers to step off of light lager terra firma and onto this solid little bridge of flavor-forward all-malt small batch diverse beers.

As I was conceptualizing Dogfish, I kept a diary. (This is pre-smart phones but I still keep an active version of this journal in the notes section of my smart phone today). I used this diary to write down the most existential and distinct statements that I wanted to build my brewery and brand around. I spent a lot of time reading about breweries and roaming to visit small breweries and artisanal companies. I focused most of my exploratory energies on locating and defining things these other breweries and companies were not doing instead of thinking of ways to copy what they were successfully doing. This is what makes Dick Cantwell's book so valuable to the aspiring craft brewer: he's written that diary for you, from the seasoned perspective and experience of decades in this relatively new industry. The second edition of *The Brewers Association's Guide to Starting Your Own Brewery* outlines what works and what doesn't, from that initial, conceptual stage on into successful growth and expansion of the business. He canvasses everything from choosing a site and differentiating your concept from the crowd to the daunting task of writing a business plan.

I wrote my business plan around what I learned in that library and visiting the few small breweries that had opened in New York and New England. There is no greater example of a work of fiction than a business plan. It's basically something you fabricate in your head and then use to try to convince bankers, family, friends, and investors to give you money so you can make your little fantasy come true. My parents recently found an early version of my Dogfish Head business plan. Our mission as stated in that business plan was to create an even smaller (much smaller considering I started with a 15-gallon) brewing system. I wonder how much easier my own experience would have been if I'd jumped in to craft brewing after having actually read this manual. But of course, things have changed considerably since then; back in the pioneering days, so few people were opening their own breweries, we didn't necessarily need a leg up on the next brewer to ensure success. Now, it's critical.

When I was working to open Dogfish in the early 1990s I learned there was a brewery opening almost every week in America—that seemed like an extremely fast rate. Flash forward to 2013 and there is a brewery opening EVERY DAY in America. There is certainly way more consumer knowledge and consumer demand today for craft beer than there was when I opened Dogfish. However, it's highly unlikely that every new brewery that opens is going to make it in an increasingly crowded marketplace; economic Darwinism will take hold and there will be winners and losers. So how will you stand out, how will you make your brewery concept unique, quality-centric, and enticing enough to sustain a long and successful run? *Starting Your Own Brewery* gets you to start asking the right questions you'll need to succeed in an ever-more crowded sector sooner rather than later. It also explains how craft brewing, while increasingly competitive, still enjoys the same sense of community, enthusiasm and selflessness its forerunners showed for one another. In fact, our industry is pretty unique in being stunningly altruistic and mutually-supportive. As Dick writes early in the book, "The collegiality and conviviality of our industry is in fact envied by those

in other artisanal industries who value individual over collective success." I think this phenomenon is set deep in the DNA of the craft brewing movement. Beginning with Fritz Maytag selling a piece of brewing equipment he outgrew at a great discount to Ken Grossman, this baton of the brewing brethren is passed between so many of us. We learn from each other's successes but we also learn from each other's mistakes. In the introduction of this book Dick writes about the pioneers of the craft brewing movement and he mentions New Albion Brewery and its founder Jack McAuliffe. New Albion was a bit before its time but it broke a lot of trail for the many pioneers who followed it and learned from it.

Before opening Sierra Nevada Brewing Company, Ken Grossman paid Jack a visit. Jack shared information about his costs and profits that would almost never be conveyed to potential competitors in most modern industries. From these conversations Ken learned that in that era and at established price points it was more difficult to be profitable as a small startup production brewery focused on bottled beer, as New Albion was. This was because there were very few bottle, cap and crate suppliers, and the few small breweries that existed paid a huge premium for these goods compared to the giant industrial breweries that had much greater buying power and economies of scale. Ken learned a lesson from Jack's experience and candor and applied it to the conception of his little brewery in Chico. Sierra entered the market initially with kegged beer, not bottled beer. In that era you could get kegs pretty cheap and with kegs, you get your empty packaging back, unlike with bottled beer where almost all your packaging expenses are sunk costs.

Similarly existential brewery lessons abound in this book and I am certain any aspiring commercial brewery in the planning phase or small brewery looking to grow her enterprise into something a little less small will find useful lessons in every chapter Dick has written. This book is written from a true brewer's perspective. For example while discussing brewing equipment choices Dick does so from chronological perspective in the order of equipment uses that occur on a normal brew day, from grain in through packaging. Dick Cantwell is not just a 25-year plus vet of the craft brewing movement, he is as accomplished a writer as he is a brewer and businessman. The most fortuitous component of the timing of this publication is that Dick is drawing on those years of past experience while recalling every painful, rewarding, enlightening phase of opening his own new production brewery start-up at the time he was writing this book. This gives the book that real time adrenaline-pumping alive flavor. He is not just offering hypothetical scenarios for aspiring brewery owners, he is giving real examples of what he learned working at other breweries, opening Elysian brewpubs and subsequently the Elysian production brewery with partners, calling on the experience and examples of his many friends in their own brewery and brand-building endeavors.

Brewers have been bringing life and vitality to the culinary world since the dawn of civilization. We are limited only by our imaginations. If you are planning on reading this book, if you are planning on starting or growing your business, then you have come to a good place. I could have searched the New York Public Library's stacks and databases for a year straight, 19 years ago when I first started working on Dogfish Head, and I would not have found half the valuable information contained within the covers of this book.

Sam Calagione
Dogfish Head Craft Brewery

FINDING YOUR PLACE
(and Your Place in It All)

No one of us invented this thing, whatever we choose to call it. Small-scale brewing has been with us—whoever "we" are—as long as we can remember. It's like a civilizational familiar, a little creature nearly always with us, and if not, close enough to come when we call. Or maybe it's like ground water, ever flowing beneath us, sometimes forgotten, but ready to burble up at our feet at times and in ways that surprise us. Whether art or science (people actually debate this stuff), it's an ancient skill. But unlike other more hunter-gatherer-type ancient skills—fly fishing and mushroom hunting come to mind—it's something that people can't keep themselves from sharing and talking about. At least in our circle. There are those, to be sure, who closely guard their so-called secrets, who because of commercial pressures from above simply smile and say, "well, you just have to try it." Try it we shall, until we get it right, even if it's different. Maybe *because* it's different. You just can't stop a culture from spreading, especially if it's more than physical, more than commercial, and particularly if it results in a mildly alcoholic beverage.

For us, the mid-1970s was the darkness before the dawn. A US brewing culture nearly forced out of existence by Prohibition four or five decades earlier found itself in the late stages of self-immolation: One by one, those who survived the storm succumbed to commercial pressures caused by concentration of corporate brewing power and either closed or allowed themselves to be absorbed by larger entities. The mid-seventies saw no more than forty extant and operating breweries in the United States, down from thousands at the onset of Prohibition. One of these, it happens, was San Francisco's Anchor Brewing, rescued from the scrapheap several years earlier by washing machine heir Fritz Maytag and maintained as a labor of love. We should all raise an occasional glass in the appropriate direction for the trials he and his company endured to provide one of the few links of continuity between then and now.

The seventies, it should be mentioned, were an odd decade for beer. Consumption was up, overall, largely because of the invention, and successful marketing of, light beer. Curiously enough, light beer inventor Joe Owades lent his expertise a decade later to the fledgling Boston Beer Company, burnishing an "old family recipe" provided by founder Jim Koch. 1976 also saw the opening of the nation's first new craft brewery, New Albion, in Sonoma, California. So like the curious and contemporaneous existence of disco and punk rock during these same years, both craft and light beer took flight together, each forever and antithetically changing brewing history.

Nor was the rest of the world in a whole lot better shape. Consolidation also ran roughshod over the brewing cultures of Germany, Belgium and England. Breweries which in some cases had operated for centuries, or at least since the industrial explosions of the mid- and late nineteenth century, were absorbed and in many cases shuttered by larger companies bent on surviving through dominance. Traditional styles were scuttled in favor of lighter, fizzier, and generally more easily-maintained lager beers. Yet at the same time a movement of resistance was born. CAMRA, the Campaign for Real Ale, was founded in 1971, uniting British beer enthusiasts against the cleansing and general commodification of beer culture. 1979 brought about the world's first brewpubs as they are today recognized: David Bruce's Firkin pub chain. Michael Jackson's *World Guide to Beer* was published in 1977, bringing knowledge and awareness of many of the world's great beers and beer styles to readers across the globe. In Belgium, Pierre Celis had exhumed witbier, a nearly extinct traditional style, at his Hoegaarden brewery in 1966. Germany—well, in Germany the Reinheitsgebot kept things pretty much the way they had been since 1516 when it was first decreed, albeit through fewer outlets as breweries there too gobbled each other up.

Sadly New Albion did not survive, owing mainly to under-production and under-capitalization (nano brewers take note). Jack McAuliffe too should by rights receive his share of California-directed toasts. But the genie, so to speak, was out of the bottle. In California, Mendocino and Sierra Nevada Brewing companies, Triple Rock and Buffalo Bill's Brewpub, and up in Washington and Oregon Redhook, Grant's, Widmer and Kufnerbrau all got on board within several years. At about the same time, beer importers Merchant du Vin, founded by Charles and Rose Ann Finkel, began bringing British and continental European beers into the US that were well beyond the pale lager variety. They offered Americans thirsty for beer of character examples to drink along with Michael Jackson's book. The timing was not incidental—Jackson and the Finkels were great friends. In addition, and probably most fundamentally, homebrewing was legalized in the United States in 1976.

This, in all likelihood, is where you and I come in; if not right that minute then certainly at the flowering of the movement that soon commenced. The waves of brewers who followed these influencers and pioneers began overwhelmingly as homebrewers. Many paused to get educations, after a fashion, at Chicago's Siebel Institute or UC Davis, or more exotically at Heriot-Watt in Edinburgh or the Katholieke Universiteit Leuven in Belgium where Jean de Clerck was a brewing professor. One fellow from Wyoming named Eric Toft landed in Germany without knowledge of the language or of brewing, stepped into some lederhosen, worked his way through Weihenstephan's brewing program and today is brewmaster at Privat Landbrauerei Schönram in Bavaria. Amazing. All of it amazing.

Aside from proper courses in brewing, knowledge and information was sparse in craft brewing's early days. Many of the texts and bibles on style and technique now sitting riffled and spattered on brewery shelves throughout the land were not yet published. Charlie Papazian's *Complete Joy of Homebrewing* brought basic brewing instruction to a generation of brewers, and continues to encourage with its unintimidating mantra "Relax, don't worry, have a homebrew." Craft brewing's first homegrown semi-serious text was Greg Noonan's *Brewing Lager Beer*, a project he undertook to convince potential investors of his gravitas as he worked to eventually open the Vermont Pub and Brewery in Burlington. This scarcity of information combined with a certain common bullheadedness often had brewers reverting to the essential superstition of their historical forebears, mashing overnight, over-sterilizing to the point of off-flavor, and improvising, always improvising. Somehow, gradually, word of reasonably standard procedures spread and the beers once best known and appreciated for their novelty began to get better. The eighties added breweries by the dozen, and then by the hundred.

Brewing was a club, and everyone belonged. Information was shared—and continues to be shared—with willingness, and with beer. The collegiality and conviviality of our industry is in fact envied by those in other artisanal industries who value individual over collective success. Coffee? They don't trust each other. Chocolate? Forget about it. If we have a legacy, this is it. It is something to be preserved and cherished, passed along as strongly and as often as can be managed. Of course it helps that our industry continues to grow. As of this writing, an ever-growing market share approaching 7% by volume (and far more by dollars, and growing,) makes it easier to snuggle, and to admit one more—you—to the fold.

It Has Happened Before, But There Is Nothing To Compare It To Now

You thought the seventies were weird? After a decade of incremental increase, the nineties saw an explosion of small breweries and contract brewing projects unprecedented in the history of everything. It was kind of like now, but unfortunately the beer wasn't as good. Homebrewers like me were pressed into professional service with even limited experience; every town you'd pass through in Colorado or the Northwest suddenly had a brewery. The business pages went from loving to hating us as silly projects faltered and independent public offerings lost money for unsophisticated and over-eager investors. The end of the Movement was foreseen; the shakeout, if you read the papers, was underway. Except it really wasn't. Growth slowed, to be sure, but quality remained, for the most part, and the number of new breweries kept rising. A lot of this growth came from the base already established, as companies opened second locations. Just the same, a wariness settled in among banks and other financial entities. The dotcom boom and bust coincided.

Sometime during this period Michael Jackson undertook to write a guidebook to American beers and breweries; a cross, I'm assuming, between his pocket guide and the excellent and exhaustive *Great Beers of Belgium*. There was so much ground to cover that group tastings were scheduled in cities around the country so that he could try as much of what was available right then as he could, in as short a time as possible. I was working at Big Time Brewery and Alehouse in Seattle at the time, and so was lucky enough to host a tasting of several breweries' wares, from as far away as Spokane. It was held at eight in the morning in order that he could fly on to Boise and do it again there. Later in his trip he visited Kansas City, Kansas, and was first dismayed to discover that three of the breweries he had planned to visit had

gone out of business, and then literally overwhelmed to find that three new ones had sprung up in their stead. He decided to abandon the project.

Meanwhile, in Milwaukee, St. Louis and Golden notice was taken. Without ever considering the loss of a few points of market share to upstart hobbyists a threat, each of the brewers spun their awareness of declining dominance into a different opportunity. Coors probably had the clearest grasp of what was afoot, devising their Blue Moon line of specialty beers to compete directly with the products of actual craft breweries. Miller ran out and bought a couple of the fastest-growing breweries in the segment: Shipyard in Portland, Maine and Celis (yep, the same Celis—long story) in Austin, Texas. Within a few years that experiment was done, with Shipyard reverting to its original owners and Celis moving its brands north to Michigan. Anheuser-Busch worked out distribution agreements with a couple of strong Northwest brands, Redhook and Widmer, in exchange for an undisclosed ownership. At the same time, they handed down word that A-B-aligned distributors were to shun all other craft brands. This was commonly referred to as "one hundred percent share of mind." Soundings in the A-B/InBev these days indicate a sort of spiritual return to such strategy, but it's too early to tell what it could mean for some of us. And by the time you read this, of course, all three of those companies have been altered nearly beyond recognition, with Miller and Coors merged in various sequence with Molson, South African Breweries, and each other, and Anheuser-Busch overtaken by InBev, the Belgian-Brazilian behemoth. Kona and Goose Island of Chicago are now variously within the A-B/InBev coil. But in the interest of concisely bringing you up to date, I'm getting a little ahead of myself.

Wheels Within Wheels— Breweries Opening Everywhere, Again

I remember a telephone conversation I had in about 1994 with Bill Owens, founder of Buffalo Bill's and the genius who resurrected the Colonial classic, pumpkin beer. We'd both noticed that up from forty-ish around twenty years earlier, there were then in the neighborhood of 400 breweries in the country. "There'll be a thousand before we know it," he observed with his borderline frantic style. Well, tell Tchaikovsky the news. Earlier this year we topped 2100, with another several hundred like yours, dear reader, in planning.

It's nearly impossible these days to keep track of the myriad openings (and occasional closings) of small breweries in America. Just within the last few months three opened in a single neighborhood here in Seattle. The Brewers Association keeps loose track of potential activity by the serious inquiries received as to how to begin going about it, and it's been a steady thousand or so (give or take a couple hundred) over the past few years. The Craft Brewers Conference is once again swollen with prospective brewery owners, and some of the most popular talks at the National Homebrewers Conference are those having to do with going pro.

Will there, this time, be an actual shakeout? Everyone wants to know. The answer isn't easy, for we all know that we can't indefinitely add breweries by the thousand and have them all survive, at least as independent entities. A great deal more opportunity exists, it seems to me, for pub breweries. Their advantage lies in literally enclosing their clientele without perhaps asking as much of the limited resources and mercantile attentions of a community larger than their own streetcorner. But a growing market, as earlier observed, creates greater opportunity for everyone, large and small, packaged and by the pint. Beer quality is paramount, along with everything else.

For relative ease of operation, availability of materials and equipment, and the acceptance by the market there's never been a better time to open a brewery. Aside, perhaps, from the fact that the word is out. The craft brewing movement was born of a spirit to buck trends, and it's only a fine point, perhaps, that the trend these days is to open craft breweries. Does this mean that conventional wisdom would indicate that the smart money is on Moroccan cuisine, or dog grooming? They're filling up, too. Passion, then as now, is what gets us into this crazy and rewarding business. I'm certainly not here to talk you out of it.

SECTION I

PLANNING

LOCATION
Born in the Country, Raised in Town

1

Possibly more than other entrepreneurial ventures, starting a brewery is a fantasy come true. Acting on a perception of opportunity is rooted in practicality, to be sure, but a great deal of the mental energy that goes into planning something so personal, so creative, so essentially warm-blooded is about honing a vision. It's the nature of the beverage, after all, to foster thought and speculation and to test the limits of a collection of ideas.

Like looking for houses or apartments, searching for a location for your brewery can be a brutal experience. No matter how unsuitable a spot, no matter how scrofulous and neglected and ridiculous for your purposes a given space might be, it's impossible not to imagine yourself pursuing your dream in a place that would be frankly awful. That's how you know the ones you like (though there's no guarantee you'll actually get them). Faced with the prospects of wastes and odor and crowds—"that after-party smell," as one of my prospective landlords said, pretty much slamming the door—some people simply don't like the idea of a brewery occupying their properties. Fortunately many do, and these are the people, along with the spaces you've fallen in love with, with whom you're far more likely to forge a harmonious relationship. Spending a lot of energy trying to talk a resistant person into your idea, especially when they might not even be aware of the realities, is probably not the best start. When you find someone who is as excited as you are by what you want to do, that's when you've found your man—or woman—but most importantly, your location.

Naturally there's a lot to be balanced. You'll want a place with at least the squinting amenities of brewing: space and adequate utility service for both production and waste disposal. Beyond that you'll want the physical necessities of doing business as a shipping brewery or a pub—a loading zone if not an actual dock, a potentially pleasant area for seating, and hey, what about location and facilities for a kitchen of some type? Would an office throw too prosaic a cast on the purity of the vision-thing? Throw in odds and ends like the general look and feel, and you've got the basic interior function covered. Don't worry, I'm being glib on purpose; we'll cover all this in greater detail later.

Of course the exterior, in terms both of what and where it is, is no less important, even adding a grain of salt to the homilies of 3L-spouting realtors. A lot is said about weighing the relative merit of any given spot, and the considerations raised are valid for the conventional way doing of business. But not everyone does, or can afford to do business conventionally. Sometimes an eyes-closed vision of a spot's potential can find something no less perfect, as long as inviting the neighborhood to come to you in a few years' time doesn't make you overly nervous. We'll take a look at all this as well.

Brewing began in the country, where its supplies were grown and processed, and where its output was mainly intended for a single farm or estate, plus the occasional traveler. There's something in the blood of every brewer that likes the idea of getting away from it all and uncompromisingly pursuing the dream in a small, out-of-the-way setting. As homebrewers our kitchens and garages qualified as such places, and as pros we're tempted. Welcome, come on in, do you like my beer? Excellent, this is how I made it. No, not so much? Well, there's another place you might like better right down the road.

Following Old World leads, the first American craft breweries of the modern era started up in places without a whole lot of people nearby. Photos from this time, appearing in places like Michael Jackson's *World Guide to Beer*, show tiny outbuildings with trucks parked next to them, a bearded brewer/proprietor standing alongside, grinning or grimacing according to temperament. As they grew, many of these pioneers eventually saw the wisdom of bringing their show to the city, if for no other reason than ease of transportation to their primary markets.

A rural brewery in fact offers wide-open spaces and autonomy. The country is a great place to make beer, provided there is adequate water from either the tap or a well. Depending on the size of the operation, there could be sewage issues as well, as places with fewer people tend to be more impacted by anomalous waste. Other potential problems have readier solutions, however, such as nearby livestock for the processing of spent grains or a garden patch for growing hops or herbs for idiosyncratic brews. But with remoteness and its benefits comes reliance on transport between source and market, whether it's you hauling kegs and bottles to sales outlets or your customers making their way to your pub at the bend in the road. Fuel and other transportation costs, as well as their environmental impacts, are of course things we all know will not get easier to bear. Hence at least an awareness of their effects on your cost and time are needed to weigh the feasibility of a pastoral location. The challenge is to find the right combination of mitigating factors, such as a ski area just up the way or an otherwise well-traveled tourist route.

The same could be said as a potential location moves closer to town and on into an urban area. The market is closer, but so are other citizens, as likely to object to odors and noise as they are to take in a joyous lungful of hop-laden vapors and simply love the fact that they've got a brewery in their neighborhood. Urban real estate costs are of course higher. In an actual city such things as foot traffic and proximity to public transportation must be taken into account, as well as ensuring that there is adequate parking. Depending on zoning, certain hours might need to be observed for garbage pickup or the filling of grain silos. And here's a funny one: you might consider all those bars and restaurants near your location to be natural customers. But once you're there and drawing from the same customer pool, they just might consider you too close to want to do business with you. Ultimately it's who you are and where you judge the best opportunities to be that determine if you are in or out of town.

There's also the in-between option, a suburban location either in a shopping area such as a mall or along a well-traveled route primarily dedicated to various aspects of doing business. These areas can offer several advantages, providing a base of customers, an overall sympathy for the needs of business such as delivery and haul-away services, a tolerance for the realities of light manufacture and food preparation and the benefits of fitting into a symbiotic community. Suitability of the suburban location may require more assessment than other models, however. How much of an existing draw is there to the area without you, and how far do people typically drive to get there? Is there a competing service nearby, almost certainly restaurant-related with of course top-notch beer, that will draw business away? Are you right on the road or front and center in a commercial nexus, or do people have to make an effort to find you? Let's not forget parking. These are questions which need to be asked of any location, no matter what its balance of market and population, but given the distances and patterns of suburbia perhaps more of a bird's eye view is required to appreciate the lay of the land.

As observed earlier, there's a difference between the perfect location with all aspects already in place, and the location that may, with time, become perfect. It should come as no surprise that the former is generally more expensive than the latter. It ought to be. It's easier to imagine. In the beginning most of us find ourselves needing to take some considered chances in order to swing the deal. Once again it's a matter of temperament and comfort as well as wherewithal. It's a speculative exercise to predict where a neighborhood will be in two or five or fifteen years. When my partners and I started Elysian, it was obvious to most people that our location was a bit off the edge. Four blocks from the quiet end of a major urban thoroughfare served by a pizza place, a venerable dive and a collection of specialty gay bars, people pretty much had to be making a specific trip to reach us. But we also knew that the area was the most densely populated part of Seattle, and at a crossroads of adjoining neighborhoods. Today those neighborhoods have come to join us, with new places even farther along continuing to spring up. It can take some time to get mainstreamed, but by taking an active role in the development of a neighborhood, you can have more control of your own destiny. Remember also that with neighborhood change comes demolition and construction; one-story buildings in developing neighborhoods are particularly vulnerable to removal and replacement. If you're going to be a part of turning an area into a place people want to come to, you want to make sure you can stick around to benefit from all that work and vision.

Zoning is one of the first things you'll need to be aware of as you weigh any potential location, for if your commercial and industrial use doesn't gibe with a residential-only designation, you're barking up the wrong tree right away. You'll also need to make sure it's even legal to conduct a business in the space you've got your eye on. A friend once called me nearly in tears, as the house in which she and her husband operated a coffee shop turned out never to have been approved for commerce—this after having purchased it from previous operators who just didn't happen to mention it.

What do you say we go inside?

So the realtor has unlocked the door, shoved an old lawnmower out of the way that someone was storing there, kicked a rat trap into the corner and discreetly flattened an upturned corner of carpet. Then he sweeps his arm in a distracting and aggrandizing way—you know, standard broker's legerdemain. You see a room probably bigger than you imagined ideal. The walls are likely not in great shape; the whole space might in fact be subdivided with stark and battered sheetrock, trimmed with the least substantial (and no doubt the least expensive) molding and frames procured at the closest big-box hardware store. The place is a mess, full of cast-off stuff: plastic chairs, boxes of unused ceiling tile, a useless old motel TV. And gosh, there's a kind of sketchy-looking guy sitting there watching a game show on it. This is getting depressing, and now you're feeling self-conscious. But mainly just to be polite you at least give the place a look.

Where size is concerned, remember that people at first tend to think over-modestly. Once you've put in your brewery and (if it's part of your plan) devoted adequate space to a kitchen, that cozy little place you'd envisioned might in fact not be able to accommodate enough customers to really make a go of it. You'll need some storage space, too. Anything else that's there you can simply get rid of—sorry, guy. But as you walk around you start to see it. That Depression-era plasterwork can simply come out; it looks as though there might be some decent bones underneath it. Suppress your natural retching instinct when surveying the yards and yards of taupe-colored paint. That can be covered over. Besides, you'll be doing some construction as well. Imagine the place empty and you can see a new focus, a counterpoint between brewery and bar, an alcove here, a cluster of tables there. That potential brewery zone looks a little small, especially if you're planning to do much with barrels. Is there a basement? What's out the back door? Sometimes, as with a lot of things, you need to look past something to start to see it.

On to practical considerations. A fantasy layout is great, but you need to make sure the place can physically support what you're asking of it. A brewery of course has some specialized requirements, having partly to do with space, but mainly with the adequacy (or adaptability) of support systems. You'll probably need an electrician to tell you if the circuit breaker (if there is one in that old building) has enough juice for your needs, or how much it'll cost to put one in that does (if that can be done at all). Water is also vital. Any main that comes in can probably be split, but you'll need to make sure, once more, that it's enough to begin with. If the place was a retail space with perhaps just a bathroom for employees, outreach to city systems might become necessary; and you may not have any idea how to even begin that process, or how much it will cost. You know drains can be put in, even if you don't know exactly how to do that right now. This may well come into the equation when you're adding rebar and concrete to the brewery zone—you don't want it all to fall into the basement. Well what do you know? There is a basement.

Okay, enough narrative. Having a place speak to you is great. It's a dialogue which, as you develop your ideas, will shape the personality and functionality of your place. But it shouldn't all be reactive. A set of expectations and needs, a checklist against which you can measure the basic facts of any potential location, will at least put a pragmatic frame around your desire to find a place you like. Soon enough you'll find out about the essential balance, the give and take of a budget. A system or two can be upgraded or changed; you'll be doing a lot of that, with and without surprises. But it's important to be as realistic as you can in assessing a potential location. Too many strikes against a place and it's out, even if there are aspects you absolutely love. You will find later that it wasn't right to begin with, especially if you watch someone else go into it and struggle.

Once you've gotten serious about a particular location it's time to test the relationship. Spend some time there, if in fact there is a "there" there. Do your emailing in the local café and watch who comes and goes and what those patterns are like. Spend some time in the bars, if there are any, and especially during times that might display less predictable flows than, say, Friday night. Is this an area where people go to eat lunch? Are there large enough office spaces or a hospital nearby to sustain daytime business? Perhaps you'll notice a lot of people in their twenties on single-speed bikes and not necessarily embedded in the nine-to-five paradigm you might find in other areas.

They don't have a lot of money, generally, but they're often free to just drop in for a beer or two (and they eventually get older). How do people get around? Do they drive? Is there a bus line? Is the sidewalk used, and by whom?

These are the concerns of an urban neighborhood, but the analyses of frequency and type can be transposed to the rural setting as well. In either case an assessment of community is what's required. Out of town, transportation becomes especially important, both for how your pub customers can find you and in connection with shipping your beer. Access to main roads seems like a minor deal when you're using them only every so often, but if you're doing frequent deliveries, major arteries can save a lot of time. If you use a distributor you'll find their schedule will be more accommodating to you if you aren't in the middle of nowhere.

Location isn't important just because people say it is. People say a lot of lazy and obvious things. It should be important because you've considered the practical implications of where your brewery will be located, and they fit with your vision. It may present itself as the extension of your vision, the perfect place, the first time you see it. Or it may alter your vision in ways you hadn't before considered, but which display good sense and draw from you a sense of the adventure on which you're about to embark. In both cases it's like the blocks of Carrera marble that, according to lore, Michelangelo would select for his sculptures. The shape was in there, ready to be freed from the surrounding stone by a combination of feeling and struggle and skill. The first you know, the second you can identify with, the third you'll develop as you go.

Chapter Highlights

Overall Considerations

- Adequate space—can you do what you want to do there?
- Electrical/Plumbing—is it adequate? What conversions/upgrades will be necessary?
- Waste removal: garbage, kitchen waste and recycling, spent grains.
- Loading dock/zone—for both retail customers and carriers in and out.
- Kitchen space—prioritize your equipment and the space each piece takes; check requirements.
- Dining space—how many seats will you need?
- Office space—how many desks are necessary? Is there phone, Internet and other necessary office services?
- Storage space—leave space for cleaning equipment, supplies, and cold and dry storage.
- General look and feel—is this your place?
- Future neighborhood development—will the people come to you? Will your building survive the next neighborhood upgrade?
- Competition—how close is the nearest business like yours?
- Room for growth—can you grow in this location?
- Foundation load/drains—can the floors support a brewery? Will drainage need to be added?
- Traffic patterns—bus lines, major arteries, foot traffic.
- Parking space—is there enough?
- Ease of transportation to primary market—how far is it to where you're likely to sell most of your beer?

Town Location

- Real estate costs are higher, but urban locations provide more people and more business.
- Neighbors may object to odors. Keep garbage and grains covered, and treated, if necessary. Consider a condenser for kettle fumes.
- Parking requirements—do you have to contribute on- or off-site spaces?
- Zoning requirements—is your location zoned for commercial business?
- Competing with potential customers—open arms, or the cold shoulder? It can be up to you.
- Built-in customer base—who frequents your neighborhood already, and who can be enticed in from outside?

Country Location

- Wide-open space—can you expand on the land?
- Autonomy—is the property zoned for commercial/industrial activity?
- Adequate water—what's the source, and is it sufficient?
- Sewage issues—how will it go away, and are you allowed to dump the by-products of a brewery?
- Spent grain solutions—can you use it? Can one of your neighbors? Can they pick it up regularly?
- Transportation and fuel cost—you're likely to be driving more than if you were in town. This needs to be factored into costs.
- Environmental impact—how can you minimize it in a location probably less able to dispose of waste materials?
- Customer base—will they come to you? How far is it to them?
- Future plans—is it feasible to grow in this location, or will you eventually be moving closer to your market?

CONSULTANTS
Free Advice and Paying for Experts

2

Breweries and their attendant businesses—pubs, restaurants, and sometimes distributors—don't often spring fully formed from the mind of one entrepreneur. More commonly they are an aggregate of expertise assembled from many different sources. Much of this expertise is free, advice enlisted from friends and others who have gone before. You'll find a high degree of willingness in your future colleagues to talk about things they did right and wrong, offered along with critiques of what you've shared of your own plans. And when your turn comes, you should expect to do the same. But an awful lot of this shared expertise isn't free. The service fees of designers, demographers and consultants, in fact, can devour your budget if you let them.

How much of this advice is necessary? It's impossible to give a simple answer. Much depends on your level of preparation, and the combination of resident talent in your team. Beyond that there's the matter of how comfortable you feel relying on your study skills, and your ability to gather and weigh information. No matter how many experts you consult, you'll still be the one making the final call. Presuming, that is, that you're going to be running the place you establish.

Take comfort in the fact that no one is an expert at the beginning. But be prepared to work like hell filling those gaps in your own knowledge that prevent you from overcoming the challenges of making great beer and running a business.

There are some things you absolutely have to hire out for. Unless you are a licensed architect or industrial designer, for example, you'll need someone with a stamp to submit the drawings necessary to get the permits to commence. Similarly, depending on the strictures of whatever loan you've secured to fund your project, you may need an approved construction company to undertake much of the work. Small Business Administration (SBA) supervision, for example, will allow you to do pre-project demolition yourself, but not actual construction or commonly sub-contracted work such as electrical, plumbing or (God forbid) steamfitting. Licenses for those skills are required all around, and it's a good thing, too. But in such cases receipts from recognized service providers are required for funding.

But beyond the basic nuts and bolts, you'll need to exercise caution. Experts will line up ready to help you form the tiniest aspects of your vision, for a price. Some of their advice will seem a necessary comfort as you prepare to take a plunge perhaps unlike any other you've previously made. But you'll find that a lot of this stuff you can do yourself. Do you need someone else to analyze the neighborhood in which you're contemplating establishing your business, or do you know it well enough yourself to make a decision? Do you have a sound enough appreciation for the market to determine which kinds of beers will establish your brand and help it stand out from others? What about recipes? The layout of your kitchen? Brewing equipment? Bookkeeping software? If these are areas you have even a basic understanding of, or even a good set of opinions, it may not be the best use of your money simply to seek corroboration. Save it for the things you know you don't know. Beware of designers and consultants who merely help you along the right track.

That said, it's still better to spend several hundred dollars for some guidance that might ultimately save you several thousand. People who have already trod the road before you should be sufficiently qualified to sift through and prioritize many of the possibly intimidating options before you. Be aware of what their perspectives are, where they've been and what their accomplishments say about the level and quality of the advice they're able to give you. As the craft brewing movement matures, the number of eligible consultants grows. There are going to be a lot of people moving away from performing the jobs they once held and into the area of talking about them. There will be, briefly put, no shortage of experts. It's up to you to determine the difference between those with valuable ideas to sell you and those who just like to tell you what they've done.

As you go, you'll find yourself learning a great deal from the people hoping to do business with you. As you compare bids for services and equipment it will be difficult not to become something of an expert yourself. Bankers, brokers, fabricators and others will want to help educate you in order that you'll choose their service or product because it's demonstrably better than other things out there. Don't worry too much about wasting people's time as you shop around for the right option; they can't expect to get your business without proving to your satisfaction that they are the best choice.

One of my partners is a master of this kind of on-the-fly education. On the prospective acquisition of nearly anything, he can (after a few conversations and internet searches) at least sound like an expert. Like many self-taught experts, he tends to impress himself with what he's found out, and can quickly get devoted to a particular thing or approach. But he will also listen to opposing opinions and generally manages to make very good choices. His is a laudable example of enthusiasm for the hunt.

The websites of fabricators and other service suppliers can provide a great deal of information before any conversation takes place. JV Northwest, for example, offers equipment specifications for prospective production scenarios as well as sample brewery layouts. Once you get to the point of pricing things you'll generally need to make verbal contact, but a great deal of research can be done without tipping your hand, entirely free of human contact. This may seem a strange course to recommend, but it is a way to move extremely fast in bringing yourself up to speed where general awareness is concerned.

Seminars and conferences can be reasonably economical places to drink it all in. The annual Craft Brewers Conference put on by the Brewers Association is one, offering an opportunity not just for established professionals to share ideas, but for entrants to the industry to seek answers for many of the questions they have, and to have new ones occur to them. It seems, in fact, that during times of booming interest in starting new breweries, attendees who are already running breweries are a sort of captive resource for those looking into it. Once you're established, Master Brewers Association of the Americas (MBAA) gatherings can be excellent educational and networking opportunities as well. There's a lot to be said for spending time amid your prospective peers learning what's going on right now in an industry segment that changes remarkably quickly.

As soon as you can, join your state brewers' guild. As of this writing there are only a handful of states that don't have them. This will immediately put you in contact with one of our movement's greatest resources: other brewers. It's a ready-made community of people eager to talk about what they've done and to share the result. Don't worry too much about being a newcomer—none of us is all that far from having been there ourselves. As long as you're willing to be forthcoming yourself, you'll be in a position to learn a lot.

The Brewers Association (BA) is our primary trade organization, a modern amalgamation of the old Association of Brewers, which served this country's smallest brewers (and homebrewers) and the Brewers Association of America, which generally served medium to larger craft brewers. Like so many of the rest of us, it has grown up into a vital, active and inspired organization. It runs our largest events, including the Great American Beer Festival®, SAVOR℠, the Craft Brewers Conference and the World Beer Cup®. It publishes magazines both for homebrewers (*Zymurgy*®) and professionals (*The New Brewer*); books like this one through its publishing arm, Brewers Publications; it advocates for craft brewers in legislatures and allied industries and it interfaces with other organizations such as the National Beer Wholesalers Association and the Beer Institute, the common trade organization of the largest brewers. Perhaps most importantly at your present stage of planning to jump in, BA provides materials to help with many aspects of your future business. Just a few of these are *The Draft Quality Manual*, which helps you to make intelligent and effective decisions about treating your beer right on its way to the consumer; the Sustainability Guides, providing guidance for issues that over time will take on increasing importance for all of us; and the web sites connected to CraftBeer.com, providing dynamic input and output for brewers and consumers. Like joining your local or state guild, BA membership puts you right in the thick of things, allowing you to benefit not only from your peers but from a trained, experienced and highly effective professional staff with all of our interests in mind.

Depending on the area of interest and expertise you bring to your project, membership in other trade and professional organizations might also make sense. If your realm is brewing, joining the MBAA is a good idea. Just joining something that serves all the Americas is appealing in itself. MBAA provides technical guidance and throws a regular and worthwhile series of meetings and events together throughout the year. If you are more closely devoted to brewing chemistry and quality control, there is the American Society of Brewing Chemists (ASBC), allied with MBAA and offering more specialized treatment. Other organizations such as the National Restaurant Association can also provide specific help for different areas of your business. If you are a raw materials kind of guy or gal, you might even consider taking a look at AMBA, the American Malting Barley Association, or the Hop Research Council. In whichever case, being a bit of a joiner can help in many pretty cost-effective ways.

Chapter Highlights

Resources to Tap

- Team talents. Realistically assess what you and your team can do.
- Research. What can you look into that will build the confidence and mastery of your plan?
- Bankers. They want to protect their investment, and will likely help you do things right.
- Brokers, manufacturers. Talk to as many as you need to in order to make informed decisions. You'll learn along the way, too.
- Industry colleagues. None of us has done this alone. Most people are busy, but willing to help.
- Seminars/conferences. There is a lot to learn in a more formalized setting from those who have gone before you.
- Professional organizations. Join the community.

Specialized Help

- Architect
- Industrial designer
- Structural engineer
- Equipment manufacturer
- Electrician
- Plumber

SIZE MATTERS
How Big Should Your Brewery Be?

3

Times change, along with the beards and behavioral fads of brewers (it may be a revelation to you, for example, that at one point we all smoked cigars), but the archetypal vision of the startup brewery has remained essentially the same during all the years I've been hearing it. It's going to be small, probably no more than five barrels brewlength (or capacity); just big enough to satisfy the demand of a local pub or a small loyal wholesale market. If it's a pub, food will probably not be served, but if it is it will be simple—peanuts, chips and salsa and maybe some really good pretzels; even a couple of sandwiches furrows the conceptual brow. It will have a rural location, or perhaps in a very small town. It might be in a suburb somewhere, but it almost certainly won't be in the city. One man or woman will run it, brewing all the beer as often as it takes, doing all the cellar work and cleaning and filling kegs. Once a week, perhaps, kegs will be offered for sale to local bars.

This was essentially the vision shared by the people with whom I attended a short symposium on the microbrewing phenomenon at UC Davis in the late eighties. Actually, when the two- or three-day event commenced most of us were uninterested in any project that required serving the public, but by the end of it nearly every concept had added food, and a place for people to sit and have a beer. And it's the core of what I've heard most often when

people ask if they can sit down with me for a few minutes and see what I think of what they're hoping to do.

I'm not really one to tell anyone they're wrong. Just because I happen to disagree with the wisdom of many of these conceptual points doesn't mean that this version of the vision can't be realized brilliantly. But there are elements of this fantasy that invite more challenges than are absolutely necessary. Take being in the country. Even a small brewing system affects the sewage balance of a rural area, sometimes requiring extra and expensive measures to comply, sometimes simply not allowed. Not serving food removes one essential element of a pleasant pub-going experience: in many locales this disqualifies families from even being able to patronize your place. And take that small brewing system. In this age of burgeoning nano-sized breweries it may seem anathema to say so, but the only way that you'll be able to keep up with demand is if there really isn't much of it; your chances for success and sustaining commercial continuance are lessened, shall we say, if you can't possibly answer the call you hope for. In addition, your cost per keg will pretty much ensure that you won't make any money on wholesale. But there are some positives.

You will belong to the club of professional brewers. You will be able to see your beer on tap in a handful of local pubs, and if you package you may see your beer for sale alongside the beers that may have served as example and inspiration. Now that that's out of the way, we can examine this and other size concepts in greater detail. It's fun, after all, to check out all the ways of putting the pieces together.

It may sound strange to say so, but not everyone cares if they make money or not. Lots of people hang onto their day jobs as their tiny little licensed brewery is taking root, with either disregard for theoretical profit from their legally sanctioned hobby or as a considered phase along the way to making it all pay. These people are tickled to see their beer on tap at two or three interested local pubs, even if it literally costs them more to make than they're selling it for. But let's at least assume a desire for profitability, and move on from there.

Zero to Sixty—Gallons, That Is

So you've got a tricked out half-barrel system, possibly made from somebody else's kegs. Maybe it's a barrel, or through the efforts of a friendly and reasonable local welder—who might in fact be you—you've managed to stretch it to two. You're making one to four kegs each time you brew. If you don't drink too much of it yourself along the way, you'll have a little beer to sell. Purchased in small-ish quantities, malt costs around fifty-five to sixty cents a pound (specialties cost more, but let's make this simple). A medium weight beer, something around 13 or 14 Plato starting gravity, will require about 65 pounds per barrel. That's 39 bucks. Let's say hops average out at eight dollars a pound. Unless you're doing something radical, you'll use about a pound per barrel. Yeast, well, let's say that's free to negligible, since you can probably beg that somewhere or grow it up yourself from a pretty inexpensive quantity. Unless you're brewing your beer in your parents' garage (stranger things have happened), you're on the hook for utilities as well. That's gas, whether domestically piped or propane, electricity and water both coming and going. Are you capturing your cooling water for your next brew or is it just going down the drain? All these things cost money. Does ten bucks seem reasonable for all the rent and utilities for a single brew day? Contemplating rent and the per-barrel-amortized cost of equipment

begins to dizzy the tabulator, so let's just leave that a sort of x-factor to be specified by individual circumstances. Oh, but wait, there are taxes. In the state of Washington, and including federal, that amounts to nearly twelve dollars a barrel. And licensing. If brewery licensing and permitting costs only a thousand dollars (and that's low), on this scale you're going to be paying three or four dollars a barrel, and that's if you're busy. That's also only your federal license (since licensing itself is relatively cheap—it's the permits and bond that cost). If it's a simple wholesale transaction, you'll probably have to put gas in a vehicle to get it to the buyer, and there's the vehicle. How much is all that? Well, leaving a lot out and assuming a squeaking economy, a one-barrel batch of not-terribly-extreme beer probably costs about eighty-five dollars to make, imperfectly considered. You can probably sell that beer for about $140 a keg (that is, if you're allowed to self-distribute; if not, maybe $110), times two, so that's a cool net of $195 (or $135, depending) once you've subtracted your costs without paying too much attention to what they actually are. Not bad, right?

It doesn't take an advanced degree in finance or accounting to poke a few holes in all this reckoning, even if only to point out its optimism. Not to mention that you're almost literally spending all of your time producing a fairly inconsequential amount of beer. From both a financial and a time/yield standpoint it makes more sense to double, or triple, or quintuple it, even considering the fixed costs pegged to production. All that other work you're going to have to do—cellaring, sales, cleaning, repair and bookkeeping—that needs attention too. It just doesn't make sense to me to begin business in handcuffs, however much you might (and we all) enjoy the processes of brewing beer.

Time and again I've watched people tune me out when I've given a version of this speech to them. Some men you just can't reach. And while I respect their confidence and independence, they need to respect themselves and the value of their time enough to be a little pragmatic. "It's the only way I can afford to do it at first," the little voice inside them is saying, "besides, that's how Sam got started."

That is how Sam (Calagione, of Dogfish Head) got started, brewing five times a day on a half-barrel system. So began the legend. That's essentially how Kim and Jeff (Jordan and Lebesch, of New Belgium) got started, too, and Ken (Grossman, of Sierra Nevada). But they had other things going for them, too, namely concepts which set them apart from the currents of their times. They all shake their heads now at how hard they worked and how lucky they all were beyond the advancement of their visions. They all also expanded as quickly as they could, in order to put those days behind them as quickly as they could. None of them, I assure you, would recommend taking that road again. Are you even listening?

Please don't consider me the enemy of so-called nano breweries. True, I've heard some among my established compatriots urge some kind of campaign to squelch all this slippery, under-the-radar stuff, whining that "they" are taking tap handles somehow consigned to "us" by divine right. I remember some of these same people taking purist umbrage years ago at the willingness of some decidedly non-funky restaurant chains to add breweries to their overall concepts. Such misguided indignation is not only small-minded but impotent. Consumer demand for small breweries, after all, only brings about more small breweries. You can easily imagine the big brewers spluttering about the market share our little craft brewing wave has eroded.

I counsel against the business model only in practical terms. You see I had the same itch to get my beer to market. The tutelage, the experience and the essential apprenticeship of the years I spent working for others in the years leading up to my own and my partners' plunge was perhaps an easier experience. Back then it was simply understood, it seemed to me, that after doing your time at someone else's place you struck out and started your own, with as proper a structure and financial plan as you could muster. Not only are jobs these days more difficult to get without training and experience, but equipment options and access to information are both better than they were twenty or so years ago. There are certainly ways that it can work, with a taproom, for example, in which the profitably priced efforts of the extremely small brewer are served to a public not overly concerned with ambiance and amenity. But is that taproom a legal and licensed place to serve beer? Do you have to pay rent on it? I just have to wonder. I know you're not paying anyone else to work there.

Our movement has always had very small brewers, with systems knee high to a grasshopper. The examples I've cited above testify to this. In the early nineties I worked on a system that yielded three and a half barrels of wort per brew, and even we shook our heads at the fact that Larry Bell's, back in Kalamazoo, was smaller. Most nano brewers avow that producing salable beer on a system of very small size is only an interim plan to establish demand, brand and legitimacy. Enough of them bear this out by eventually building bigger facilities, perhaps even leveraging a loan or otherwise securing financing by gaining attention through their efforts. Allowing a little conjecture, it's almost certain they don't finance their expansions from cash flow. But where there's a will there can absolutely be a way.

There's also a certain amount of ear-stopping inherent in doing what we've all either done or aspire to do. It's a little bit nutty to drop whatever it is you're doing and take a left turn into beer, and some of us hear that from others even as we take steps to do so ourselves. Take a look at some of the blogs presenting, examining and popping off about the nano brewing phenomenon. In addition to the bare facts, in addition to the enthusiasm and wonderment, there's a fair representation of fringe opinion: such things as reference to the government ripping us off by taxation and the assumption of a mantle of purity, even superiority to rival breweries, based on size and hard work. Taken to logical extreme, these are things which could bring trouble to a project. I've also seen categorical reference to the "lies" that are told aspirant nano folks about not being able to make it under seven barrels. I don't recall being quite so self-righteous. I just wanted to make beer. No lie.

Seven to Ten Barrels—the Divine Path

There's a reason many American craft breweries (and especially brewpubs) begin their lives in multiples of seven; actually, there's a word: Grundies. These UK-manufactured, dish-bottomed tanks were produced in the decades following World War II by a few different companies, and in later life they were readily and inexpensively available for serving and cellar use by a whole wave of new breweries starting out in the 1980s and 1990s. One brewery, Four Peaks in the Phoenix area, even made use of them as an entrepreneurial tool to finance their project, tapping a source of many hundreds and re-selling them to other brewers. The original (and secondary, for the most part) English supplies have at this point dried up, but they are still out there, taking their lumps and blowing their tops over time in cellars throughout the land. Their volume—seven UK barrels, which with headspace is close enough to seven US ones—dictated the sizing of brewhouses manufactured for the craft brewing movement's earlier boom times. That's why a lot of brewpubs in particular have brewlengths of either seven or fourteen barrels.

Another bit of size-related ancient history is that many other systems produced in the UK, in Canada and to a lesser extent on the European Continent were just a bit larger—10 hectoliters, or about 8.2 US barrels. As the brewpub craze lurched into motion in the mid-eighties and early nineties within such seminal entities as David Bruce's Firkin chain in England and Paul Hatfield's Spinnakers pub in Victoria, BC, fabricators built what were essentially metric-sized Grundies to answer the demand of economy-minded brewers not necessarily trying to take over the world by sheer volume. American fabricators (and brewers) tended to bump it up just a bit more to 10 US barrels, but whatever the reason—a little bigger and better, or close enough to be able to use a size mix of tanks with a little draft or cask drawn off here or there—these were the sizes with which brewing's pioneers of rediscovery chose to move out into the world.

As a potential startup today, you are in no way bound by such conventions, but it's tempting to consider seven to ten barrels the perfect startup size. Like the almost providential-seeming establishment of the 90-foot baseball basepath, which all but ensures a close play on a fast runner and a sharply hit ball, this size range just works. Seven barrels of a flagship ale will satisfy the demand of a reasonably busy 200-seat pub for a week, with supporting ale brands settling into a 1 ½-, 2- or 3-week rotation. Or it will provide 14 kegs for wholesale with each brew. With four fermentors and say half a dozen conditioning or serving tanks (with some kegs to empty tanks in order to make room, in a pub setting), a four-brew week pencils out to just under 1,500 barrels capacity. Cut that a bit if it is only one person working it, in order to allow for cellar work and other cleaning, and/or sales and delivery. Assuming other factors are in accord, this can be a profitable level of business.

Doubling the size of the brewhouse doesn't necessarily double its price, as the cost of stainless is not the only determining factor in manufacture (or resale) of equipment. In all likelihood you will need more serving or conditioning tanks. But you've also increased the efficiency of your single brewer by going to two brews a week, allowing him or her to work it pretty well alone. Notice also that I've specified ale for the harmonic perfection of such sizing. Lagers and other styles will no doubt queer the dynamic (but that's kind of what we're here for, isn't it?).

More than This...

Of course you can start out bigger than seven or fourteen barrels. It's a free country, right? At least in most states. Taking this kind of plunge requires a pretty specific (and flexible) plan: probably a hybrid of in- and out-of-house sales; or a commitment (or legal requirement) to exclusively wholesale; and the notion that expansion will take the form of multiple brew-sized fermentors. When we opened Elysian with a 20-barrel system, it seemed huge for a pub, and to be honest it took us a while to grow into it, even doing some wholesale business. Twenty barrels of wild rice ale, for example, tended to hang heavy on our hands at times. But we did grow into it, and the capacity that at the beginning seemed excessive made it possible for us to steadily grow wholesale.

Then there are concepts that start out grand, with adequate financing and gutsy vision, undertaken either by industry veterans or otherwise cold-eyed observers. These are all-in projects beyond the means of most startups. Most likely, they have an awareness of marketing, equipment and how the industry works built into them. Rather than join wary, well-served craft beer markets (Seattle, Washington or Portland, Oregon, say), startups these days are moving into possibly underserved markets such as the Southeast, Arizona and southern California. You won't find me second-guessing this approach. They leave the spirit of DIY (which I've generally tried to treat here) decidedly in the dust, but that makes them no less legitimate and honorable, especially if they have it all together and actually succeed.

Another trend I've noticed lately is the matter-of-fact thirty-barrel startup, generally intended for strictly off-premise sale and sometimes allowing for the possibility of some level of cooperative production.

Many of these folks, because of time spent in the industry, truly have the resources, the wiliness and the experience to make such a plan work. You, as a presumptive starter-upper, should be wary of this school of thought, however. It is no more "the only way to go" than the teeny-tiny startup model. The system that works for you is the system that can go with the flow.

The sky's the limit, naturally, given demand, financial wherewithal and the strength of your concept (and the quality of your beer, which these days is just table stakes). It's also possible, given the right model, to be as small as small can be. It's simply valuable in planning to run some simulations on what life will be like for any given vision once it's taken a turn for the practical. Go with God.

Chapter Highlights

Advantages to Extremely Small-Scale Brewing
- Can generally be run by a single person
- Low overhead
- Can get started right away
- Can do it anywhere

Challenges to Extremely Small-Scale Brewing
- Extremely labor-intensive (see one-person advantage above)
- Can't make much beer
- Difficult to make money
- Unsustainable over time—what's next?

Advantages to Larger-Scale Brewing (30 bbl. or more brewhouse)
- Can make enough beer to make a splash and supply a market
- Won't have to expand right away
- Lends itself to contract/alternating proprietorship brewing (see Chapter 5) to fill out production
- Costs of equipment not proportional to size increase

Challenges to Larger-Scale Brewing
- Expensive to start
- Requires experience or advance understanding of market to be able to sell that much beer
- If contract/alternating proprietorship brewing is involved, administration is required

NO PRESSURE
Committing to a Concept. Or Not.

4

From the first chair you buy or the first paintbrush you pick up, indeed from the first thought you have of what your place is going to be like, you are forming the concept of your brewery. Oh sure, there's a lot that will be dictated by safety and service standards, the physical facts of a place and the requirements of various government agencies. You can't live in an imaginary universe. Unless you decide to make that your concept. You laugh? You've obviously never been to Bardo Rodeo.

There was a time when concepts were simple, merely the outgrowth of function, the identity and look of any given place taken from the ideas and objects closest to hand. Even names were simply those of families, or perhaps that of the hill on which the brewery stood. But the woods are crowded these days, as moving and mutable—some would say as threatening—as those at the end of Macbeth. Mountains and creeks, Smiths and Joneses, resin chairs from Home Depot—you've got to do better than that if you want to be memorable and differentiate yourself from that other brewery down the road. The one named after the owner or his dog, tricked out with resin chairs maybe from Lowe's.

What's In A Name?

Amusingly enough, brewers these days think of themselves as outlaws, trendbuckers and iconoclasts. The identities and names of their places and their products show this, with references to pirates and other bandits, the rough-and-tumble side of American expansion, race cars and ribaldry—this coming from a newly-formed group of over 2,000, governed by more laws than most other industries are, and capable of debating the finest points of classic styles. The rebellion is real, but in most cases it's embedded in personal history—lots of personal histories—a reaction against the status quo rather than society at large. We're daring but responsible. We're bass players and drummers, not self-destructive lead singers, or pyrotechnic axemen. But we're still a little out there. In some ways we are classic American reinventions. We're still in the band. We may as well make the most of it.

Even we used to be more conservative. Names were often taken from the tumbledown (historic when it suited us) old buildings we saved from the wrecking ball and general lack of interest. An old-timey spin was borrowed from brewing's past and pasted on something that to us felt brand new. I blush to point out that my own company has the words "and Public House" appended to the mere facts of the matter, a hippie-ish genuflection to other eras of nostalgia, when people thought it was brilliant and hilarious to call a barber shop a tonsorial parlor. What's a barber shop? Never mind.

These days it's more likely to be Spike's or Big Al's; names, but less corporate-sounding names.

Or Two Brothers; but not which brothers, and not burdened with an archaic qualifier like "and Sons." Garden-variety fauna like the White Horse or the Fox and Hounds have given way to horrific experiments and poetical constructs like Duck-Rabbit and Bandersnatch. The eminences giving their names to bars and beers are as likely to come from Hunter S. Thompson as Samuel Coleridge, and more imaginary than real, like Magic Hat, Flying Dog or New Belgium. There was a time of heedless silliness in the mid-nineties, when both the wisdom of projects and the names given to them hit rock bottom—forgive the inadvertence. I remember consoling a fellow complaining that his beer, Red Ass, was being cheapened by a rank newcomer, Big Ass, by assuring him that his name was much more clever.

Of course your name is only part of your identity. It is a start, however, and an opportunity to put some thought into what kind of place, and what kind of beers, you intend to put your hand to. But names can be confusing, too, like the generic-sounding, one-of-us-type names given to modern-day think tanks conservative and progressive. I'd stay away from political references. We may be a secret society, but we'll spill all the details once we've had a beer or two.

Speaking of politics, there are some divides to consider when fleshing out concept and identity. And though beer and brewing seem to exist happily apart from party politics, we can still use words like "radical" and "conservative" when describing a brewery's look and feel. A stalwart porter, a crowd-pleasing pale ale, lots of wood and perhaps a fireplace, with names referring to outdoor recreation or bygone local industry—that's conservative. It isn't boring, necessarily, it's merely very safe, and it is hopefully very comfortable to a numerous and responsive clientele, to whom such nostalgic and place-specific values are meaningful. But it won't work everywhere. There are hipsters among us, after all, who might be more comfortable in an unapologetically uncomfortable wire chair, sipping tongue-wringingly bitter IPA and rocking out to thrashy music playing from the bartender's iPod. Or, in the case of a packaging brewery, with labels designed by Ralph Steadman.

In general this divide is a matter of baseline and trajectory. Do people in a given area have any idea what a brewpub or craft brewery is? Probably, at this point. But is the local market already saturated with established breweries, with one or more of perhaps regional scale? In that case it may be less important to occupy the role of pioneering evangelist than to make more of a devil-may-care statement of individuality and opposition. Much of it of course has to do with your personality and level of comfort where a potential course is concerned. We're practically past the point of filling in the blanks on the craft brewing map, and the challenge these days, while still that of the explorer, is more a matter of role and concept.

Don't think that I'm opposed to the idea of a theme, or that the post-post-modern slacker thing is where I think it's at. Craft brewing has worked its way so pervasively into everyday life and commerce that it doesn't seem odd at all anymore to have a small brewing system over in the corner of an ordinary-seeming restaurant, sports bar or casino. At a local guild meeting not long ago, raised voices called to put a legislative stop to such places coopting what we'd worked so hard to establish. My reaction was a shrug: come one, come all; when clothing stores and gas stations and bowling alleys start putting in breweries it'll only prove how complete our victory has been. To scorch the earth behind us as we gain territory simply because the types of places putting in breweries don't always correspond to our sensibilities is to mimic the industry we rebelled against in the first place. We need protections because of our size, to be sure, but none of us should consider ourselves more equal than others.

Sometimes we are literally custodians of beer culture, in its merchandise as much as in the beer we make. Brewpubs in particular have a tendency to display the signs and trays, the bottles, mugs and promotional materials of the history not just of beer and brewing but of advertising itself. The walls of our places lend themselves as de facto museums, sometimes to the extent of looking like some kind of revival ice cream parlor or the psychedelic retro zoo of the 1970s Oakland A's. And Public House—touché. I enjoy these collected remnants as much as the next fellow, but you'll need to decide how much of a museum your place should be. There are wonderful examples, such as the phenomenally appointed museum room at the Pike Pub in Seattle or the well-chosen artifacts adorning the Russian River brewery in Santa Rosa, California, where not only are beautiful new beers crafted to general acclaim, but priceless objects such as signs from New Albion are displayed for the knowledgeable. Russian River also occasionally resuscitates extinct local brands for reinterpretation and release. I mention all this not at all as a criticism but as a caution; we can't all successfully play the nostalgia card.

And since I've mentioned history and psychedelia, a few words need be said about the McMenamin's western empire. This chain includes some 50 pubs, almost precisely half of which produce beer on rudimentary brewing systems, according to local tied-house law. Along with hotels, movie theaters, ballrooms and other historic edifices, a distillery and winery and various other conceptual afterthoughts, the McMenamin's group is the quiet giant of collective concept and self-reflected reinterpretation. Other large brewpub chains take a blander route, perhaps coopting a filigree of local culture for seamless application onto a stolid corporate look, or making their primary goal to look absolutely the same. With the McMenamin concept it's as though there is an actual biological culture, a collection of ambitious and creative organisms eager to latch onto a location or project. They are then turned loose to see what combination of the bizarre, the funky, the historic, the fractally nostalgic, and even sometimes frankly the uninteresting, will be brought to bear on the agar of whatever spot has been secured. The classic McMenamin's look is decidedly trippy, with pulsing-patterned wallpaper and brewing vessels painted to look like grinning totems. They've converted classic Northwest edifices like the Spar in Olympia, Washington, the Crystal Ballroom in Portland and the old poor farm in Troutdale, Oregon which now breezes along as the Edgefield, a hotel/winery/distillery/par 3 golf course/movie theater. There are so many McMenamin's pubs that no individual need serve as flagship. Rather, each concept is content to serve as an otherwise nondescript joint serving local need, like Seattle's Roy Street pub. The resilience of the McMenamin's vision is something to

be remembered when crafting a concept, and especially when considering additional locations.

Like the decision of whether to run with a brewery nostalgia theme or put in a dozen TVs for sporting events, there are lots of ways for the water to run when the creative rains of concept are allowed to fall. High-tech, celebrating the nerdier and more technical aspects of brewing? Maybe. Funky but chic, with old couches and mismatched lamps? Or maybe you want the place to look like the space station in "2001," or the bar in "Deadwood." Maybe you're into Danish modern (careful, though, that stuff's fragile). Quite likely your concept will take its personality cues from the array of beers you brew or a food theme you've got in mind, such as really good pizza or barbecue. But it's got to be your place and show a personality not even necessarily your own yet one that differentiates and says something: come in here, get a feel for what we're doing, get a beer, eat some food and come back. Or, in the case of a packaging brewery: you liked this beer? Trust us, try our others. Keep in mind that themes and concepts are based on consistency, if not slavishness. Like the house flavors of your beers, the look of your packaging should share conceptual lines between its various labels, carriers and cases. You want to trigger a recognition in the roving consumer that causes them to make the turn or to stop in front of your little half-acre of shelf space. Anomalies are tolerated—it's funny how many breweries have a rogue brand (not the same as a Rogue brand) with a different look from the others—but all in all customers seem to appreciate picking up on the clues. It may not all be a game, but we may as well have as much fun with the creative parts as we can.

Nuts and Bolts Brewing Co.—
Some Basic Choices

Like the first of a new car model that roars down the street and turns heads as it goes, a distinctive and creative new tap handle in the alehouse array attracts the attention of more than just the cognoscenti. Tap handles are arguably the most totemic of concept and brand statements, and not just because of the way they are shaped. Like other recognized art forms given to individual interpretation—the sonnet, the pop song, or the dunk—a tap handle carries a specific message within the requirements of function and the space it is allowed to occupy. It needs in some ways to be the same as the others, but it's got to be new, distinctive, bold and fun. Why else would so many places have exhaustive displays of our collective property adorning designated walls and rails? It isn't simply to keep them on hand until the next time we manage to crack the lineup. Like other physical extensions of our brands and ourselves, tap handles most often bind together elements of whatever it is we've chosen to represent us. Bicycles or racing cars, the aviation industry, knights, baseball or the Church, wherever you've decided to run with your imagery and themes, your tap handle is a little piece of folk art. It stretches back to a grand and whimsical tradition that includes the Guinness shillelagh, the Budweiser football and the Mickey's buzzing bee. This is another thing you may as well have a good time creating.

Tap handle wars aren't just about securing space in a bar or restaurant. They can be aggressive, reactive, battery powered, beautifully machined or hand-carved. They can also go to ridiculous lengths, literally. More than a decade ago, I remember a Northwest (and likely beyond) trend when tap handles got longer and longer, outdoing each other like the skyscraper race in 1930s New York City, getting to the point where they were hitting bartenders on the head and even opening the untended tap by their sheer top-heaviness. It's one way to sell beer.

What you do with the physical facts of your brewery (and its brewers) is another opportunity to make a statement. How prominently placed, first of all, is the brewery itself? Some early brewpubs were so proud of their equipment that they put it literally in the middle of the bar or restaurant space. Operating during opening hours was deemed part of the show, but watching a pump running hot caustic from four feet away made me a little nervous on a couple of occasions, not so much for myself as for general

liability. The necessity with this kind of placement was to have all brewing-related work done invisibly and in the middle of the night, like the shoemaker's elves, presenting each morning some foaming new evidence of labor. It's pretty safe to say that whatever romance or mystique imparted to the customer was inversely proportional to that enjoyed by the brewer having to begin work at two a.m.

Sometimes the concept is so low-profile as to be barely evident. One of my places, I'll admit, is this way by necessity, with a very small brewing system tucked away in a storage room. Never mind the prominence of identifying signs and the presence of our sixteen beers on draft, lots of people don't get the fact that we brew on premise. It's always a bit of a tug-o-war between brewery and restaurant as far as space is concerned, of course. As long as it's more like a two-handed saw, with enough space and prominence devoted to each side, the job gets done.

Beyond all this there's style. Is yours to be a German-looking brewery, with bells and whistles ($), gauges and shinily functional equipment ($$) and copper vessels ($$$)? Perhaps it's a funkier and more bearded English-style outfit (¢¢), with funny and archaic-looking widgets and gadgets, and homey wooden slats around the brewing vessels. (They aren't much fun to clean around though.) Much of this will suggest the styles of beer you want, and are able to brew. And what about your brewers? Do they wear lab coats, logoed coveralls, or t-shirts from other breweries? The same goes for your floor staff.

The point to all this is that everything you do, every choice you make toward look, feel and identity reflects who you've decided to be in your little fiefdom. This includes extensions into the wider world as well, the ways you've chosen to interface with your community and the charities and non-profits you pick to support (for in truth, if you build it they will come). It doesn't all need to be a box that confines you and what you do, but it may as well be recognized that it is a package.

Chapter Highlights

Questions to Ask Yourself

- What does your name mean?
- Are you focused on geography, theme or character?
- What is the personality of the brand?
- What styles of beers will you make?
- How do you differentiate yourself from others?
- How do you fit into the traditions and movements of brewing?
- How do you define your brand identity?
- How does that identity translate to your Point of Sale (POS)/pub?

CO-OP BREWING
Putting Your Heads Together

5

One way to start a brewery is not to open a brewery at all. There are many creative ways to brew your beer in someone else's brewery. This can be either a temporary solution to the challenges of a limited budget or a sustaining model with no plan of eventual physical independence. In one such model, you could purchase finished beer and sell it as your own. In another, you could license outside premises for your company's use. Either you or your employees would staff those premises, or you might temporarily employ the staff at your host brewery. Depending on your resources, whether of money, energy or expertise, and taking into account the scope of your plan, there are many models for undertaking what we'll call cooperative brewing.

Nor is this a one-way street, it taking two to tango and all. You and your brewery may—even from the get-go—undertake with other commercial entities to produce beer in your facilities eventually to emerge under the auspices of an outside brand. It is not at all uncommon these days to hear of breweries planning to open with this model in mind. It can serve as a great way to make use of excess production capacity for the first indefinitely numbered years of existence, as home-generated brands totter to the edge of the nest and contemplate full flight. I get inquiries all the time from prospective brewers eager to dip a tentative toe into the market; everything from a hands-off nano willing to commit to a half-barrel a week to more ambitious projects involving thousands of barrels and more.

I'm Not Judging—Contract Brewing

Many breweries start as a brand. It doesn't have to cost money, after all, to dream up a name, to design a logo and fiddle with a recipe. Homebrewers are infamous for the lengths to which they'll go to create their own non-commercial brands, with a name for their brewery and beers, labels for their bottles, and business cards for the simulacrum of their hobby. It's therefore not surprising that many of them are going ahead and applying for licenses to take that last step to legitimacy. But some of the brands we know as fairly large players began their lives as companies without their own breweries, and in some cases with ideas and imagery before actual beer. Steve Hindy of Brooklyn Brewing writes in *Beer School*, the book he wrote with his co-founder Tom Potter, that one of the first challenges he faced was finding a designer to graphically display the company's identity. That designer, famously, turned out to be Milton Glaser (of Bob Dylan's Greatest Hits and I ♥ NY fame). Jim Koch of Boston Beer (Sam Adams) is proud of the efforts that went into coming up with a recipe for his flagship beer, Boston Lager, tapping both his own family lore and legacy and the services of Joe Owades (incidentally also known as the father of light beer). And who among us now remembers the very Spuds McKenzie-like cartoon dog on the original labels of Pete's Wicked Ale, a remnant no doubt of at least the sensibility of Pete Slosberg's days as a homebrewer?

What these three craft brewing pioneers have in common is the fact that their first years of brewing took place in other breweries, under contract. Slosberg never deviated from that model, in fact. They agreed on a recipe with the production brewery, then their companies, which existed primarily for sales and marketing, purchased the finished beer for resale. Brooklyn then became a successful distributor, offering other craft and craft-like brands to the clientele they built.

You too can do this. You can hit the pavement, in actuality or, figuratively speaking, on-line, with a folder of ideas to present to breweries which may be in the market to peddle some of their extra capacity. You can have your idea fully formed, with a recipe, a label, packaging concepts, a sales plan and all the rest. Or you can show up with sufficient desire and cash to make it happen using the services provided by your prospective manufacturer. Usually, it's a mixture of both these extremes. Some breweries, for example, will insist on using their house yeasts for all production (so much for your sour cherry lambic, as conceived); and of course packaging equipment is configured to accept bottles of particular size and dimension. A successful contract cooperation seeks to provide good beer, as jointly conceived, in the appropriate package, for stand-alone marketing and sale.

It used to be that fairly large regional breweries were the only ones available to undertake contract brewing. There are reasons for this, not entirely felicitous, having mainly to do with collateral damage inflicted by the biggest American brewers. These regional breweries, in short, were generally running under capacity with their own brands, and hence were willing to entertain the possibility of brewing for others. Some of these breweries were already producing dozens of brands for a hodgepodge of commercial entities—what was one more? Not that this inspires confidence. In any case, these were the possibilities, and because these brewers were often identified with a down-at-heel segment of the market, producing industrial-style brands of

subordinate prominence and price, there was something of a stigma attached. One interesting thing is that sometimes these contracts of convenience turned into fruitful partnerships. Both Brooklyn and their contract partner, FX Matt in Utica, New York, for example, have benefited greatly from their combination of long experience, marketing savvy, personality and intellect, and are both more vital because of it.

But following the mantra of this book and this movement, things have changed. Breweries of all stripes and sizes are entering into contract arrangements with each other in order to bring more beer to an increasingly craft-thirsty public. The mid 1990s were a boom time for craft brewing, mainly due to startups. The early 2010s are a boom time as well, for that same reason but also due to unprecedented expansion. Dozens of breweries have undertaken extremely ambitious growth plans, building breweries that will, by their capacities, leapfrog them out of small brewery status and into regional. There are now far more breweries with at least the capacity to entertain the contract possibility; indeed some of them have financed part of their growth by building into their plan a percentage of their (at first) unused capacity. It remains to be seen, in fact, whether all this expansion can be sustained without some cooperative component.

On the other side of the deal, breweries that brew under contract can use the opportunity to brew in someone else's facility as a way to expand. 21st Amendment, a good-sized brewpub in San Francisco without the in-house capacity to take their popular Watermelon Wheat and Brew Free or Die IPA to the market they command, has maintained a contract relationship with Cold Spring, a venerable regional brewery in Minnesota, in order not only to make more beer, but to ship to much of the country from a more central location.

And there are contract surfers. Years ago I met a Dutch brewer, Marcel Snater, who made a practice of employing the excess capacity of a succession of breweries in the Netherlands in order to brew his recipes and offer his beer for sale under a consistent label. At the time he had brewed in several breweries, and I know by my most recent trip to Holland that he's still at it, under his company name de Snaterende Arend.

You'll note that I said Marcel did his own brewing, and that's what Dann Paquette does as well, he of Pretty Things Beer and Ale Project, based in Somerville, Massachusetts. Perhaps not as nomadic as the Dutchman, Dann has produced his beer in three different breweries in Massachusetts, performing the work himself. Pretty Things refers to itself as a gypsy brewery, and has managed to negotiate a pretty free rein, employing Belgian and other less definable yeast strains in the guest production of its distinctive beers. With the eventual aspiration of having their own brewery, Dann and his wife Martha have managed to pursue commercial viability with limited resources and the cooperation of their production partners.

A Parallel Universe— Alternating Proprietorships

In some states it is possible to pursue what is essentially a contract production arrangement with greater autonomy and control, as well as the maintenance of the unbroken aegis of the branding company. This is called an alternating proprietorship, and does exactly what it says, alternating the management, supervision and production of the beer from one company to another and back again depending on the brands produced. This sounds more complicated than it is in practice, and implies a repeated schedule of replacement by staff members, along with the attendant payroll and other issues. In actuality, it is the figurative donning of special glasses, like those worn by the inhabitants of Oz in the L. Frank Baum books, which ensured that the Emerald City would always appear green. When wearing the glasses, so to speak, the employees of Brewery A, who yesterday were producing beer for their own company, are today working for Brewery B, making beer for sale under its brands. Record-keeping must be maintained separately, and in fact there must be separate and ongoing warehousing space in order that the products of the two breweries be plainly discreet and available for inspection. The responsibility for taxation and licensing falls to each brewer depending on its side of the arrangement. One important and highly justifying reason for following such an apparently convoluted path is that if the guest brewery's total production falls below the 60,000 barrel threshold of the Treasury Department's definition of a small brewer, they qualify for the reduced excise tax rate of $7.00 a barrel. To put it another way, should the host brewery's total production exceed 60,000 barrels on its own, for the production of its own brands, then any beer produced under a straight contract arrangement would be taxed at the large brewers' rate of $18.00. Confusing? Perhaps, but the last point made should serve as justification for at least finding out whether such an arrangement can work for you.

Like contract brewing, alternating proprietorship can be a way of expanding without actually expanding, or of building production and demand to the point at which it makes sense (and perhaps provides the resources) to build a brewery. The case of my own company, Elysian Brewing of Seattle, comes to bear on nearly every facet of what I've described above. We began our cooperative production arrangement with New Belgium by brewing small batches of beer for them in Seattle under an alternating proprietorship. At the same time, because Colorado did not yet allow alternating proprietorships for breweries (just wineries, oddly enough), we brewed large batches of our beers at the New Belgium brewery in Fort Collins, Colorado under contract. We all spent time traveling between each other's facilities, engaging in brewing our beers on each other's equipment. Along the way we added other locations of ours to the alternating proprietorship. Once the Colorado legislature was successfully petitioned to change the law (with the cooperation and shared lobbying expense of Elysian, New Belgium and the Colorado Brewers Guild), we switched to alternating proprietorships all around. As of this writing we are undertaking the building of a new brewery, and once it's operational, New Belgium, in an expansion mode themselves, will be happy to have their production capacity back. It remains to be seen what types of cooperation we'll put together for the future, but it's likely we'll be doing more brewing for them.

Collaboration between brewers is all the rage these days, with friends in the industry getting together to produce a joint project combining the creative energy, expertise and branding of both houses in one beer. It's like Superman and Batman joining forces in World's Finest comics, a chance for fans to enjoy something unique and probably short-lived, combining a convivial surfeit of talents. In its way it's indicative of the general good fellowship of the craft brewing movement, a fractal of the ingenuity of fruitful cooperative brewing arrangements.

The possibilities are endless where the cooperative production and branding of materials for later sale are concerned. Producing wash for an outside distillery is something my company is just now getting into, with all attendant cooperations of barrel-aging and tasting room serving; materials and expertise employed in one area will eventually yield something from another. Providing no yeast is pitched and fermentation does not occur at the brewing location, all tax issues are transferred to the distilling partner, as well as all regulatory concerns connected to the generation and distillation of alcohol. I also know of a brewery in Ontario, Beau's All Natural, which began its life leasing space in its brewery to a water company, which also incidentally supplied all brewing liquor (water for brewing). The brewery now uses more water than the little spring water concern can draw from the earth, and has effectively become the sole customer of this semi-autonomous Lichtenstein.

Goin' Up the Country—Real Cooperatives

A lot of conversation—some of it drunken—goes into taking the steps necessary to start your own brewery. A lot of it comes to nothing. A spirit of egalitarianism at first generally presides, expanding the theoretical plan to include everyone in the room, whether it's a group of longtime friends or everyone who happened to show up for that particular meeting of the Brews Brothers. "We should all start a brewery," goes the proposal, "we've got the best brewers I know right here in this room."

We'll let most of those conversations natter on, to be forgotten until the next meeting's revival, or to serve as the next step on the way to becoming the hottest new brewery in America (according to *Beer Advocate*). The ones I want to listen in on are the ones that use words like cooperative and collective, even perhaps communal, to describe the commercial entity under discussion. It might be a group startup, a bunch of people looking to share the financial impact of investment along the way to providing a springboard to a number of fledgling brands. Or it might arise from discussion among those already professional, at a brewers' guild meeting, for instance, outlining a collective expansion into a facility able to accommodate the needs of a few.

Of course there are snakes in the garden. Who's in charge of this thing, to begin with? Who pays for it, up front and as it goes merrily along? How is production allocated, and what happens when one brand takes off as others languish, hastening the day when an expansion may be required, begging all questions all over again? And what happens when somebody doesn't do the dishes, figuratively speaking? Perhaps such an arrangement is only intended as a collective springboard, to provide the participants with a convivial, Sooner-esque start to their careers, after which they leave the nest and take individual flight. With the plethora of startups these days both proto- and actual, it doesn't sound so crazy to implement facilities which specifically nurture and bring to fruition the ideas of those out there just busting to do it.

There are a lot of other, interesting aspects as well. As with other plans more centered and selfish, the key is in the vision. Rather than have the individual brands of the collective don their armor on their way out the door to do battle in the marketplace, perhaps the whole entity could be bundled together, taking advantage of a new approach to marketing and sales. A revolving door of brands may seem like an administrative nightmare, but it's also a ready-made culture of cooperation and can-do spirit, as the list of successes and also-rans lengthens. Remember Smittybrew? Smitty wasn't much of a businessman, but that was the best double IPA I ever had. You never had it? Bummer.

All that may seem too "Easy Rider"-ish to you. Contract brewing may seem too removed from the process and passion that brought you to this point. Like Baby Bear's porridge, an alternating proprietorship might seem just right. As more and more of us embark on this crazy journey, there will certainly be a lot of creative solutions to the challenge of getting it all done and out there.

Chapter Highlights

Contract Brewing

- Use others' extra capacity
- Benefit from the expertise of established industry professionals
- Perform sales/marketing
- Expand brands while staying small
- Pursue commercial viability
- Geographic separation of production sites can aid in efficiencies of shipping

Limitations of Contract Brewing

- Control over recipes (e.g., house yeast, raw materials)
- Limited input to process
- Packaging styles

Alternating Proprietorships

- Separate record keeping
- Separate warehousing
- Separate licensing
- Responsibility for taxes

Advantages of Alternating Proprietorships

- Expand production before building/expanding
- Potential tax advantages over contract with a larger partner

Real Cooperatives

- Collaboration: group of misc. brewers/brands
- Who is in charge?
- How is it paid for and when?
- How is production allocated?
- How do you deal with successful brands, or a revolving door of brands?

WEATHERING DELAYS
When Time Stands Still

6

The midterm congressional elections of 1994 brought change to the political landscape in America. In addition to other conflict and confrontation—much of which we've seen since, but which at the time was particularly acrimonious—there was a standoff about the federal budget, resulting in government shutdowns for a couple of stretches totaling about three weeks. I don't bring this up because I'm still mad about it, but because the Small Business Administration was one of the agencies suspended by the shutdown. My partners and I had just taken possession of the space that would shortly become our brewery, and we watched nervously as the stalemate stretched on. With the SBA out on furlough we couldn't access any of the money we needed to begin construction; we couldn't even contract to begin construction. We found we had no control over a situation that affected the health and vitality of our project in its earliest stages.

Planning for delays is an oxymoron, but every project encounters them. Even if you manage to open on time (and we did essentially—a scant week late) it's almost certain that it won't happen precisely the way you planned it. There will probably be a little give here and some take there, a surprise or two you'd never expect, but that won't turn out as bad as you think. That's the key right there: trying to think of as much as you can ahead of time, so that when things pop up, they merely happen; they don't floor you. Easier said than done, of course. Still, there's research to be done in your planning phases—right now, for example, before you're paying rent or for the services of experts—that can make you better prepared for some of the things that have a habit of surprising people.

An industry as heavily regulated as the production and sale of alcoholic beverages puts the fledgling participant right behind the eight ball where control is concerned. This may sting, but you'd better get used to it. It doesn't mean that you sit there passively waiting for your calls and emails to get returned and your permits to get reviewed, but it does mean that you have to recognize who's in charge and adopt a strategy of both doggedness and diplomacy. Today more than ever before, a lot of people are thinking of opening breweries. While it's important to ask for help where compliance is concerned, it's best not to needlessly or prematurely appropriate people's time. This includes your own. Do as much background research as you can before you stand in line or make an appointment. Know as much as possible before you start talking. Amid the thicket of projects, you want to be the one that gets noticed as having a chance of proceeding to completion, the one that deserves to be taken seriously and is worthy of help. You're about to move from talking to doing, after all. Don't jade some bureaucrat by chattering on about your project unless it has bearing on what you're there trying to secure. This goes for all those other permits you're going to need, too.

A lot of this will rest with experts you've paid to bring on board—electricians, plumbers, builders and other tradespeople—people familiar with codes and other requirements as well as the work they're there to do. But you are still the one in charge of the project, and if you don't have a daily awareness of where you are—not just with the work but in the permitting process—it's you who's going to be paying for more of your peoples' time and perhaps not opening on schedule. It's their job to work in the area for which they're trained; it's yours to clear the way for that work while satisfying the requirements of inspectors and bureaucrats. People often shrug philosophically about the inevitability of delays. Nothing is inevitable, even if it nearly always happens. How much money do you have to lose?

In general, codes and permits can be described as statesman Winston Churchill characterized the complexities of Russia: a riddle wrapped in a mystery inside an enigma. This isn't just a cynical take on the labyrinthine tendencies of bureaucracy, but a recognition that there can be seemingly endless layers of compliance. Some make sense and some don't, but all of them have to be checked off in order for your project to proceed. The obvious ones? Regarding your physical space, there's electrical, plumbing and structural, and each of these can be further subdivided to address specific areas of your project. For example, the concrete pad for your silo, or the fact that not only the water line to the brewery but the soda gun behind the bar needs a separate backflow preventer. Also obvious are the layers upon layers of permitting relating to alcohol. The less obvious? How about the size and type of the signs you plan to have on the outside of your place? Awnings and lighting are regulated in some neighborhoods, too, especially if it's an historic district. The benefits of locating in a cool old neighborhood or building sometimes come with a price. Where is the steam from your kettle going to go? Up a stack to the roof or with some kind of condenser which allows you to deal with it all less conspicuously?

Bathrooms alone can throw you for a loop in myriad ways. In Seattle, for example, trough urinals aren't allowed in new projects. That one cost us a thousand dollars. Of course you know that there need to be a certain number of stalls and combinations of fixtures for spaces based on seating, but what about all the things specifically related to the Americans with Disabilities Act (ADA)? These will affect the rest of your space as well, at times requiring ramps and lifts for access. All that space in bathrooms, which may seem wasteful to you as a casual customer, is required so that a wheelchair has room to move around and turn 360°. If you don't delve into the laws affecting your planned business, these are the things that can stop you in your tracks and make you spend valuable time and money to re-think.

It may seem obvious, but what you need is an overall project plan, plotted like one of those civilizational timelines of the history of the world. For you are creating a world, represented by the progress of all that must come together to create your dream. Plotted, drawn and prominently displayed, this timeline will presage the progress you'll need to see as construction, plumbing, wiring and all the rest take shape. Such a schedule can even serve as a motivational tool, pointing inexorably to the day when all work will be completed and all appropriate permits are fulfilled.

Different elements of the project will take different lengths of time. There will be days and weeks when it doesn't seem that much is happening, when a lone tile setter or electrician is just plugging away; there will be others when people can barely stay out of each other's way. Your plan will be one tool that tells you it's happening the way it's supposed to. In addition, it's an aid to scheduling peoples' time. You'd think that a downturn in the economy combined with the coolness of what you're putting together would have tradespeople clamoring for your business, but these are skilled and busy people. You can't assume they'll open-endedly make time for you when you're not sure when you're going to be ready for them. Tell them when you're going to need them and make sure that works for them. If you aren't firm about your needs and schedule, they'll find other ways to fill their time while you get it together.

Many of these project lines will be dictated by what has to come before them. For a brewery control panel to be wired, for example, sufficient electrical preparation needs to be in place. Fill in the blanks for plumbing, construction and concrete. Inspection appointments and deadlines will also dictate when work has to be done. There are hurdles both early, such as the Master Use Permit, which establishes the legal appropriateness of a proposed project, and late, like the Certificate of Occupancy, which takes all other permits into account and gives the go-ahead to admitting the paying public to the space. Your plan will have vertical lines in it, drawn across all those horizontals, which make no mistake about when a particular phase needs to be complete. Regardless of the careful planning though, don't be surprised when things don't fit; when phase C is supposed to start but phase B isn't yet complete. There will be rescheduling, and the opportunistic diversion of labors to make the best use of all resources. Keep telling yourself that's the fun part, one of the aspects in which you'll take pride once you get the doors open, that you didn't know you had in you when you got started on this whole crazy mess. In order to keep on top of all this you'll find that you need to continually redraw your plan, to reconfigure schedules and budgets based on where you are this week, today, right now. Think like basketball great Larry Bird, not with frustration and disappointment about what just failed to happen, but about what you have to do to get the job done.

Most of the foregoing models and scenarios have to do with avoiding surprise; making yourself aware of requirements, how long they will take to fulfill, and asking the right questions for each process. But what about the things that just plain come up, like that SBA/government shutdown we experienced as we were getting our project going? What if a permit just isn't coming back, even though you gave it more than what you thought was ample time? What if your electrician's band unexpectedly heads off on a European tour?

Well, where the SBA thing was concerned, there wasn't a lot we could do, aside from finding other ways to fill our time that would ultimately help in the larger effort. If the government had never resolved its differences, we never would have opened. Somehow, though, the term "hill of beans" is what occurs to me when thinking of the relative importance of a brewpub opening in Seattle compared to the mess we'd all be in right now (and still could be). If the permit process sticks, try everything you can think of, but keep in mind that what bureaucrats hate above all else is to be annoyed by people who want special treatment. You might get lucky while you're sitting there in that office. The right person might happen to walk by you, desperately needing a zinc tablet and unexpectedly becoming your friend for life because, against all odds, you happen to have one in your pocket. Good things happen to those who are prepared. And the electrician? He's got to reach for the stars, too. All you can do, once you've arranged for a replacement (and likely with his help), is recommend great places for him to drink beer in Prague.

Scenarios of the unexpected mainly point out that you are dependant on a great number of people to bring your project to fruition. People can let you down, either by not coming through for you, or by simply by not being the puppets you often wish they were. That said, it's better to stick with one person than have to retell your story and basically start all over each time you encounter a different face behind the desk. Politics happen. Be aware of what's on the horizon, and have an inkling of what might come up—it can go a long way toward dealing with crisis or disappointment. Oh, and having a budget flexible enough to weather the occasional surprise without shutting you down helps too.

Horror stories abound of municipalities deciding they'd better take a last-minute look at brewery piping, of basement tanks and other hidden toxicities surfacing, or environmental rethinks dawning on you only after most of the work is done. It's possible, for example, to discover in the course of your own permitting that your space should have been built a certain way, but wasn't. Take two steps back as you bring someone else's mess up to code. Remedies for all of this? Know your space the best you possibly can, and know the people you hire to work on it, not just for the necessary construction, but for all required permits and inspections.

Chapter Highlights

Planning for Delays

- Think of as many things as you can that could go wrong.
- Prepare well for compliance meetings and shepherd permits through.

Pay Special Attention To:

- Electrical permits/inspections
- Plumbing permits/inspections
- Structural permits/inspections
- Health and safety inspections
- Air quality permits
- Wastewater restrictions
- Local sign ordinances
- Historical neighborhood/building restrictions
- Americans with Disabilities Act (ADA) compliance
- Master Use Permit
- Certificate of Occupancy

Scheduling

- Plan for contractors and the arrival and installation of equipment.
- Continually reassess progress.
- Adjust schedule as needed.
- Don't assume your contractors are as flexible as you want them to be.
- Expect the unexpected.

HUMAN RESOURCES
Finding the Perfect Fit

7

For most startups, the duties of a Human Resources department are practically limited to arranging for trash pickup or thanking the mail carrier when they come through the door. It often doesn't feel as though hiring and managing a staff is something that will ever be necessary or, if it is, more than obvious. But jump the timeline of your company ahead even several months and the wisdom of figuring a few things out at the get-go will become apparent. Take your corporate philosophy or mission statement, for example. It might just seem like words on a page placating the most sensitive of your partners, but in even a raw form it can determine how you treat your co-workers as you bring them on and what you stand for in the landscape of striving, sometimes struggling small business. For in so many ways, it's important to have a plan—from figuring out which products to put forth in the market, to managing a distribution network, to deciding which pieces of equipment to add or improve along the way. Planning to hire and develop a staff can be an easy thing to neglect amid all the hubbub and emergency, but it can also be fundamental to determining the type and timing of the steps you take as you move forward.

Many companies begin in a spirit of altruism, intending to provide competitive wages, full health benefits and humane and generous retirement plans. Sadly, and especially in this country, where such things are rarely a birthright, implementing even one of these ideals is a challengingly expensive commitment. This certainly doesn't mean that it shouldn't be attempted and planned for, perhaps in stages, as the situation permits. Government occasionally and variously steps in, such as today's gradual health care plan development, or simply in the enforcement of a minimum wage. This last might seem a no-brainer in its inadequacy, but take a look at some of our western states contrasted with the East's general pittance mandated for say, tipped employees; the payroll philosophy of even a small western pub must take into account that servers and bartenders are often paid what kitchen workers are, and get tipped besides. Being forced to bankroll certain things, after all, constrains other programs that might be considered elective.

Setting aside philosophical differences for a moment, consider that in a generally expanding segment of business you are competing with other companies for your workers. Imbuing your workers and workplace with the passion, decency and rightness of what you're doing may inspire staff loyalty all by itself. But as workers on strike often say, you can't eat prestige. People need to be treated at least fairly or they will leave. The place that at least makes an effort to recognize their security and happiness has a better chance of winning their loyalty. This can mean offering them anything from higher salaries to a share in the company. We'll try to take a look at many of these possibilities later on.

Timing, Wage and the Management of Expectation

Perhaps the first formative decision of an HR director, even if that person is also the brewer, bookkeeper and bartender, is when to bring in extra help. Having your hands full is obviously one of the first considerations. Having them so full that bringing in someone else might mean your own increased effectiveness in an area where your talents and inclinations lie is a more practical way to look at it. Division of labor in a growing company is an essential part of the process, on up to the top levels. The CEO who supervises each broom stroke or insists on being on hand for all equipment maintenance is a person who perhaps can't decide whether to keep his or her hands clean or dirty in the administration of the company. Conversely, it's foolish to delegate critical tasks that demand your expertise. Being able to afford help, well, that's kind of up to you. You might decide the best use of resources is to bring in an HR director part-time to help sketch out the rest of the plan in the time you can afford to pay them.

But first, a word on the unpaid intern. Many companies enlist people who are paid nothing for their labors, but commit to showing up and slaving (almost literally) for the experience of it all. Many times these people come affiliated with an academic-styled program such as the American Brewers Guild, in which case the internship period of their instruction serves as a crowning practicum to a course designed to provide an array of formal classroom and on-line coursework and hands-on experience. I view this type of intern, connected as he or she is with an essentially vocational program, as a duty for those of us able to take them on. The unaffiliated, unpaid keg washer or delivery driver I consider an exploitation of the eagerness of many to get into our industry. In fact there is some indication that the Department of Labor may take steps to prohibit such non-academic "internship". Refusing to pay such a person a fair price for their labors is not only unfair, it sends a message

of lesser valuation to those who either do or would do such things for an actual wage. If they work for you, pay them a fair wage.

This being said, there is a range of wage appropriate to each task in the brewery. The keg washer (or even cellarperson or shift brewer) who continues for years in an unexpanded and unchanging role should not expect to rise above a certain wage ceiling merely on the basis of longevity. Increases in pay need to be justified in terms of a broadening responsibility and expertise. It's more common, of course, for the professionally inexperienced worker to begin in a menial capacity and eventually "graduate" into a role of greater responsibility and compensation. It's also appropriate to reward loyalty and longevity with increased pay, as long as it all makes sense in the larger payroll picture.

This larger picture, though, is sometimes hard to grasp. I've heard many in the past several years describe their staff expansions as being, because of sustained growth in our industry in general, ahead of the curve. This is fine for the most wildly successful among us. For those of us growing more moderately or even slowly, this kind of extravagance can result in overpaid staff or over-staffing, a period of awkwardness to be weathered as the company gambles on growing into a need for its new people. No template or survey can tell precisely the right time to bring on additional staff or what to pay them, but the BA salary survey outlined in the biannual *Brewers Resource Directory* is a good place to at least build an awareness of what our industry pays.

Of course there are strategies for easing people into job responsibility and the wage that comes with it. When I was offered my first brewing job in the early 1990s it was at a preliminary wage of five dollars an hour. My duties at first were mainly demolition; when I started actually brewing I got a 40% raise, to seven dollars an hour. Could I realistically live on this, with a one-year-old child and a struggling marriage, even given the almost antediluvian timeframe? Could I afford to get a haircut? I did it, however, mainly (but not always) cheerfully, because as a homebrewer of not much more than a year's experience it gave me a shot. Soon I was brewing my own recipes, living, I guess you could say, on prestige. In that same job hunt I visited nearly every brewery in town and the environs. Showing up at what then was the largest production brewery in Seattle, I got an audience with the brewmaster and announced, without quite knowing what I was saying, that I wanted to work in the brewhouse. Appropriately, he laughed politely and encouraged me in my search as he didn't at the moment need a keg de-bunger.

Even the experienced brewer at a small pub cannot expect to vault into operating an automated system on the brewdeck of the largest brewery in town. He or she may be able to start in the cellar or on the packaging line and prove his or her worth, perhaps eventually moving into a position of greater trust, control and authority. Recognizing the potential and drive of prospective staff is a good way to start a working relationship. I know of top executives in successful and highly regarded breweries who started as tour guides and on the bottling line. It can be gratifyingly corroborative for people to grow in their roles and find new ones as their lives change and their company grows.

It's so obvious as to barely be worth mentioning, but hiring your friends and family will change your relationships with them. It's not easy to suddenly take on the role of employee or boss, especially when that role requires making difficult decisions. Even equal partnerships change relationships, frequently cooling them to mere functionality. Realistically, however, the employment pools of startup companies usually overlap with at least acquaintance. My best advice would be to go into the process with eyes open and eventualities weighed.

Sometimes there isn't time to bring people along from within. Such cases as precipitous expansion often require advertising, recruiting and considering people from farther flung geographies perhaps more skilled and experienced than those one might find closer to home. In such cases it's likely you'll need to pay more than you might for an internal move upstairs, and offer travel, lodging and perhaps moving expenses for the deal to proceed. All this needs to be taken into account, once again, in the overall payroll scene, and perhaps managed within a company which has grown beyond just bringing existing staff along.

Not everyone thrives or keeps pace with a changing company. It sounds harsh to say, but the person who can run a department proficiently when a company is small isn't necessarily the best qualified to take it to the next level, or the one after that. Sometimes people simply burn out. Sometimes they feel threatened by what they see as fundamental change. Sometimes the solid shift worker doesn't turn out to be a good manager. These are tough situations to navigate. Of course there are solutions less draconian than simply giving up on a co-worker of years' standing. It's important to recognize, without judgment, that a job and a role doesn't necessarily come with a trajectory; it can be okay to stay where you are, or to move sideways into another role, or even to settle into a position of less responsibility.

Salaries both hourly and fixed are generally discussed in sort of a blanket way, but there are important differences to be considered in the way people are paid, from the standpoint of both workers and management. Hourly wages, with appropriate paid overtime, work well in many cases, as they correspond directly to the time worked. Weekends, holidays and overnight shifts can have augmented pay built in in a predictable and systematic fashion. The move to a flat salary sometimes works well too, as long as it benefits all concerned, and as long as the job in question is legally appropriate to be salaried, as defined by the Department of Labor (DOL). The purpose of such a change should not, from a management point of view, be to wring another twenty hours a week out of a devoted employee. It should bring greater flexibility in both directions, contracting at times and at others expanding to accommodate crunches and increased demand. It can also render less untidy and onerous such things as dropping by to check gravities or heat brewing water. Times of extended work should be paid back with a little time off. A person on salary is generally a person with some prestige, who can be trusted to manage their own time and organize their own priorities with the greater good of the company in mind. As defined by DOL, he or she is involved in critical business decisions, managing other people, or making sales transactions. But not everyone functions as well under salary, or is as happy as they might be in a more tightly structured pay arrangement. Salaried positions carry additional rights and rewards along with increased responsibility. Moving into such a tier is often an earmark of management or quasi-management status. It can also trigger certain benefits not always offered to hourly staff, such as health insurance, extended vacation time or the establishment of a retirement plan. There are ways to put it all together that make sense, and that benefits rather than exploits those entering into it. As base wages are established you can consider how benefits and potentially some form of bonus or profit sharing plan can balance the needs of the people.

Health Benefits, Retirement Plans and Employee Ownership

As earlier observed, benefit plans are expensive to maintain. They are also an excellent way to reward and care for co-workers beyond simply paying them, especially as in the early days of many businesses actual cash is tighter than deferred compensations. The decision to implement such a plan should be based on your long-term vision of corporate identity. Not all of us do a great job with this, especially in contrast with companies in our industry renowned for employee satisfaction and devotion. Success stories like New Belgium and Sierra Nevada have been profitable enough to reward their staff with impressive and laudable benefits, thus acting as role models for business and industry at large. It can be argued that such lavish benefits are in most cases contingent on the success of the company, but conversely, starting out with your employees' best interests in mind may go a long way towards achieving success. Everyone has to start somewhere.

Some health protections, such as those mandated by state departments of Labor and Industry, are built into the relationships between workers and employers. Injuries sustained on the job are thereby taken care of through insurance carried by the company. Health care undertaken outside of work is of course a whole different story, as is coverage for any missed time at work. It is impossible to generalize about plans, coverage and balances of arrangement, especially as our country continues to wrangle about the best ways

to handle it all. It is the responsibility of any company to be aware, at the very least, of plans available for the protection and care of its workers. Whether it can afford to undertake such coverage on its own, or in cooperation with and copayment by its workers, is truly something to be weighed in each individual case.

The issue becomes particularly thorny for brewpubs, which often have, especially in their servers, a young and transitory group of workers who often don't see a benefit in the kinds of things deemed essential by families and older workers. Many restaurant employees are also part-time, and so may not even qualify for present-model plans regardless of interest and engagement. Possible scenarios requiring blanket coverage of all staff may necessitate the consolidation of working hours into full-time blocks, thereby placing pressure on the few-shifts-a-week employees. I bring these things up not to editorialize, but to put a few things before you as you contemplate which route to take on a challenging journey.

Nearly as many options exist when it comes to retirement plans. Probably most common—aside from not offering anything at all—is some kind of 401K, in which employers may augment some level of employee contribution. Employee savings accrue, and can be cashed out or rolled over into some other plan if they leave the company. Once again, a young workforce may not care about such plans, or may regard them as yet another paycheck deduction. As a company grows and matures, however, so do its workers. Retirement savings will eventually take on value, even if it's simply to redeem them.

In the old, traditional, paternalistic way of doing business, there are owners and there are employees, period. Different models involving cooperative or employee ownership have also appeared here and there, providing life-sustaining benefit to workers; and they are not all modern. The mainly Quaker founders of Victorian chocolate works, for example, held as a cornerstone of responsible business the care and housing of their staffs and their families, even the locations of their factories in places salubrious and considerate of their workforce—this in the face of widespread Industrial Revolution-era exploitation. In addition to generally being an industry founded and sustained by progressive and large-hearted people, ours is fast maturing to the point at which succession will become a fairly loud and frequent refrain. What this may mean, on both counts, is that various schemes of cooperative ownership are sure to be increasingly discussed and undertaken. For not only does a measure of employee ownership engage those participating in it and reward loyalty, longevity and performance, it can serve as a way of compensating founders as they move toward the next phases of their lives.

An ESOP, or Employee Stock Ownership Plan, is a larger construct than will likely be considered for even a forward-thinking startup brewery or any other fledgling business. Its administrative demands are relatively large, both in terms of cost and oversight. It also requires the participation of a large percentage of company employees in order simply to exist. Once a company grows to a certain point, however—and as Craft continues to grow there are more such companies each year—an ESOP or some variation on its themes may become a viable option for co-worker reward.

An ESOP provides a vehicle for employee ownership through a trust. To initiate an ESOP, an owner of a company will sell all or a portion of his shares to the ESOP trust. To purchase the shares from the owner, the ESOP trust will take out a loan. The shares and typically some cash are held in each participant's, name until he leaves the company. On the surface, the structure is similar to that of a retirement plan including a vesting schedule. However, the assets of this retirement plan are substantially or fully invested in company stock, providing a type of long term incentive plan where accounts will grow as the value of the stock grows. This creates the ownership attitude and the incentive to see a retirement asset grow as each person invests his time, energy and talent in to the business.

So if an ESOP isn't a realistic option for a fledgling brewpub or packaging brewery, why treat it here in such detail? First, because as a responsible founder and owner of a business of any size, it's important to know some of the different ways that business can work. Next, they can act as an incentive to engagement. In short, the arc of the growth of your business might sooner or later take you to the point at which such a construct is an option. Finally, and perhaps in some combination with the above, there are lessons to be learned from the ESOP model that can inform other programs of employee ownership.

One of the benefits of the C type of corporation (see Chapter 13 for the finer points of this designation) is that different classes of stock can exist. This means, for example, that in addition to the shares purchased at the outset by investors in the company, another group of shares can be issued and distributed to, say, co-workers of long standing and a high level of involvement, as a benefit to ongoing employment. Voila! It's possible, even on a smallish scale, to put together programs of ownership for the employees of your company. Why should you share your success, you may ask, if you don't actually receive cash for these shares? I'm going to leave that to you and three in the morning. The point is that there are many custom options to give your co-workers a personal stake in the company should you decide to engage them as partial co-owners.

Naturally there are tax ramifications that make such a scenario too good to be true in its simplest iteration. What sometimes happens in these cases is that the company budgets for and undertakes such responsibility as part of greater compensation, for which, of course, there is still individual tax responsibility. Sometimes the better solution is to create a share value or profit-pegged bonus pool, distributed proportionally by wage, stature or longevity—likely a matrix of these and other factors—as a means of sharing the wealth (should you be so lucky), as well as creating shared value in the company—building a bigger, better pie. In any case, there's advice to be taken from our more mature and successful siblings when we seek to reward the loyalty and effectiveness of our staff.

Chapter Highlights

- Be aware of industry salary ranges
  (*Brewers' Resource Directory*).
- Recognize and reward potential with moving up/
  greater responsibilities.
- Salaried personnel are generally considered
  management.
- Ensure compliance with state mandated protec-
  tions and insurance.
- Weigh the benefits of providing, well, bene-
  fits—401Ks, health insurance, etc.
- Retirement plans add value as employees mature.
- Employee ownership rewards loyalty, longevity and
  performance.

STARTING UP/ GROWING UP

WRITING YOUR BUSINESS PLAN
Speculative Nonfiction

8

A business plan is like a treatment for a screenplay. It outlines the workings and gives a feel for a complete project, which if supported and financed, could actually come to pass. One could argue that it's a work of fiction, since much of what it describes is not yet real; many of the characters depicted are only nameless sketches, to be hired and fleshed out later, and the monies described as disbursed are as fantastical as treasure in the Arabian Nights. It is a creative work, to be sure, and it needs to be gripping and entertaining, evocative and inviting, but it also needs to display seriousness and understanding, to engage the analytical and not just the narrative reader. Like any piece of good writing it needs to be credible. It should also be original, displaying to the reader why this plan above others deserves to be financed and brought to fruition. In this time of booming expansion it's likely yours won't be the only brewery plan to cross the desks and coffee shop tables of potential investors. So you've got to make the most of it without being overly ambitious.

But even though you need to get your reader's attention, a business plan must follow a fairly rigid template. Properly executed, it should present both sides of the brain of a project, the part to get excited about and the part that shows an understanding of the market, and business in general. Its writing should be spare and straightforward, explaining

and elucidating without bravado. The validity of your plan, after all, should be evident by your analyses and presentation, and not because you have a killer recipe for a beer (we've all got those). Its numbers as well should explain the workings of the project, expressed in pro formas stretching out for the potential first few years of doing business, expressing in reality-based terms the financial ins and outs of making and selling beer and perhaps other products within the framework of your ideas. It needs to bring the reader up to speed where the brewing industry is concerned, and if you're planning a pub, the restaurant industry as well, so that your specific ideas have some meaningful context.

However little actual writing there may be in it, it does take time to write a business plan. This is because while it is primarily a tool for raising money, it's also an exercise in focus for you, requiring competence and understanding of each aspect of your potential business. You'll probably need to do a lot of research in order that both your words and your numbers present your ideas accurately, and then you'll need to hone your presentation of them, cutting out extraneous expression but still telling the whole story. Unless you somehow manage to hit an easy home run where finding investment is concerned, you'll need to satisfy different types of investors: the kind that skip straight to the numbers and the kind that want to get a feel for the concept by absorbing the more narrative statements. There are different psychologies for this. It's a bit general to say so, but most numbers people—the ones who evaluate business prospects for a living, for example—wouldn't even be looking at your plan unless they've already made some decision based on what they know about you. They may not feel they need to read your statements of concept and operation; they just want to see if you know what you're talking about. But then there are people who decide things with their heart. They'll want the numbers to make sense, but what they really want is to have a good feeling about where, and with whom, they're putting their money, and to sense the validity of a project in the way it's presented in words.

Again, it's a bit general to say, but these are probably going to be your friendlier, smaller investors.

Baring Your Soul: A Business Plan with the Advantage of Hindsight

What follows is the entirety of an actual business plan couched in the offering circular that my partners and I wrote during 1994 and '95 for what would become Elysian Brewing Company. It has been amended with comments and insights we've accumulated since then and this, coupled with the sample business plan in the appendix, should assist you with outlining the plan for your own business.

Elysian Brewing Company, Inc.
Offering Circular
April 30th, 1995

THE UNITED STATES SECURITIES AND EXCHANGE COMMISSION DOES NOT PASS UPON THE MERITS OF OR GIVE ITS APPROVAL TO ANY SECURITIES OFFERED OR THE TERMS OF THE OFFERING, NOR DOES IT PASS UPON THE ACCURACY OR COMPLETENESS OF ANY OFFERING CIRCULAR OR OFFERED SELLING LITERATURE. THESE SECURITIES ARE OFFERED PURSUANT TO AN EXEMPTION FROM REGISTRATION WITH THE COMMISSION; HOWEVER, THE COMMISSION HAS NOT MADE AN INDEPENDENT DETERMINATION THAT THE SECURITIES OFFERED HEREUNDER ARE EXEMPT FROM REGISTRATION.

This, of course, is the front cover of the document. It isn't particularly jazzy; a later version bore a photograph of the location which we had by then secured, and for which we still needed to raise about twenty percent of needed funds. The main thing here is the disclaimer of any perceived or sanctioned legitimacy. Essentially: Abandon all hope of legal recourse should this simply turn out to be an unsuccessful investment.

PROPOSAL FOR THE ELYSIAN BREWING COMPANY, INC.

The Elysian Brewing Company, Inc. is to be a brewpub/restaurant, serving hearty, intriguing and value-conscious fare with a brewing capacity of 5,000 barrels. In addition to Elysian's in-house sales, outside distribution of beer will constitute up to 60% of production, thus positioning Elysian as both a tavern and a production microbrewery. While no location has yet been secured, the area in Seattle in which we have decided to establish our operations is the Capitol Hill/First Hill zone. Elysian's three officers are Joe Bisacca, currently a vice president with Seafirst Bank; Dick Cantwell, head brewer at Big Time Brewery and Alehouse; and David Buhler, president of Brix° Marketing, a company dealing with imported and Northwest specialty beers.

This statement of intent and trajectory could hardly be simpler. It states the concept of a distributing pub, which oddly enough, in those days, was something that hadn't been tried all that much, and not at all in Seattle, save at the aforementioned Big Time Brewery and Alehouse. At Big Time I had managed to increase production by a few hundred barrels by undertaking some (extremely) limited outside sales. This seemed to us an idea worth expanding upon. In very few words it states the restaurant segment it intends to serve: "value-conscious", suggesting somewhere between high-end and bare bones chips-and-salsa. It admits that while it has a neighborhood in mind, it hasn't found a location yet. Finally, it presents the three people putting the plan together, with the briefest mention of their qualifications.

It's interesting (to me, at least) to be struck by the fact that prior to our most recent expansion to a production brewery, the output at our original Capitol Hill location was at around 5500 barrels for the past few years. We have stuck to the value-conscious thing, and the three original partners are still involved in day-to-day operations, albeit in somewhat different roles.

The principle of the brewpub is one probably familiar to most people aware of the brewing renaissance in this and other countries. In a brewpub the beer served is brewed on the premises, and may be distributed as far afield as production practically allows. Though brewing sets the brewpub apart from other restaurant operations the food remains an essential part of the equation—the successful brewpub is also a successful restaurant.

The principle of the brewpub is of course even more familiar these days than it was back when this was written. Washington state law allows for distribution (including self-distribution) by brewpubs, but such is not the case everywhere. The hybrid model we outlined in our business plan would be illegal in many states. A number of brewpubs went out of business during the movement's early days because of a lack of attention and seriousness where food was concerned. We state here that we won't take our food for granted.

It will come as no surprise to anyone in the Northwest that the craft brewing movement is well along in the process of taking the country by storm. Some 470 pub and production craft breweries are operating today in the United States. The market share of craft breweries has steadily increased while nationwide overall beer sales have flattened and begun to decline. Since the beginning of the movement, the Northwest, along with Northern California, has constituted its most active region: nationwide, craft breweries account for approximately 1% of the total US beer market; in Washington the figure has topped 4% in total sales. Recently Miller Brewing bought 51% of Celis Brewing, a Belgian-styled craft brewery, and Anheuser-Busch is test marketing a hefeweizen under their new craft brewery label Crossroads. Anheuser-Busch also has a marketing agreement with Redhook for national distribution.

Where to start? We've come a long way since then, with even more strictly defined craft beer market share well above 6% nationally as of this writing. Every region now boasts hefty numbers of craft breweries. The number of craft breweries in America has more than quadrupled the number stated here, which was intended to goggle the eyes of potential investors. Big brewers who took notice back in 1995 continue to do so today, spawning craft-competitive brands like Blue Moon and Shock Top, and agreements between Anheuser-Busch and Widmer Brothers, Goose Island, Kona and others, to say nothing of Inbev.

Elysian proposes not just to be another brewpub (although it is our feeling that this type of business remains inadequately exploited in Seattle), but to be three related businesses: a brewpub serving top-quality ales and lagers, both of our own production and those available on the wholesale market, and offering simple and value-conscious, yet artfully-crafted fare; a 20-barrel brewery with a yearly capacity of 5,000 barrels; and a wholesale distributor which supplies the needs of selected taverns in the local market. This triumvirate of related businesses is something that has not been explored in the Seattle market, though combinations of the various elements have been carried out in other areas of the country, most notably with many of Colorado's 43 craft breweries.

In a state allowing distribution of a brewpub's products, this may seem a fairly obvious model. Still, I think it shows an awareness of the market gained from within it. It might seem that we were then proposing to be a craft distributor along the lines of those established by Brooklyn, Stone or perhaps Two Brothers in the Chicago area, but such a plan was not in fact on our minds. We meant only to distribute our own beers. Colorado, well, they've grown, too, and continue to be one of craft brewing's leaders in business innovation.

COMPANY OWNERSHIP

The Elysian Brewing Corporation will raise $750,000 for the construction of the brewpub and first year of operations. $250,000 will be from equity investors and $500,000 in the form of an SBA loan.

We will be organized as a Washington State sub-chapter S corporation under federal rule 504 and Washington State offering small-offering exemption, which limits us to a maximum of 35 investors of which 20 may be non-accredited.

50,000 shares of common stock will be authorized and 10,000 issued. Of these, 3333 will be offered for equity ownership at $75.00 per share. The minimum subscription is 100 shares, and maximum subscription is 600 shares, though both minimum and maximum subscriptions are subject to waiver by the company. These funds will be escrowed in an interest-bearing account prior to the formal application to the SBA. Of the remaining 6667 issued shares, 500 shares will initially be allocated to each of the three officers upon opening. The Elysian officers will retain voting rights to the 5167 outstanding shares and this remaining equity ownership will be transferred to the officers in direct proportion as the SBA loan is paid down.

These shares are restricted for resale by the Washington State Department of Securities and will have restrictions placed on them by the Corporation. There is no guarantee that a resale market will exist for Elysian's shares. If more shares are issued or a secondary offering is made, shareholders will have preemptive right to maintain their percentage of equity in the Elysian Brewing Company.

An advisory committee made up of shareholders, industry personnel and friends from the community will be established to provide objective input to the board of directors.

Well. $750,000 turned out to be within just a few thousand dollars of enough to get the doors open a week or so later than a year after the date of this circular. We didn't have a sign and mice lived in the couches, but we made beer and served food, and we paid ourselves and our staff. We did raise $250,000 from equity investors, and we did secure a $500,000 SBA loan.

One of the decisions to be made in forming a company is which way to go on the road that determines corporate structure and classification. The most commonly taken options are S and C corporations, as referring to the respective sub-chapters in Internal Revenue code. There are several differences between them, but the one most often used in making a decision is the way dividends and losses are treated for taxation. S-corporations pass gains and losses on to their investors for tax responsibility, thereby eliminating the need to pay corporate income taxes. It makes for simpler organization within the company, and ensures that taxes are paid only once, and beyond the ring of direct corporate control. It does come with some restriction, such as the necessity of all investors being US citizens, which is specifically why we ended up going the other way, as a C-corporation. As things shook out, a couple of our investors were British. A C-corporation is required to pay income taxes, and any benefits passed on to shareholders are taxed at their personal level as well. There are benefits to organization as a C-corp, such as the ability to have different classes of shares and greater flexibility when it comes to selling the company. It makes things more complex within the company (though with greater overall control), but relatively simple where the shareholders are concerned, especially if the company chooses to grow. Profits are reinvested rather than paid out, perhaps extending the eventual shareholder benefit in favor of paying taxes on those profits twice—at least for the moment.

Another option is to become a Limited Liability Company, or LLC. Like both S- and C-corporations, LLC provides protection from risk to operators of the company. It is less restrictive in that more than a hundred investors can take part and there is no citizenship requirement. It does generally come with more involvement by shareholders, and it is less easy for principal operators to draw a salary as an employee—compensation is generally more closely tied to operating profit. Like the S-corp, tax responsibility is "passed through" the workings of the company to individual investors. LLCs also often have a term for their existence, and so must either be disbanded, re-formed or merged into another corporate entity.

Confused? The good thing is that these days it is easy to ask questions without embarrassing yourself, on the Internet. The SBA provides good definitions of the differences of corporate organization, as do the websites of many legal service organizations and firms themselves engaged in steering their customers through it all.

The next paragraph covers the numbers of shares and their control and disbursement. It may seem like a morass, but it both ensures control of the directional ownership decisions possibly encountered as the company grows, and most importantly, it describes how ownership of the company will be gradually transferred to the principal partners. It establishes expectations as to the size of individual investment but does not absolutely restrict them. This became useful in the late stages of fundraising, when we still needed money but felt confident enough about the closeness of the goal to be able to welcome investors smaller than 100 shares. It also provides both structure and incentive for the transfer of stock to the three of us who started the company, assembled the investors and took on the risk of the loan. You may have noticed that we put in very little money for the initial investment—only a few thousand dollars each, truth be told, when gaps needed to be closed. This was something that a couple of prospective investors objected to (and because of this chose not to invest, feeling that without actual "skin in the game" we might not take the whole thing sufficiently seriously). But it showed that we planned to stick it out, investing a substantial chunk of our lives in managing a company that we would not actually own until we'd been running it for some time.

Then there's that last bit, in which we assume the willingness of everyone else in the world to get together for a couple of beers and tell us how great we are. We eventually expanded our board of directors beyond just the three of us, thereby formalizing what would otherwise have been a fairly loose arrangement. I suppose we convened our "advisory committee" anytime we talked business with our friends.

CONCEPT

Treating the three elements of the business separately:

In addition to pouring five to seven of the beers produced on the premises, Elysian's **Brewpub** will offer the best and most popular import/specialty and craft beers available on the wholesale market. In this way the pub will be able to draw not just on the loyal clientele devoted to the beers produced on-site, but on customers interested in the beers available in the movement at-large. Elysian's in-house-produced beers will answer the demand for aggressive Northwest ale mainstays (India Pale Ale and a heavy Porter or Stout) as well as departing from a regional trend to date by offering at least three lager beers at all times (a Pilsner, a Dortmund-style Export and a Munich dark lager). In addition, two or more seasonal specialties will be served.

The Elysian menu will offer both good value and innovative cuisine. An array of soups and stews, including vegetarian offerings, will provide the core of the menu, along with sandwiches and salads. More involved main courses will available as specials. Beer will be emphasized not just as an accompaniment to the food, but as a recipe element in many of the menu items. The Elysian will be as much self-service as possible, with food orders taken at a window and food served either directly to hand or delivered to tables by a runner from the kitchen. In this way a rustic and unintimidating style can be established, while maintaining efficient labor costs.

With the 20-barrel brewhouse, the **Brewery** will be large enough to have an ongoing presence in the wholesale market while still amply supplying the taps of a successful brewpub. Too often breweries are designed too small to serve an expanding need for their products. Both Pike Place's (4-barrel) and Big Time's (14-barrel) brewhouses, for example, are inadequate to supply local demand for their beer. With a larger brewhouse, Elysian will commence operations with the ability to claim and hold an everyday presence in the local wholesale market, as well as offering beer styles previously unavailable. We will have an exciting array of beers on tap at the Elysian pub and supply the wholesale demand for our products. Because of the profit margin, it is in our interest to pour as much beer as possible through the taps in Elysian's pub; the larger brewhouse will enable us to exploit the wholesale market as a complement to seasonal and consumer trends in the pub.

The **Wholesale/marketing** aspect of Elysian will coordinate brewery production to make the most efficient use of our capacity, both in-house and in the local market. This department will have a substantial voice in brewery operations, responsive to consumer demand and preference. Moreover, as each Elysian handle in local pubs represents not only a sales outlet for our beer but also acts as a direct advertisement for our brewpub, an essential aspect of the marketing department will be establishing and maintaining rapport with our wholesale clients. The marketing/wholesale department constitutes a key voice in the coordination of Elysian's production power.

As presented, the brewpub concept is fairly straightforward, even somewhat innovative for 1995, even if things didn't work out exactly the way we thought they might. Take pouring outside beers. It was nice to pay homage to our friends in other breweries by buying and then offering their beers for sale. The night we opened, in fact, since we had only one beer we had actually brewed, we poured beers from all the breweries any of us had ever worked at. But aside from imported kegs that came into town in very small quantities, and which aroused the interest of those paying attention—and this was before Facebook, and Twitter—some of the best beers being produced in the Northwest languished in our lineup. The good news was people were there for our beer. This doesn't expose the concept as flawed; it just didn't work for us precisely the way we had envisioned it.

The description of our food is general enough not to be worth analyzing, but the notion that we could get people to essentially serve themselves was discarded early in the planning process. Places like Big Time succeed in getting customers to submit to ordering at a counter and then having their food delivered. But Big Time is in Seattle's University District, where people are used to standing in line; to register for classes, for example, to eat in cafeterias, or to find a seat in the lecture hall. It was not going to work in our freer-spirited neighborhood. We had table service from the start.

Though we encountered more resistance in our own neighborhood than we thought we would—our pub competed with other bars and restaurants even if we were the neighborhood's only brewery at the time—the advertising aspect of having tap handles around town in our minds justified the lower margin of wholesale price. Or did I just say the same thing twice?

MARKET ANALYSIS

Since 1983 when Redhook Brewery first opened in Seattle, the craft brewing movement has evolved from a fad to a fixture. From a handful of pioneers to 471 craft breweries as of September 1994 (according to figures compiled by the Institute for Brewing Studies), the current national market share of 1% is expected to double in two years. Four straight 40% growth years have brought craft brewing industry sales close to one billion dollars. This is still only 1% of the national beer market. In the state of Washington, the craft brewing market share has topped 4% total, with a draught share of 17%. Within Seattle, both these figures are significantly higher. So far the main impediment to growth, both within individual breweries and the movement at large, has been production capacity.

A couple of bar graphs accompanied this paragraph, showing the steady progress, over the previous handful of years, of craft sales in Washington. They, and the gist of the above verbiage, continue to compel, as their general trend has continued onward to today. Sure, there have been a couple of "landings" along the way signifying periods of slower growth, but it's clear we collectively occupy a market segment that keeps on growing. Whatever problems and challenges might beset craft brewers in the future—availability of raw materials, access to market, infighting, succession—lack of demand will almost certainly not be one of them.

CAPITOL HILL

With over 17,000 households and 40 units per acre, the Capitol Hill/First Hill area is the most densely inhabited in the city. Seattle Central Community College and Seattle University contribute upwards of 15,000 students and staff to the area's economy, and between Swedish, Providence and Harborview Hospitals, over 10,000 more people are employed. With relatively few taverns and clubs (and the tendency, to date, for the places that do exist to cater to specific segments of the population), it is our view that neither its needs nor potential is being met. It is, however, a changing market. Moe's on Pike Street and Linda's Tavern on Pine Street have opened to provide an alternative to the insular atmosphere of the Comet, and the retooling of Ernie Steele's and the makeover of the 5-0 on 15th indicate a refinement of the Capitol Hill style. Most of the places along Broadway, conversely, are indicative of a corporate, cookie-cutter approach to doing business drastically at odds with the funkier, street-life, common-ground hipness that is Capitol Hill. Elysian proposed to provide a focal point responsive to the various groups represented on the Hill.

Specific sections of the Capitol Hill commercial area have also, in past decades, been home to car dealerships and light industrial enterprises, businesses requiring the kinds of space and use requirements compatible with relatively easy conversion to a small brewery. It is further felt (and demographically indicated) that as the success of such places as the Wild Rose and Café Paradiso presses change on the Pike and Pine corridor both east and west of Broadway, further space will open up for an undertaking such as ours. The departure of REI from three buildings and the development by QFC on the SW corner of Broadway and Pine, will help continue to transform the area of our proposed location.

Competition for the restaurant is primarily along Broadway (Capitol Hill's main business route) which offers a variety of fast food and sit-down dining. With regard to our pub operation, not only is the Capitol Hill area underserviced, but the existing taverns tend to be exclusionary and specific. Moe's, Linda's and the Comet Tavern constitute Elysian's most direct competition, as well as the Latona Pub's occupancy of the 5-0 space on 15th Avenue East. The competition for the brewery so far consists of the array of craft beers currently available on the wholesale market as well as plans by the McMenamin's chain of brewpubs to establish operations at 300 East Pike Street. With our capability to sell beer to go, we also consider any grocery store with a reasonable selection of craft beers a viable competitor.

This is a cogent and pretty clear-eyed analysis of the neighborhood where Elysian ended up. If you know Seattle at all you might call it prescient, especially considering the basic facts of our history. Truly enough, while the main drag of Broadway has developed to offer more choice, it has since this 1995 writing been plagued by increased vacancy. It has in fact been the Pike and Pine corridor which has developed as a far hipper and more active locus of restaurant and nightlife. When we eventually opened in part of an old Packard dealership four blocks away from Broadway, people had a hard time envisioning where we were. Now we help hold down what has become arguably one of the most active neighborhoods in the city.

There's a subtext in some of this analysis that I'm a little ashamed not to have more explicitly addressed. While we concentrated on the taverns that were most like what we proposed (but without breweries, of course), we only allude to the fact that most area watering holes were gay bars. At the end of the first paragraph of this section we, fingers crossed, hoped to attract "the various groups represented on the Hill." I'm pleased to say that we have. The location we occupy sits at a confluence of major streets feeding inward from the area's different neighborhood divisions, themselves already a diverse blend of gay, straight, university, African-American and gentrifying. Before we even opened, we hosted the campaign kickoff of Capitol Hill's state representative, as his people told us that there wasn't a public space on the Hill as big as what we were putting together. That right there told us we were doing something right. We continue to be proud of the diversity of our clientele.

MARKETING STRATEGY

There are two facets to the marketing of the brewpub having specifically to do with pub and restaurant operations. The pub will have a selection of 6-10 beers produced in-house, as well as 8-12 of the craft brewing movement's finest beers. In this way we will appeal to both the aficionado and the casual beer drinker, encouraging sales of our beers without restricting our clientele. Since the profit margin on our own beers is substantially higher than those purchased wholesale, our pricing policy will encourage consumption of Elysian beers. Pending space and licensing constraints, we will offer limited live acoustic music. The restaurant menu will highlight soups and stews, hearty fare to complement the broad range of beers offered at Elysian. Rather than waiter/waitress table service, we envision orders placed at a central location, with a service window and runners to deliver food when necessary. Like Elysian's beer, all menu items will available to go, with soup/beer and stew/beer combinations emphasized and strategically priced.

One thing that will define Elysian's brewery operation is the plan to brew both German-style lagers and Northwest ales, something which to date has not been consistently executed by any local brewpub. We plan to offer 3-5 lagers and 2-4 ales supplied by Elysian's brewery, including seasonal beers such as Oktoberfest, a pale Bock and a Christmas ale. The brewery hardware will be such that we will be able to produce top-quality examples of each of these beers, unlike the more simply conceived brewhouses of many competing breweries. Moreover, the capacity of Elysian's brewhouse and storage facilities will enable us to be responsive to demands and quality expectations of the wholesale market.

With Elysian's projected product line, we expect to be able to offer wholesale accounts an array of beers which to date has simply not been available. Because of expectations based on the contacts and experience of the partners, we anticipate a high degree of market interest. Some of the general shortcomings of the craft brewing movement have had to do with product inconsistency, personnel turnover and inability to keep pace with demand. With key staff members in positions of ownership, we ensure commitment to the project and consistency in our product. Once more, the capacity of the brewery will enable us to answer local demand on a consistent basis.

Beyond the individual strengths of Elysian's departments, there exists a collective dynamic which truly makes the whole greater than the sum of its parts. The mutability of the balance between the retail and wholesale marketing of Elysian's beers constitutes a strength not within the capabilities of either a brewpub or a purely production brewery. By keeping all possible sales channels open, we ensure a stability able to weather seasonal change and fluctuations in demand, while keeping the brewery and kitchen working as close to capacity as possible.

The typical brewpub in the period immediately prior to our opening in 1996 served a scant handful of ales of safely American or British type. Midwestern craft brewers were more likely to produce a lager or two, and few breweries anywhere in the country produced more than an occasional Belgian style. For us to run sixteen lines (plus one beer engine) at opening seemed a trifle radical, but really no more than what we thought everybody wanted. Like a lot of good ideas it seemed obvious, after the fact. Within a couple of years, a dozen house-produced beers became de rigueur in the same places that once had coasted on the simple novelty of a brewery on the premises. We were never a particularly successful music venue—though we did put on some memorable shows, particularly on Halloween—but we paddled that boat upstream for five years before finally giving it up, as much for the kitchen business we lost as the difficulty of managing it all. I've previously observed that the order window didn't make it past the earliest iterations of concept, and I don't know about you, but I'm feeling more than full with all this talk of soup and stew.

We did in fact install a three-vessel brewhouse capable of the step mashes desirable for the production of lagers. With only three fermentors to start it was all we could do to keep a couple of them on hand due to the maintenance of both an ale and a lager yeast. No matter; we had begun with the capability, once we grew, to go in any number of conceptual directions regarding style and outside sales.

The less said about the next two showboating paragraphs the better. I suppose we were puffing ourselves up for the benefit of potential investors who knew little of who we were or where we had worked. Suffice to say that we had to work as hard as anyone else unproven in a new venture to convince people to sell our beer.

COMPANY ORGANIZATION

The three officers of Elysian are: Joe Bisacca, chief financial officer, currently a vice president with Seafirst Bank, managing Seafirst's West Seattle branch; David Buhler, pub and marketing manager, currently president of Brix° Marketing; and Dick Cantwell, head brewer, currently head brewer at Big Time Brewing.

Joe Bisacca is the coordinator of Elysian Brewing's financial affairs. Joe is currently a vice president at Seafirst Bank and manager of Seafirst's fourth largest branch, with extensive experience in commercial lending. At Seafirst, Joe has run a pilot program on SBA and other small business loans and a series of seminars to increase profitability in business. Since graduating from Gonzaga University in 1987, he has spent eight years in the banking industry, including three years as a commercial lender at Chase Manhattan Bank before joining Seafirst in 1990.

As president of Brix° Marketing since 1991, David Buhler has represented such clients to the Seattle area market as Rogue Brewing, Scottish and Newcastle Importers, Wyder's Cider and Stewart and Yamhill Valley Vineyards. With some eight years' experience in the areas of sales and marketing of imported and specialty beers and wines, as well as management in the restaurant and hospitality industry, David brings a broad range of skills to Elysian.

Dick Cantwell is head brewer at Big Time Brewery and Alehouse in Seattle's University District, the city's most successful brewpub. Now with nearly five years' professional brewing experience, Dick was the first head brewer at Duwamps Café/Seattle Brewing Co. on Lower Queen Anne and spent two and a half years at Pike

Place Brewery. He is a nationally published reporter, columnist and feature writer for the brewing press and is a nationally recognized beer judge. He is regarded as an authority on historical and traditional brewing practices, and is currently overseeing the expansion of Big Time's operation to a capacity of over 2000 barrels per year.

The main strength of Elysian Brewing as a project is its core personnel. In Joe, Dick and David it has a trio of highly qualified people whose areas of expertise overlap, and whose duties will expand and change as the business changes and grows. Beginning, for example, as the person in charge of staffing, ordering and management for both the kitchen and bar, David will move increasingly into marketing and distribution of Elysian's wholesale beer as the brewery's capacity expands. Having overseen the implementation of Elysian's financial systems during start-up, Joe will move into day-to-day bookkeeping and office management with a high degree of involvement with the staff. Dick will be primarily involved at the outset with bringing the brewery on-line, but will work closely with David on distribution, and with the bar staff on proper coordination of Elysian's beer availability and service.

Judge for yourself how qualified we were for the jobs we proposed to fill. You may notice that none of us had professional or vocational degrees in any of the areas in which we were essentially presenting ourselves as experts. Joe majored in psychology and art, Dave in German, and I in a sort of mish-mash of American studies. We all had BAs, which at best qualified us for occasional spirited discussions having nothing to do with the business we started seventeen years ago.

One thing the above anticipates is the alteration of roles as the business grew and departments solidified, sometimes beyond the capability and interest of our core group. We recognized early on, for example, that we needed a kitchen manager, and later another manager to oversee the floor staff. As we've continued to grow, our functions have continued to change and change again, with administration of three restaurants, four brewing locations and wholesale operations serving ten states. One thing is certain: we aren't done re-defining our roles or re-balancing our priorities.

RISK FACTORS

START-UP COMPANY. With every start-up company there are inherent risks involved. As a start-up Elysian does not have an operating history. The current failure rate for U.S. brewpubs is 1 in 6 according to the Institute for Brewing Studies. While this is substantially lower than the failure rate for all start-ups, as the microbrewery industry becomes more competitive the failure rate is bound to increase. Further, there is no public market for the Company's stock, and the Company will be controlled by and dependent upon its majority stockholders.

MICROBREWERY GROWTH. The microbrewery industry has seen dramatic increases in the sales and consumption of specialty beers in the past several years. To meet this demand new breweries are being built and production capacity is being increased by existing breweries. There is no assurance that demand will keep up with the growing supply of specialty beers.

COMPETITION. The beer industry is highly competitive. The company plans to compete with regional breweries primarily from California, Oregon and Washington. The national breweries are venturing into the specialty beer market and have greater financial, production and marketing resources. While we believe that this will bring more consumers into the specialty beer market, there is no assurance that the competition from larger breweries will not affect our growth.

GOVERNMENT REGULATIONS. The manufacture and sale of alcoholic beverages is regulated by both federal and state authorities. The Company has not obtained the required federal and state permits, license and bonds to construct or operate its brewery. Although the Company does not expect the brewery to encounter any difficulties in obtaining the necessary permits, the application and approval process requires considerable lead time. Failure to obtain such permits and licenses would prevent the brewery from engaging in operations. Furthermore there is no assurance that the Company's operation will not become subject to more restrictive regulation or increased taxation by federal or state agencies, which could adversely affect profitability.

DRAM SHOP LIABILITY. Serving of alcohol beverages to a person known to be intoxicated may result in the server being held liable to third parties by injuries caused by the intoxicated customer. The company plans to serve beer and wine at the brewpub. If an intoxicated person is served beer at our establishment and injures a third party, the Company may be held liable for damages to the injured party. The Company plans to obtain host liquor liability coverage and continue such coverage if available at a reasonable cost. However, future increases in insurance premiums could make it prohibitive for the Company to maintain adequate insurance coverage. A large damage award, not adequately covered by insurance, could adversely affect the Company's financial performance.

What we predicted in the first paragraph certainly came to pass, as the spell somehow seeming to protect brewpubs from failure dissipated and the rate of failure by brewpubs drifted more into line with the restaurant industry norm. This was not difficult to predict. We'd all like to believe that beer protects us all, but in this and many other ways it just isn't the case.

The rest of the material outlined here mainly states that the future can't in fact be predicted. The craft beer phenomenon might peter out; the big brewers might decide to make it a higher priority to squeeze the smaller, more charming players from the market; the feds and state authorities, well, you never know what they're going to do when money gets tight; and it's hard to predict the effect of bad luck, poor decisions and rising insurance premiums. This page is intended to take a much-needed break from the swagger of competence and manifest destiny and recognize, in a potentially sheltering way, that things can go wrong.

SOURCE OF FUNDS

Equity investments $250,000
SBA Loan $500,000
TOTAL **$750,000**

USE OF PROCEEDS

Brewery Equipment and Installation $250,000
Restaurant Equipment $100,000
Construction $250,000
Working Capital $100,000
Startup $50,000
TOTAL **$750,000**

TIME SCHEDULE

Equity Offering begins .... April 15
Initial SBA Loan Submission .... April 30
Site determination .... May 30
Brewery Construction upon deposit .... 16 weeks
BATF Review .... 10 weeks
Construction and Permits .... 24 weeks
Brewery Install .... 2 weeks

Well, everything adds up to $750,000, for sure. For a trio of guys with undergraduate degrees in the humanities, that must mean that we were geniuses,. We did of course work hard, and we did get lucky. A key element was doing everything we could in advance—applying for such permits as we could without actually having secured a space, or once we did, before work had actually begun; having SBA documents ready to go pending only the pesky acquisition of the last $75,000 or so; having the brewery space ready to receive equipment when fabrication had been completed. As I look at the above dates, I know we were later than this getting the site, for example, but come January 1 of 1996 we were in our space tearing down lath and plaster. We opened May 10.

ELYSIAN ORGANIZATIONAL CHART

DICK CANTWELL **Head of Brewing**	**JOE BISACCA** **Head of Operations**	**DAVID BUHLER** **Head of Hospitality**
Assistant Brewer 1	Bar Manager	Kitchen Manager
Assistant Brewer 2 (6 mo -1 yr after open)	Waitstaff (7-12 employees)	Kitchen Personnel (6-8 employees)
Keg Washer (6 mo- 1 yr after open)		Wholesale Delivery/Sales
Driver/Sales 1 Driver/Sales 2 (6 mo- 1 yr after open)		

RESPONSIBILITIES

Dick:	**Joe:**	**David:**
Lead Brewer	Financials	Food Ordering
New accounts	Budgets	Inventory Control
Wholesale	Books	Floor manager
	Bar	Marketing
	Inventory	Catering
	Beer to go	New accounts

How accurate was all this? It was our best guess at the time, and it assumed a couple of things. One was that our wholesale business would take on a bigger part of Elysian at large than it actually did, and that we would continue indefinitely to self-distribute. The fact was that, especially with the distractions of running a fairly large restaurant (and actually, now that I remember, getting into a second sort of franchise retail arrangement within only several months), wholesale took a bit of a back seat for some time. This was due partly to naiveté and the assumption that accounts would want our beer so much that it would sell itself. We did self-distribute for a few years; by the time we might have taken on that second driver we decided to go with a distributor. I did have two assistant brewers for that first year, but not because of growth. My first accepted a job as a head brewer in California only two weeks after starting work at Elysian, and as it took the better part of a year for that position to be close enough to ready for her to actually leave, we had an informal trainee who soon worked himself to a level of competence to be able to take over. He's still with us as our senior brewer.

While the responsibility of the brewery was an easy skill group to assign, the rest of the place was more nebulous, with duties apportioned mainly to keep staff lean. Not all of this construct worked. Within several months bar, floor and kitchen staffs had come under more direct control of managers. This was because that structure made more sense, and also because the three of us didn't want to do it day-to-day anymore. We soon devolved to the main areas of brewery, financial and general operations, and sales and marketing.

What do the three of us do now, you might ask. I still run the breweries, but with four locations and other duties I've become an unreliable shift employee. I do research and development of recipes and themes, mentoring of the brewers, and marketing strategy, as well as public appearance and writing most copy. Joe is now CEO, acting as project manager for our production brewery; he continues to oversee operations, and still handles the financial stuff that first brought him in. Dave is no longer sales director, but manages compliance such as taxation and permitting for developing projects, and contributes to marketing strategy and development.

I'll spare you an analysis of our résumés. In addition to experience in the core skills that brought our project together, I notice a common theme of restaurant work. The skills we proposed to bring to the formation and operation of the company, we had to hone over an average of about six years for each of us.

ELYSIAN BREWING COMPANY, INC.
Pro-Forma Balance Sheet

ASSETS

Current Assets	
Cash (working Capital)	$80,000
Beginning inventory (brewery & pub)	45,000
Other (organizational expenses)	5,000
Total Current Assets	130,000
Noncurrent Assets	
Brewery and Wholesale Equipment	260,000
Kitchen Equipment	75,000
Pub & Restaurant Equipment	55,000
Leasehold Improvements	230,000
Total Noncurrent Assets	620,000
TOTAL ASSETS	**$750,000**

LIABILITIES AND EQUITY

Long Term Debt (SBA Loan)	$500,000
Total Liabilities	$500,000
Stockholders and Equity	
Capital Stock	$250,000
Total Equity	$250,000

TOTAL LIABILITIES AND EQUITY	**$750,000**

Spreadsheet Noir—It May All Be There in Black and White, But It's Still Speculative

The Excel worksheet in Appendix A is not a reflection of the original speculations we did in an attempt to raise the money for our project back in 1995. Rather this is a tool—perhaps even a toy, but a simulation in any case—put together by my business partner, Joe Bisacca, as a way of looking at the balance of incomes and expenditures for a brewpub business. It is based on empirical knowledge of having actually run such a business, and while its amounts and proportions are reasonably true to practical form, it is intended that they be adjusted to reflect differences in model, opinion and experience. A strictly packaging brewery, for example, could simply eliminate all fields pertaining to restaurant operation. In its presented form it represents operations for a business worth a bit less than 1.5 million dollars in annual sales. This number too can be adjusted to reflect more or less. All other expenses—and all other incomes—can be adjusted as well. The point is that it is a dynamic spreadsheet, written, programmed and ready to receive theoretical numbers in any field to reflect an unending number of possibilities. The dynamic version is online at BrewersPublications.com/SYOB_spreadsheet and you will be prompted to download and save a file. When you do, you'll immediately see its variability. If not, it can still serve as a template not necessarily to fix anything in stone, but to use as a springboard for your own ideas and specifics. A static version exists in the appendix.

You'll notice some zeroes in there as well, most obviously in the area covering taxes. This is mainly due to state-to-state variability. The adjustment to these presently very round numbers will no doubt affect theoretical profitability, but call that a lesson in just how much effect taxes and their differences have on the bottom line. Other unsupplied numbers are similarly subject to differences of business model and operational style. What you will see is a month-by-month breakdown of operations, speculating on a seasonal flow of business and showing changes in profitability based on fixed costs and other variables. It's possible to get a feel for the cost of goods where both beer production and restaurant operations are

concerned. If you disagree with them, so much the better. Just plug in your own numbers and fiddle away until you get a balance of factors that seems more appropriate to your model, your individual and idiosyncratic concept and other stuff you either know for sure or think you do. Like I said, it's a toy, er, tool.

Chapter Highlights

A Business Plan Is:

- A treatment for a functional business.
- A tool to raise money.
- A market analysis.
- A statement of prospective revenue/expense and profit/loss.
- A presentation of principal owners/operators.
- An assessment of potential risks and rewards.
- Concise.
- Not written in a day.

RAISING MONEY
Filthy Lucre

9

When it comes to money, people have differing levels of comfort. For this reason alone it often takes a partnership to turn a creative endeavor into a commercial enterprise. Most brewers I know aren't necessarily "money types," and while modern times in general may have seen an increasing incidence of the artist-entrepreneur embodied in a single person, that probably has more to do with confidence than any particular fundraising talent. Any after-the-fact mastery of getting blood from a stone tends to be more important to salesmen than raisers of initial capital.

Not that raising money isn't salesmanship. It's taking the tools at hand—climates, ideas, potentialities and reputations—and gradually building a structure that takes on greater solidity as its founding goals are approached. Sometimes all it takes is a single sale: the sweetheart investor, the big bank loan or the venture capitalist willing to front the full amount. In other cases it's like selling vacuum cleaners door to door, approaching friends, acquaintances and three-times-removed hookups one at a time, cobbling together a whole from perhaps dozens of coralline parts. Most often it's a little of this and a little of that, pulling from multiple sources to assemble the bits that will eventually become a business.

It's not my job to scare or intimidate you, or to tell you how difficult things are to pull off. That might seem to build a wall around the industry as it stands right now, today, with two thousand breweries and counting, thank you very much. This book isn't about that wall, which in this industry, thank Annubis, mostly doesn't exist. It's about different ways that maybe you can get it done.

Try, first of all, to look at your pitch from outside, as others will see it when it's presented to them. Who are you? What's your level of experience in the area you plan to take on, to spin, with all other parts, into a successful business? Ditto your other principals. And how do you plan to cover the (inevitable) areas which aren't adequately covered by credibility and faith? What combination of capital and collateral do you and yours bring to the project? Is it realistic to assume you'll be able to secure what you'll need to pull it all off? What's your credit and other business history like? In today's boom time, what does your analytical gut tell you about your prospects for success?

Some people start with their nest egg and put it to work, but a lot of small brewery projects start with very little actual money in hand. To think that one can start such a project simply on the strength of a concept or a fistful of recipes is at best naïve, and in most cases egotistical. But sweat equity can work: since you're the one putting the deal together, you'll be the one logging the hours in the brewhouse, as well as behind the broom, the bar, and in line at the bank. It's perhaps the most compelling way of showing your faith in your own project, and assuring potential investors that supervision will be maintained in the closest possible way.

This chapter presumes that you'll need to raise money from outside sources, and that you plan to enter the economy at large prior to taking the plunge of opening your doors for business. There are as many different ways to do this as there are to purchase a house, for example, or fund a college education; different routes to take, each with its own contingencies, responsibilities and commitments. None is necessarily better than another, and it's important for you to ask yourself a few questions first, for just as there is variation in one's level of comfort in dealing with money, the ways in which you raise it can determine the future structure of your business. Public and private funding prescribe their own courses, for example; the first is perhaps more black and white, the second more nuanced and negotiable. Is your ultimate aim to own the business outright, or are you comfortable sharing ownership with the people who helped you get it off the ground? Do you plan to regularly disburse profits back to your investors, or reinvest in the business, either for continued operation and maintenance or for improvement and expansion? How much do you feel comfortable offering potential investors as incentive for their involvement? Voting rights, a seat on your board, or discounted beers at the bar? There is precedent for each of these models, just as there is precedent for every permutation and combination thereof.

Borrowing from Peter to Pay Paul— Banks and Other Lenders

It's difficult to characterize climates of lending. As of this writing, in the current economic climate, money is cheap but tight: it's difficult to convince a bank of a startup's worth, but it's worth taking as much as they'll give you, if only they would. It's far easier to borrow if you're well into the deal, and have a location or two to show for your efforts. But of course that isn't startup. Banks like it better if you've got something they could (grudgingly) take in case of default—a house or two,

the assets of another business, something accessible and of value, something you can't easily spend. They don't necessarily want to go that route, however; they are much happier when paid on a schedule, when the business remains solvent and viable.

They also like it if you have a plan. It isn't enough to put on a tie, like actor Warren Beatty in the movie *Shampoo*, and look handsomely earnest, fumbling around about what a great idea you've got, a fistful of jargon-laden can't-miss this and that. A business-plan-in-miniature, at the very least, should be flourished and referred to, showing that you've got a schedule for profitability and a way to pay back the money. Acumen, experience, talking a good game; these things don't hurt, but what any lender wants to see is what's in it for them, with minimal risk.

Similarly cagy—and perhaps colder-eyed—are the considerations of the venture capitalist. His or her priority is profit, on schedule, whether it's the whole ball of wax, with interest, x number of years down the line, or y amounts on z schedule, for the undifferentiated life of the deal. Or perhaps they want to maintain equity, and the control it implies, as they reap their share of the profits of your venture. It's more likely these days that venture capitalists would prefer established businesses desirous of acquisition, which could then be resold a few years down the line. But there didn't used to be small breweries, either. Venture capitalism comes in all sizes, and from surprising sources. You may even find a little altruistic elasticity. The portfolios of investors are often balanced; perhaps you'll find someone in the mood for a flyer.

Times and climates change, and they change back again. Twenty years ago money was more generally available for brewery projects, since at that point not many of them had gone out of business. Plus, there weren't that many. Today, once more, we're in a period of expansion. Now the challenge is showing any potential investor what it is about you and your project that makes it a uniquely worthwhile investment. Just as it takes patience in finding the right location, you'll probably shoot a few blanks where funding is concerned. Getting started is the best way to learn how to do it.

The SBA, Entrepreneurial Helper

Fortunately, there's help available. The Small Business Administration is a government agency which, while not actually providing loans, offers guarantees for approved loans to the financial institutions that do offer them. This makes these institutions—typically banks—feel more secure about supporting projects like yours that are solid, well conceived and responsibly enacted. In addition, they provide help and information through the whole process of conception, planning and application. Their website (www.sba. gov) is an excellent place to start. Application materials for their various programs are there, of course, along with useful tools like a soul-searching questionnaire to help you evaluate the state and development of your project, and information on programs to help women, minorities, veterans of the military and people with disabilities borrow money. Naturally there is oversight. Disbursement of SBA-guaranteed funds needs to be tied to receipts for equipment and materials, and certain models need to be followed. You can demo yourself, for example, but you can't act as your own contractor. You will need to follow certain protocols in order to insure that you're spending the money the way you say you will, that you're on schedule to complete the project, and that ultimately you will be able to pay it back. While necessary, certain commodities like the grain and hops to make your beer and the foodstuffs to stock your kitchen do not constitute qualified expenses. This isn't an Easy-Bake Oven you're cranking up here; not everything comes in the box.

So if the SBA doesn't cover everything you need to get started, where does *that* money come from? I'll break it to you: you're going to have to do a little work. Typically, the SBA sponsors loans in which a proportional amount of project funding is supplied by the borrower—you. If you can raise a third of the money you'll need to get off the ground, say, taking a certain amount of direct risk yourself and ponying up for some of the things that the SBA typically won't cover, the SBA and your bank are in a position to swing the rest. It's not a guarantee, of course, but you have to show a willingness to lift a finger in order to borrow money from anyone, right?

Having said that, here's a hint: that earnest-seeming money doesn't necessarily have to come from you, yourself. Money raised from people who trust you can serve as this initial stake, which you, with or without the SBA's help, can then parlay into the bulk of your loan. Yes, properly executed, it's possible to swing this deal without any financial contribution of your own. It's to be assumed that having achieved this, you won't be sitting back and watching the money of others work—you'll be right there, on the front lines day and night. More on some of these scenarios later.

The SBA sponsors loans other than start-ups, too. Expansions can be undertaken with its help as well, and the limits for those are higher, presumably commensurate with the wherewithal and track record of the potential borrower. They even have a micro-lending program with a $50,000 limit, and some of these funds can be used to purchase inventories. I'm not a lender, but to me this screams nano. Check out their list of services and programs, suggestions and guidance, and see if any of it might work for you.

Alchemical Prestidigitation — Alternative Financing

There are many creative ways to secure financial credit, subsidization and deferment which aren't dishonest, coercive or what's-yours-is-mine hippie-ish. It may feel like the long con to convince neighborhoods, municipalities, landlords, vendors and contractors to come into your deal, but depending on the character and circumstances of your project, these can all be perfectly legitimate parts of the puzzle. A lot of it might not appear in the form of cash up front (though some of it can), but the effect can be the same as you alter the terms and types of the responsibilities you undertake.

Many brewery projects start their lives on the so-called wrong side of town. Neighborhoods fallen on hard times and zones of industrial contraction can not only be cheap to get into, they can also be ideal locations targeted by civic entities for rejuvenation. Even the soundest projects are often eligible for funding or incentives as compensation for neighborhood improvement, job creation and general economic stimulus. Sometimes these benefits are deferred in the form of credits for taxes and land acquisition. Other times there can be cash up front, for perhaps the joint improvement of a waterway or historic building façade. It's definitely worth asking around as your project takes shape; it could even help you in choosing a location. Successfully employed, this incentive-based strategy can not only help you in realizing your plan, but in integrating it into the community and forging alliances which may well serve you in the future.

Somewhat along these lines, landlords can help realize your project through the shrewd negotiation of your deal. You are, in many cases, putting labor, love and investment into a piece of property that they own, theoretically enhancing its value and helping raise the value of other properties (which they may also own) nearby. Getting them to come in on an improvement like increasing electrical capability or the replacement of decrepit and inefficient windows can be a relatively easy sell. Other more general allowances for tenant improvements can come either as an outright deduction from what you might otherwise owe, or as some kind of deferred loan, perhaps to be paid off over a timeline less urgent than upfront and right now. They may even, either initially or as your project develops, come to see the merit in some kind of partnership or investment arrangement.

Sometimes financial partners can be found among those providing equipment and services to a developing project, or even among distributors. The average manufacturer of brewing equipment or your local arm of a national construction firm might not be terribly interested in swapping part of their billables for equity in your fledgling brewery, but the right combination of size, character and personal connection might make the matter worth exploring. Stranger things have also happened than financing arrangements with materials suppliers. One thing's certain: you won't find investors if you don't ask.

Equipment for your brewery will likely be the single largest line item in your budget; throw in what you'll need for a kitchen in a brewpub and the proportional amount is even higher. Though more often used as a tool for expansion once a track record has been established, leasing rather than initially buying equipment can be an option as well. It's another deferred debt,

of course, putting further burden on cash flow during your vulnerable first few years, but it's worth considering as part of the picture. It may also help get you open faster, thereby not only enhancing but helping to originate profitability.

The Jerry McGuire Maxim—
It Has to Come to This

Perhaps the most important thing to keep in mind where raising money is concerned is to get that money in hand. It's ridiculously obvious, of course, but you'll find that a lot of conversational interest in your project will turn out to be just that. If you're trying to raise, say, thirty small chunks of money—several thousand dollars apiece, for example, with maybe a few larger ones happily thrown in—you'll need to talk to an awful lot of people to get the job done. You'll also find not only differing levels of interest and engagement but different levels of comfort. Some people are fine about being asked for money for an investment that may or may not appeal to them, while others regard it as a request for a handout. I recall a friend of fairly long standing with whom relations cooled for some years simply because I mentioned to him that I was raising money for a project. I also remember—though not so much in my own experience—people willing to write checks and hand them over without even looking at the business plan concerned. Looking for investors is a process that can be compared to a lot of things involving cajolery and salesmanship—looking for a job, perhaps, or dating. You need to assess the solidity of a prospect and follow up without hounding. Easy to say? Definitely. Not so easy to accomplish, but do-able, with proper preparation.

Who are these people, you may ask. Whoever. Friends and family are a nice core group, especially as they tend to trust you, and may be more familiar with your vision than the average stranger on the street. Chains of acquaintance can bring others to your door, or you to theirs. When it comes to people handing over their hard-earned money, be realistic about the likelihood of their inclination. Friends with more money are far more likely (duh) to sign on than those with less. They may also know others with the wherewithal to work you into their portfolios. Have documents ready to assure them you won't simply run off with their cash, that it will be placed in escrow pending successful completion of your fund-raising campaign, and be returned, with interest, should it fall short within a prescribed time. Success breeds success, and imparts momentum; to be able to report eighty percent fulfillment of the plan can make fruition inevitable. It can also, perversely, represent a wall seeming to repel potential contributors of fainter heart. There's a psychology, in short, to be apprehended with each new pitch of your proposal. An impersonal circular may be enough to get you started, but it's highly likely you'll need to get down in the trenches in order to move your lines forward. Perhaps your style is more comfortable with presentation to a group, combining social occasion with investment opportunity. Best, in my view, to make such a gathering known as such in advance, but perhaps I'm fainter of heart than you are where it comes to working a room. Think of it all as practice for when you're out there on the street, your brews percolating away back at the ranch, trying to secure handles and shelf space in a marketplace as variably enthusiastic.

Chapter Highlights

**Things to Keep in Mind
When Trying to Secure Financing**

- Be bold, but not too bold.
- SBA is a good place to start.
- Be clear about what people get for their investment—repayment, buyout, a share of profits, equity in eventual sale of the business, free beer.
- Municipal money is sometimes available for historical or restoration projects.
- Landlords will often give allowances for tenant improvements.
- Vendors and even distributors are sometimes willing to invest.
- Leasing equipment can spread out payment.

PRODUCTION PLANNING AND SALES PROJECTIONS
Going with the Flow

10

P assion for brewing may have been your impetus for taking it on professionally, but selling your beer is what will make that continue to be possible. Your business plan will no doubt include an analysis of the market you intend to enter, and while this in itself will establish credibility for your project with investors, be ready to use what you've learned from your analysis as you truly do enter and begin to claim your share of that market. How large a percentage, first of all, does craft beer in general command in sales within the market in question? What sort of competition to your brands is already out there, and how much of that can you reasonably expect to take? These are the first questions to be asked in planning production and forecasting sales. Without having a sense of their answers you are likely doomed to a reactive existence: doing the best you can as the data comes in, and running this way and that rather than plotting a course and following it on your own terms. The history of craft brewing is littered with failed breweries that either under- or over-produced, that essentially had no idea what they were doing; many functioning breweries, in fact, manage to stay open because of luck and favorable market factors. But luck is becoming less of a factor as competition becomes more intense; those without a plan cannot expect to be in control of their own destinies.

Counting Beans and Bottles— Inventory Control and the Forking Paths of Production

It might seem that by starting extremely small it would be easy to keep track of your beer and its production, track inventory and forecast sales, and know the status of each keg, case and tank. The reality is somewhat different, however. Factors as small as the beer you and your staff take home or consume on the premises and as large as potential systemic missteps like making too much of a particular brand for the time in which it is intended to be sold affect inventory control. Whole departments exist in large craft breweries to map and predict such things, so don't feel bad if at times it seems difficult to get your head around it all. Just don't expect it to take care of itself.

The first and most solid maxim for planning production is that you shouldn't make beer you don't know you can sell. On a pub level, this might be as simple as gauging whether a particular beer is likely to be popular enough to sell through. That kind of thing can be chalked up to testing your market and perhaps risking beer getting a little old—really no big deal. But once you're feeling fast and furious, particularly in a packaging brewery, and it seems as though you can't keep up with orders, it's easy to get a little heedless and over-produce for your flow pattern. Developing a sense for this flow is one of the keys to succeeding and making it all look effortless, and more importantly, for keeping your customers satisfied. And by customers I don't just mean those loving your beer one at a time. I mean your retailers and distributors, too. Uneven supply is one of the easiest ways to cool the interest of those ordering and re-selling your beer. You can count on only so much indulgence, even though our industry segment expects such things occasionally. To manage and maintain consistent supply is a professional necessity, not only to make sure that there is enough, but to ensure quality and freshness.

One good thing about the imposition of taxation on brewery production is that it requires accurate record keeping. Any brewery project approved for licensing necessarily carries with it a planned point of taxation, whether at racking, packaging or specific transfer; it must be proven that amounts are accurate, both of beer and the taxation it incurs. It should therefore be fairly simple to track production inventories, and by extension the inventories of where it all goes down the line, as long as everything is written down. A well-designed brew sheet (see Appendix) should carry all the information associated with a particular batch of beer, from processes employed during its production to the type and container it all went into: pint, bottle, keg or drain. A well-trained brewer or cellar person should be able to provide this information. This is the most basic of inventory reporting: telling the story of the contents of a single tank of beer.

Most breweries have more than one tank, however, in order not just to increase supply but to provide selection. It's therefore necessary to have an overview more general than the one-thread narrative provided by the brewsheet. A simple timeline map of each tank, aggregated to show schedule and contents, will provide information for production planning. It may also eventually show you the necessity for expansion. Schedules of all types can deviate from the ideal, of course, but to have a reasonably predictable pattern of production flow tied to transfers, shipments and sales will take the first vital steps toward effective management of all these systems.

Say you operate a brewpub in a state in which you're allowed to distribute outside your own premises. Given the higher margin associated with retail draft beer sales and the fact that you don't want your pub or restaurant to run out of beer, you'll want to take care of your own taps before you even consider selling outside. If you do have "extra" beer for outside sales you probably have some idea of where it's going to go. Predicting when to brew more of any given brand is where the challenge lies. If you self-distribute, all it takes to maintain a sense of your inventory is to saunter through your walk-in and count kegs and glance at the sight glasses on your tanks. If you have distributors, you need them to report their inventories to you. By establishing pars, or levels of inventory intended to remain constant in order not to jeopardize supply for a determined period—say thirty days—you can build a schedule for brewing based on the reality of sales. If sales pick up or lag you can react by brewing particular beers more or less often in order to keep realistic production needs rather than what you wish were the case. Go ahead and wonder why a particular beer is selling more or less well than it was—or than you wish it were—and adjust other factors such as your sales force or the time you spend on it, or perhaps the appeal of the product itself; but don't make beer that doesn't yet have an evident home.

In addition to delivering and perhaps selling your beer, distributors provide a number of other services, but only if you ask them to. Warehousing is one such service, making it possible for you to use the space in your cozy little confines for making rather than storing beer. Inventorying is another. Regularly reporting depletions to you, as often as weekly if you need it, can go a long way towards helping you feel sure of maintaining appropriate levels. Establishing systems and expectations with your distributors will make it easier for them, and you, as you all work together to sell your beer.

It might at times be tempting to play what you feel is a hot hand, to produce more than what your depletions tell you is prudent; increased sales might even occasionally condone this gut impulse. For example, you might have just added some tanks to increase production to a level that you feel you can manage to sell. Or maybe you've just landed a splashy new account or two and have a pretty good idea that previous production levels aren't going to get the job done. Great. I applaud you. Just be careful. Your production eyes, after all, might prove bigger than your sales stomach. It's stomach-turning, in fact, to have to destroy out-of-date beer or fire sale it (and your brand) by discounting it to brokers who do business selling old stuff in the Third World. Among the worst horror stories is of breweries that, having actually landed some floor space, say in a big box retailer, then must buy equipment to keep up with demand that eventually proves fickle and fleeting.

Remember that sales should drive production, and not the other way around. It's simple enough to compensate for increased demand by ramping up. Easy enough to say in a climate that seems to have no abatement from sunshine. The fact remains, however, that having a plan is essential to the successful navigation of all eventuality. Having a system that checks itself by institutional integration of supply and demand protects against surprise.

A Word from Our Sponsor— Extremes Need a Plan, Too

All this pragmatism momentarily aside, concepts arise which would seem to fly in the face of sense, safety, and the wisdom of mapping it all out. Michael Jackson himself advised the founders of New Belgium not to attempt the model they envisioned, of producing nearly exclusively Belgian-style beers in the US. Dogfish Head came into existence producing literal museum pieces such as Midas Touch, made with honey, raisins and saffron, and adding hops to other beers every single minute for various durations of boil—how much in the way of sales legs could something that odd be expected to have? Closer to my home, the boys at Hair of the Dog in Portland, Oregon, made intensely unique beers, generally of prodigious strength, in an institutional soup kettle. I used to say that I was so glad they did what they did, but that I was happy it wasn't me doing it. But there's a big difference between indulging what might seem a crazy concept and taking it all as it comes. The operators of all three of those breweries may not have been able to predict their own futures as they left the gate, but they had strategies, plans, and effective (if unconventional) business models in mind.

Such apparent extremity of concept requires the kind of custom planning that any business should craft for itself. Not only is the risk of catastrophic world shortages of saffron something to be taken into account, but the likely reception by retailers unaccustomed to mind-bendingly unusual beers. Education is key: both yours as you quickly adjust to unforeseeable production and sales variables, and that of the people you hope will become your loyal customers, distributors, retailers and servers.

Fifteen or so years ago, when there were only several hundred small breweries out there, it was possible to simply call up malt and hop suppliers, and order what you wanted. Providing your money was good, you could get just about anything on the next truckload out of the West. Today, with increased competition not only in markets, but for the simple attentions of these raw materials suppliers, realistic planning is essential to the production of consistent products and the maintenance of their consistent supply. If you produce a beer that the whole world loves and wants to buy, but you can't continue to get the hop variety or specialty malt that makes it what it is, you're constrained, shall we say, from succeeding. Conversely, if you contract for malt or hops so specific to a particular beer that it can't be shuffled around to something else should sales prove disappointing, you've got yourself boxed in a whole different way. A realistic sales projection will help secure what you need to make the whole thing happen.

E-Tools of the Trade—Informational Aids

Keeping track of where everything is and where you want it to be starts with conceptualization beyond simply counting kegs and measuring sight glasses. Those observational tools are of course important in generating the data that informs more general awareness, as are the kinds of charts I've mentioned which give a view of the larger picture of your whole operation. These days nearly all of us have basic office and accounting software at our fingertips to help us document and store data on what we're making and selling; it's a fairly simple matter to have it report to us in ways that make variegated sense, whether in the form of specific packages or the raw barrelage that helps gauge production volumes and determine taxes. For small operations with limited staff, this can often be sufficient. But when business gets more busily underway, when brewery personnel and production increase, it can be both more important and more difficult to keep track of it all. This is when departments are formed and more specific duties assigned, when more information is sought and more sophisticated analytical tools are required to not only give a moment-by-moment look at where things are at any given time, but to set priorities and plan strategies.

It should come as no surprise in this age of information that there are programs and services that can either be bought or subscribed to that will help with both inventory management and sales. As with so many of the areas and general products touched on in this book, brand specificity is forbidden me, but it's just as well: even a span of months would outdate anything I might mention or even be aware of. And for the purposes and resources of those getting started now, awareness is enough. When you are ready for such things you will shop for them. Simply be aware of some of the types of things out there.

We all have different tastes for and thresholds of information. One's personal analysis of the industry and how it informs strategy might first come just from day-to-day experience. A magazine or two might later appear in the mailbox—material or electronic—whether from one of our trade or professional organizations or from a more commercial entity along for the ride. Weekly and even daily newsletters are available, for a price, that can keep us all abreast of trend information down to the tiniest detail. It's possible to spend a great deal of time and a fair amount of money keeping up with what everyone else knows who makes the commitment. It can be valuable, or it can merely be entertaining.

More directly practical are the services that inform the flow of our own businesses. Programs which track raw materials as they are converted into saleable beer, then monitor that beer from our premises on its way out the door can help our entire operation run more efficiently. The more information we have, the less we guess, and the better our feelings are informed when we consult them to make decisions. Sometimes

circumstances dictate actions, such as when all tanks and cold storage are full. At such a time you probably don't need to make more beer. But when operations are continually running to and fro, creating clots which hamper smooth operation, what might seem either unmanageable demand or frustrating lack of it can often be understood and objectively analyzed by an information-based system of decision making.

Similarly, sales information comes in many forms, and in many levels of detail. It can tell you how much of a particular item has been shipped, period; or it can break it down in more detail: where it went, in what specificities and increments, and where it went after that. It's possible in this way to keep up with the inevitably changing picture of how and where your beer is selling, and to inform every aspect of your operations, from where salespeople should be spending their time to how often a particular beer needs to be brewed. Such information is available both as it specifically pertains to your business and in its brand-by-brand and package-by-package description of the industry. It's certainly possible to lose yourself in it, but appropriately consulted and considered, it can show you, for example, where exactly you are in reference to any given wave.

It may seem over-analytical and tedious to consider the use of such tools in putting together your own sales strategies and forecasts. It might seem scarily like what the big brewers probably do as (you imagine) they lose sight of their products and the inspiration that originally brought them about. Many of our sub-industry pioneers would never have imagined, as they loaded their pickups with the lovingly crafted results of their days' work, that they would be consulting such things and placing themselves not just in the passion-driven current of craft beer but in the framework of the brewing industry at large. But like it or not that's where we are, and where you will be as you face the challenges of survival, if only as a member of the collective.

Chapter Highlights

Don't Make Beer You Don't Know You Can Sell

Analyze your market
- Who is the competition?
- What market share can you expect?

Keep track of inventory in all aspects:
- Tank, keg, cold room, distributor

Track and plan for production

Maintain pars for a specific time period

Consider software programs and information services for:
- Keeping track of the market.
- Keeping inventories of beer and raw materials.

Use Your Distributor For:
- Warehousing.
- Sales, as far as it goes.
- Reporting of depletions.
- Co-oping of promotions and point of sale materials.

Have a Plan
- Project sales and allocations.
- Have confidence in your concept.
- Tell your story, and the story of each of your beers.
- Be sure you can get the materials needed to continue producing a successful beer.
- Be prepared to change your plan.

PLANNING NEVER ENDS
Maximizing and Adding Locations

11

In some ways the craft brewing movement is an iceberg, with perhaps its largest part—breweries yet to open, or at least in planning—lying submerged beneath those that so far have managed to begin operation. For this is a phenomenon in planning. Each year its trade organization, the Brewers Association, tracks serious inquiries relating to brewery startups in the several hundreds; each year scores of prospective brewery owners attend the Craft Brewers Conference. And each year a varying number of those previously submerged creep above the water line to join the professional ranks.

It's sometimes easy to forget that the planning process never really ends. There are always systems to improve and developments to be undertaken. And for an increasing number of craft brewers who have realized their dream of doing business, planning for a new brewery is something that will be undertaken more than once. Tiny, seat-of-the-pants operations will seek to put together brewing systems larger and perhaps more commercially viable; brewpubs will open second and third locations, and demand willing, production facilities to expand brewing operations. Established packaging breweries will need bigger breweries capable of taking their message and their products to more outlets.

Firing on All Cylinders—Making the Most of What You've Got, and Then Some

Before shedding your skin and moving into an entirely new facility, you'll probably want to maximize the space and the equipment you have to make more beer than you ever thought you'd be able to. This is often the way it goes. Maximum capacity remains a fixed number for years—then demand forces some creative, efficient way to set a new upper limit. It's a bit like the marathoner's wall—struggle suddenly gives way to strength, and new potentials are achieved. For the small brewer, this may even include profitability. It's a gratifying feeling to finally locate that sweet spot, but the day eventually comes when something more needs to be done.

When demand starts exceeding capacity, it's time to identify bottlenecks. It comes down to two choices: getting creative with staffing or investing in a larger system, providing you have the space to do so. Identifying obstacles appropriately is the key to getting bigger in a meaningful way. The first barrier likely to fall is working on weekends. It can be a bitter pill, especially if you're the one doing all the work, but those two days, previously only good for the occasional keg filling or gravity taking, force decisions and generally slow things down. Schedules can be adjusted, of course; weekdays off are a refreshing alternative to what most of the rest of the working world does. A second shift is another possibility, but this is where we begin to get into the limitations of equipment and the times involved in its employment.

What to add first to enhance the capability of your equipment? It depends on the type of brewery you run. A pub dependent on tanks for most of its on-site beer service will need more conditioning or bright tanks, especially if beer is whittled away piecemeal: half a dozen kegs here, maybe a hundred cases of bottles there, leaving what's left to be served at the tap. This isn't an efficient method, but it does allow flexibility and keeps a good variety of beers on hand. But with a brisker wholesale business, you'll find your cellar generally empty of beer as you wait for fermentation to catch up. The bright tanks you thought you needed back when things were more sprawly suddenly become unnecessary; now what you need is more fermentation space. Those beer-lonely brights will be used soon enough, once multiple-brew-sized fermentors are sending product their way. Unless those fermentors are tricked out as unitanks, able to ferment and condition all in one, which will again render your extra bright space superfluous.

The point, of course, is to empty tanks all at once as soon as beer is ready to move. By doing so, a large number of fermentors and a small number of brights can unite in polygamous efficiency, spending the least amount of time necessary in any given place. That is if packaging, or kegging, or filtration can keep up with the increased flow. You get the idea. If only those single-walled tanks in your cold room were jacketed you could do whatever you want with them. If only you had another vessel in your brewhouse. These are the things that occur to you when you're trying to wring the most out of the space you probably thought at the outset was going to be just fine. The covetousness that comes of wanting to improve other systems all at once is something that just comes with the territory, as is the wish that you just had a little more space, or perhaps another location.

The Golden Goose—Doing It All Again

When putting together a first brewery, the possible variations seem endless. For the second brewery, this is no less true. The difference is that now you are informed not just by the experience of having been through it before, but by changing times and markets, developing tastes and talents, as well as the simple inward stirring of perceived opportunity. In such cases it's almost as though—in a funny, time-warp kind of way—you're granted a second chance, armed with knowledge from the first time.

This is where it gets fun. Now you have greater resources, greater flexibility, and a clearer idea of how this project will evolve, guided by the same vision and personality of the first. Do you want to do essentially the same thing, bringing your look, products and strategy to an area you think will embrace them with the same (or greater) enthusiasm than you've experienced in your current seat of operation? Or does this new location speak to you in a way that suggests modifying your message? Is the assignment so different this time around that everything you've done up till now has essentially served as training for the real assignment? Or perhaps your business model has morphed to accommodate new partners, or even another brewing company, eager to contribute to the personality of the project. We will here consider all these possibilities.

Following a proven paradigm is perhaps the most obvious way to pursue expansion to a second location. And let me hasten to say that obvious does not have to mean boring. Many of the best ideas, after all, seem obvious only after they are accomplished. To take something successful, transfer it, and see it flourish again is to have created the perfect model for success. Still, it's at least good form to consider what elements or circumstances made the original a success, in order to make sure they also apply to the new space. Are the demographics of the new location, for example, tolerably similar to the original for the unaltered concept to work there? If so, do you intend this new place to stand on its own like some kind of parallel universe? Would a customer of the original, walking into location number two, feel at home, or would it give them the creeps?

That isn't intended to be a joke, but I will tell a funny story. A Seattle brewpub I worked in for a couple of years, Big Time Brewery and Alehouse, is in many ways a duplicate of its elder sister pub, Triple Rock, in Berkeley. This was especially true in their early days—the same wainscoting, the same style of gorgeous Brunswick back bar, the same type of shuffleboard table in the back. The same guys, in fact, up from California, did much of the work on the new Seattle interior space. One night during the Big Time buildout, after a couple of beers amid the stowed tools and the sawdust, they deciding to call it a night, put on their jackets, locked up the doors and walked out onto the Seattle street to wait for their bus home—in Berkeley. So similar was the feel of the space they had just left that they thought they were home. Very "Twilight Zone," right?

The familiarity and comfort these workers felt, even in the unfinished new space is testimony to the conceptual success of applying the original look and feel to another spot, and presaged the commercial success Big Time enjoyed when it opened. But even the largest and the most successful brewpub chains, some of them numbering in the dozens of locations, are careful to bring elements of familiarity to the new stores they open without making people feel they could be in any one of them. Whether customers are new to the joint or loyal and established, you want to welcome them in, not lock them in.

Another story involves another roving contracting crew, this one engaged in building out one store after another for a national restaurant chain I will not name. These guys were charged with literally and endlessly duplicating a single model deemed optimal by the designers in the home office. They'd bang one out, head off to the next, and do it again, exactly the same, down to the curve of the bar and the placement of the mirror just inside the door. Well, even this kind of immortality bridles after a time, and the designers decided to mix it up a bit. Freaked out by the alteration of the floorplan they had numbly—and to them, comfortingly—reproduced, the entire crew quit. Now that's what I call creepy.

Sadly, and for various reasons, these chains are the neighborhood bars of much of America. In fact this is what much of America has facilitated through short-sighted development. That's why America needs us. For example, one unintended consequence

of municipalities' limiting of liquor licenses in the supposed interest of moderation can be a free-floating (and often independently brokered) price so high as to remove entrepreneurs like you and me from the running. That, however, is a side subject. Suffice it to say that degree of duplication is something to be weighed in expanding an empire even to a second location. And naturally there's more than the look of a place to define it. The repertoire of the beers offered and the menu are key elements to be considered when carrying a successful concept to the next step.

Departure from a Theme— a Whole New Animal

Perhaps more challenging and engaging is the new location that stands as an intentional departure from the original. Whether responding to a markedly different type of town or neighborhood or in an effort to appeal to a specific crowd perhaps outside the bullseye of the original concept, the challenge with this expansion concept is to seem new while still harking to the best of what has come before. And this is most definitely a challenge. I'm continually amazed at the frequency of confusion where one of Elysian's pubs is concerned. The company name is on the sign outside (though not part of the name of the place), a six-by-six-foot window with our logo on it hangs in the middle of the dining room, and the bar offers fourteen to sixteen of our beers, but many people still don't get it. Are they stupid? Certainly not. More delicately put, we could no doubt have done a better job of helping them along. The brewing equipment, for example, is not visible from anywhere in the restaurant, and the decorating scheme is less rollicking than our original, definitely more beer-centric location. But to some degree that's the neighborhood. We got seven smell complaints the first time we brewed there, despite the presence of a coffee roaster, a hair salon, a doughnut shop (organic), and a sausage restaurant within half a block; the (pretty well muffled) roof fan for the heating and ventilation system elicited noise complaints because of its variation on the usual nighttime crickets; and on one visit a guy sent back three steaks while his wife turned up her nose at seven glasses of wine. But despite the occasional thorniness of the residents it's a great neighborhood for the business. They may be resistant to change, but once it's established, they are hugely loyal.

There's a lot to criticize, in fact, about taking a new direction when branching out. It's complicated. A radically different menu, on one hand, might disappoint diners wanting their favorite item from your other place, but it also brings the core of your concept to a different crowd. A different lineup of beers, similarly, might occasionally send someone grudgingly to their second or third choice, but it will also often pleasantly surprise. I know I leave myself open to skepticism by saying so, but I've always felt that making it tough to choose between your places is not a bad thing; the key is making sure that both places are great.

Reward and Risk

Even if it isn't possible, legally and logistically, for you to offer the products of one of your places over the bar of another, the research and development possibilities of having a second brewing system are boundless. Not all states allow the shipment of beer between locations within the same company, and some require the use of a distributor to do so. But if this is not the case in your state, you'll be able to put a far greater variety of beers before your customers. They will appreciate your ability to recognize their love for variety. Invariably, one group of regulars has a penchant for a particular beer when across town or thirty miles up the road they prefer another.

It's also possible to take advantage of different-sized brewing systems; use the larger system for your well-established, popular beers, and the smaller one for pilot beers. The successful experiments—meaning your customers like the beer—can then be moved to the bigger system, to be made in larger quantities. And on to the next experiment. The only problem you'll find over time is that with so many beers in your quiver people will continually be clamoring for the one you haven't brewed in a few months or a year. But you knew that already from your first location.

Flexibility of staffing is an advantage when having multiple locations, whether it's brewery or restaurant personnel. People tend to prefer working in a single place, and there's something to be said for the continuity of familiarity where the customers are concerned, but to find the right spot for particular people to work is a nice additional management touch. For the brewing staff it can be a nice reward to get off the site of most of their labors to be a part of an experimental new beer, or when needed, to pitch in for a particular beer-related event (like filling a lot of kegs, you're thinking—you're not fooling me).

Perhaps more than anyone, managers need to be flexible, too. It's possible with more than one place, with perhaps one larger and more demanding than another, to use a less hectic setting to bring people along with a training hitch in one spot for eventual flowering in another. And even managers need days off. The ability to have them covering each other in rotation makes the whole engine run smoother, and binds together the otherwise potentially disparate entities within your company.

Also consider economies of scale. Even a modest-sized group carries more negotiating weight than a single location. Like managers, vendors can be brought along, auditioned here and rewarded with the whole there. Creative solutions sometimes suggest themselves. I am able to purchase larger quantities of malt at a lower per-pound price, for example, which can then be split between the silos of two of my brewing locations. The more potential business you bring to a vendor the more they are willing to work with you.

Naturally every potential reward has its risk, for each time you extend your empire you truly roll the dice. Unless your locations are so numerous as to have built in the philosophical and financial support to sustain isolated failure, a single bum location can bring the whole thing down. Like the management shuffle above, seasonal variation can be a saving grace if the ups of one mesh with the downs of another—stadium locations come to mind—but cold winds tend to blow pervasively. A drain by definition is a remover of material, after all. Expansion of a brewery/restaurant group is not like a well-orchestrated game of Risk—your Irkutsk location, however apparently protected by your rampart in Kamchatka, can still be attacked from all sides.

Cooperation and Merger

Sometimes breweries, even in a single market, find a reason to work together in expanding their concepts and production capacities. Sometimes they go so far as to become one company. Merger of companies is of course a corporate decision, and probably not something you're thinking of as a way to begin a business. Working cooperatively, however, under whatever rubric, is a possibility that may at some point make sense. Say someone else has just undertaken an expansion and temporarily has capacity they aren't using. This could be an excellent intermediate step for you as perhaps you gear up for an expansion of your own. You can create and even answer demand as you build the structure of a market that eventually you'll be able to get into more robustly. Another scenario, with probable implications of joint ownership, is the combination of a brewpub company and a production company expanding in both ways, closing the circle of production and retail on a larger and perhaps more profitable scale than either would be able to achieve independently. The subject of cooperation between brewers is more completely treated in the chapter devoted to it. Suffice it to say that expanding your brewery, its capabilities and concepts is a subject which almost universally sprawls across the current consciousness of our movement.

Chapter Highlights

Maximize Efficiencies

- Identify the weak link preventing growth within existing facilities.
- Evaluate what is working well.

Duplication or New Identity?

- Avoid customer confusion—Is it too similar? Too different?

Growth Allows:

- A chance to benefit from your experience.
- Experimentation.
- Cross-training employees.
- Economies of scale.
- Cooperation.

Growth Risks:

- Everything. Be sure to do a realistic evaluation.

SECTION III

LEGAL/
REGULATORY

THE TAXMAN
Let Me Tell You How It Will Be

12

As it must for all men, death may eventually have come for Charles Foster Kane, the main character in the movie *Citizen Kane*, but the taxman likely didn't gain frequent entrance to Xanadu, the estate where the snow globe finally fell. Xanadu Brewing Co., however, would never be left so unmolested. For there's one expense where you can't cut corners in the business of brewing: the taxes you'll owe to the feds, to your home state, and in some cases to more finely-pared governmental bodies. It may seem silly to state (and re-state) the necessity of following through on this—and of regularly maintaining the flow of revenue once begun—but breweries (and businesses in general) are shuttered and chained more often than you'd think owing to tax delinquency. I always find this surprising, but perhaps I'm naïve. I always find it surprising, too, when bars are closed because of storerooms full of guns, untaxed tobacco, or weed. Because if you fail to pay your taxes in a reasonably convincing way—two days late might be okay, but don't quote me—they will surely shut you down.

Altered Agencies and Tiers of Taxation

The post-Prohibition Federal Alcohol Administration, formed in 1935, was reorganized into the Bureau of Alcohol, Tobacco and Firearms (BATF) in 1972, an arm of the Department of Treasury. Thus were morphed the intrepid "revenuers," hunting stills and busting barrels during the glory years of Prohibition, into an oddly-configured agency devoted both to auditing the taxes of brewers, distillers, winemakers and tobacco manufacturers and laying their lives on the line for the occasional armed standoff. The post-9/11 world saw the ATF reinterpreted in 2003 as the TTB, or Alcohol and Tobacco Tax and Trade Bureau, spinning the more active functions of law enforcement off to the Justice Department, where they probably should have been all along. It still may seem a little odd, as you're filling in forms and calculating rates of taxation, to see spaces devoted to tracking amounts of raw distilled spirits and numbers of cigarette papers, but that's the way history and government interpretation have seen fit to organize it all.

As much as we all may complain about the taxes we pay as small brewers to the federal government, it is only through the advocacy of our trade organizations that we pay as little as we do. It was in 1976 that the Brewers Association of America (BAA, a precursor of today's BA, or Brewers Association) succeeded in obtaining a differential rate of tax of $7.00 a barrel for the first 60,000 barrels of production, a rate which stands today in contrast with the $18.00 a barrel paid by larger brewers. As I write this an effort is underway by the BA to further lower the rate of tax to $3.50 a barrel as a way to further stimulate the specific economies of small brewers and allow them to reinvest in equipment and create jobs; by the time you read this, the measure will either have succeeded or not. The point is that these organizations have your back, and particularly through the institution of the 1976 differential, have as a result kept many of us in business.

Compliance, the Prequel

Before being admitted to the joys of filing federal tax forms, however, there are other hurdles to clear. Information and forms for all these processes can be requested from the National Revenue Center in Cincinnati (800-398-2282 or www.ttb.gov/applications/index.shtml). In the packet they'll provide will be guidelines and requirements for everything you'll need to get started on establishing what is essentially a contract between you and the government (as represented by the TTB and the IRS) requiring taxation and compliance for the production and sale of alcoholic beverages. The contractual aspect of the arrangement is important to remember when pondering the appropriateness and classification of all the things they ask you to present and do, and in recognizing the authority held over you, a newcomer to the industry, should you stray from the path of requirement.

Most over-arching and descriptive is the Brewer's Notice, which outlines the site location, size and layout of your brewery (including legal description of the property), as well as its corporate structure and such property- and revenue-protective things as security on the premises. This includes diagrams of the brewery layout which, while perhaps conceptual and a trifle inexact, are still subject to inspection and verification. Like a lot of things, this needs to be close enough to show seriousness and subjugation. You need to prove your operation isn't some fly-by-night shadow plan and that you have nothing to hide. Along similar lines, matters of corporate structure include questionnaires for all key ownership personnel in order to present them as suitable for TTB-regulated business (based on age, citizenship and legal history), as well as a clearly defined statement as to whether yours is a company either independent or aligned with another licensed producer. This last bit might seem odd, but

remember: ours is an industry in transition, with such mergers and partnerships becoming more commonplace all the time. Responsibility/stewardship issues are also covered, such as water quality both in and out of the brewery, as well as solid waste removal and operating noise considerations.

The cherry on top of all this is the Brewer's Bond, generally filed with the assistance of an insurance company. This ensures the payment of taxes and potential penalties and interest, and amounts to an agreed-upon dollar value anticipating yearly tax revenues (remember that beer is currently federally taxed at a rate of $7.00 per barrel up to 60,000 barrels of production). With a minimum amount of $1,000 on up to a maximum of $500,000, this once more demonstrates seriousness and commitment, and provides recourse to the TTB and IRS in cases of delinquency and slackness. It is increased as production increases. This is pretty straightforward and grown-up, but I'd recommend making sure the insurance entity you employ understands the importance of maintaining amounts and schedules as the bond needs to be updated and otherwise amended. I once temporarily lost the ability to pay after the fact of production (requiring prepayment based on anticipation and later correction—a real and easily avoidable nuisance), simply because the agency we used didn't get it (or our continued business, once this occurred). A form giving power of attorney to this engaged agency also needs to be attached to the bond.

You'll notice in all of the above a certain concreteness of concept necessary in even proceeding with application. You can't, in short, pre-apply for a license to operate a brewery-in-planning, site-to-be-determined, investment-personnel-not-yet-fundamentally-secured, etc., etc., etc. And with government staff cuts in virtually every agency not directly involved in national security, fewer people these days look over a greater number of applications than before, resulting in far longer processing times—as long as four to six months, in fact. E-mail and the Internet in general have hastened many processes, but (I'll say it again) you can't really move forward with this aspect of government paperwork unless you're pretty far along in your concept and its execution.

Oh, and by the way, should you decide down the road to open another brewing location or fundamentally alter the terms of your original Brewer's Notice (such as a change in ownership), you need to go through all of this again, from the beginning. Re-statements abound in such cases, by way of assuring the TTB that this is in fact the same company, with the same primary shareholders and bylaws, as well as the same well-maintained and unflinching devotion to compliance and timely payment of tax owed. And with all this paperwork, it's worth suggesting that each page of everything filed be signed and consistently dated in order to bind together all parts of any given document.

It Isn't Just About the Money

While we're at it, the TTB governs many other aspects of the business you're likely to do. Any kegged or packaged beer removed from the premises, whether sold to a private citizen, on- or off-premise retailer or distributor needs to bear a label approved by the TTB: that means it must contain a government warning written in specific language (and type-size) and cannot contain any verbiage or illustration deemed inappropriate. This could include the word "strong" for example, or a cute little cartoon which might be construed as an attempt to appeal to children. Cute little cartoons are not explicitly prohibited, by the way, but like many aspects of the label approval process, it is left to the interpretation of the examining officer. Copies of each label must be submitted for review and eventual Certification/Exemption of Label/Bottle Approval, or COLA. Happily, this can be done electronically, which speeds things along considerably.

The application of specific procedures such as filtration employed to alter character or appearance, the removal of water or other concentration of beer, as well as the use of unusual ingredients also needs to be approved. This last may not once have been much of an issue, but in this age of extremes and experimentation, it is now commonly required to provide types, amounts and even sources for many of the ingredients you and your brewers will want to put into your beer. This includes spices, herbs and alternative fermentables. SOPs (in this case standing for Statement of Process) must be submitted and approved, and

verbiage concisely revealing what's in the beer (e.g. ale brewed with spices) needs to also appear on the label for consumer evaluation. Once again, the level of understanding on the part of examining TTB officers varies. Once they have ruled, however, your course has been determined, whether it makes sense to you or not.

A quick and fairly harmless example: Pretty early in the history of my company, when we were going through the label approval process for our kegged beers offered for wholesale, my partner sent in an approval form for our Porter. For no particular reason in the course of other applications he had included either the word "ale" or the word "lager" in a designated spot on the keg ring. Other labels so treated had been approved, but the porter label came back rejected because, in ATF reckoning, porter was not an ale, but was its own unique thing. You and I know that porters are generally ales, of course. Research discovered that other styles, such as Dortmunder, Bock and Stout, were held inviolably unclassifiable, not to be described as ales or lagers on associated labels. Of course we sputtered, but finally re-submitted the porter label without the word "ale". I could observe on the other side of the scale that so many non-traditional ingredients and processes are being used these days that use of the word "winter" on the label of a seasonal offering doesn't even raise an eyebrow as it once did, when it might have been code for "spiced." Now it's just business as usual.

One key item that needs to be proposed and approved as part of the Brewers Notice is the point at which you determine the volume of beer to be taxed. This can be at the point of transfer from fermentor to conditioner or serving tank, at kegging or at packaging, but whichever method you use must be cleared by the TTB so that they can check up on you and your procedures, if necessary. The measurement system you adopt could affect the design and orientation of your brewing equipment, so it's best to resolve it early. Still, as mentioned above, it isn't possible to gain approvals without a specific site and plan. You had some idea there would be mild paradox involved, didn't you? One further quaint little requirement specifies that tanks be clearly marked for volume, whether in gallons or barrels.

Once you're up and running, the TTB reserves the right to drop in and check the compliance of your production site, and to check your beer in the market for stated alcoholic content and fill level conformity. In addition, they devote a fair amount of oversight to advertising and web materials, a sort of extension of the label approval process, acting as a monitor of comportment and compliance along interpretive lines. Pet peeves include the narrative use of descriptive terms not included on actual labels (such as "strong") and the omission of a website entry page screening entrants for legal age.

Ah Ah, Mr. Wilson, Ah Ah, Mr. Heath

So you've brewed a single seven-barrel batch of beer and processed it to the approved point of taxation within the last two-week period. You fill in the blanks on the TTB form appropriate to the production of beer, assign a serial number pursuant to your system (mine runs something like 1,2,3, and so on), sign and date it with your title—this is the only place I ever refer to myself as brewmaster—and send it off within the allowed ten or so days following the taxation period with a check for: let's see, seven times seven is $49.00. Seem simple? It actually is. As long as you stay on it. It's also possible to file electronically, once methods of transfer have been approved. Don't assume, just because you don't hear anything, that they haven't noticed if you're late. They almost certainly have, and if they decide it's worth their while they'll come after you. And yes, they will fine you.

While paying seven dollars a barrel may be painful, its reckoning is reasonably straightforward. Even eighteen is simple enough, should you rise above 60,000 barrels. This is why the TTB is so exacting about when exactly it is you determine your tax: it's easy for you to figure, and easy for them to check. Similarly simple on the surface is the Brewer's Quarterly Report of Operations, as it balances wort production and the racking of finished beer. It may just be me (though I don't think so), but this is the one I've always dreaded; the one that keeps me sitting with brewsheets and calculator far longer and far more often than I'd like to admit, trying to make it all fit, for every barrel to balance. It can be simple enough, if your situation is simple enough. A one-brewer brewpub with no outside sales, brewing a reasonably set amount a couple of times a week—that's simple. A brewpub with a wholesale component, with a variegated combination of tanks of different sizes between which transfers (and losses) occur and from which bottles and kegs are taken with perhaps (perhaps) sometimes imperfect record-keeping…that's not so simple.

The Quarterly Report is not, strictly speaking, a tax form. It is however required by the TTB to chronicle amounts of raw materials used to produce specific amounts of wort, which are then in turn processed into beer, to which water may or may not be added, and some of which may be wasted or diverted for samples—even destroyed, both "under supervision" and frankly by mistake. Lest you forget the point of the whole exercise, there's a section that gives you one final chance to re-examine the tax returns you've filed over the previous three months and set down the results, once again and for the last time, in black and white. Unless you need to go back and correct something. For while the TTB—and by extension the Treasury Department—is a jealous agency, it is forgiving when it comes to recognizing that we are brewers and in most cases not Nobel Prize-winning mathematicians. If you've found you've made a mistake after the fact, there are spaces on the forms for that, too. You can be fined for this, of course, but incrementally (and of course there are such things as large increments). I'd recommend getting some guidance from someone who's been doing it for a while to get a feel for the workings of the Quarterly Report.

You're Not Done Yet—
State and Local Taxes and Permitting

Generally speaking, state and local permits for opening and operating a brewery are primarily dependent on federal approval. This isn't so much to indicate that the approval process on the local level amounts to simple rubber-stamping, but rather that local permitting concentrates on different areas, such as the fitness of the physical space and the changes wrought on it in order to allow safe occupancy. Electricity, plumbing, health and the adaptability for use by handicapped patrons and workers; these are the kinds of things municipalities need to assess and sign off on before that shiny new license to operate can be put to good use. And while the upfront cost of federal licensing is, aside from the cash or instrument necessary to enable the Brewers Bond, fairly negligible, state and local permits can be expensive. Licenses to operate different kinds of pubs, for example, can run into many thousands of dollars depending on where you are and what local laws and other constraints apply. Simple production facilities are, well, simpler to certify, but add in even the merest of taprooms and legality may immediately be challenged. An awareness of all local regulation, permitting and licensing requirements may at first discourage you and slow your process, but it will prove critical to staying in business.

The scary thing about even attempting to set forth amounts you can expect to pay in state taxes is that in today's economy, and especially on the state level, beer taxes are frequently targeted to make up for other shortfalls. It often seems a good idea to legislators, for example, to tie an increase in beer taxes to alcohol or drug education programs or to other categories that in the minds of some would seem to mitigate some moral wrong allowed by what we are permitted to do by law. These bills and initiatives very often don't pass; the nickel and dime a drink that are sometimes presented as piddling would after all translate to an increase in taxes paid of twelve to twenty-five dollars a barrel, instantly skyrocketing that particular state into the comparative stratosphere of tax burden (and, because of resultant markups, beer price). And thankfully, state senators and representatives often recognize the impact of steady tax revenue from businesses which might cease to exist following draconian tax hikes. Often, but not always. As it is, states vary wildly, from less than a dollar a barrel paid in Wyoming to over twelve in Alabama and Alaska (no, they aren't ranked alphabetically). And by the time you read this, some of them have probably changed.

It's also impossible to generalize about the ways in which state taxes are tabulated and paid. Multiple forms sometimes chronicle shipments to distributors and break sales down by type (in-house, direct-to-retailer, if allowed, or to a distributor), or differentiate in-state and out-of-state sales. Some states also require

a breakdown for draft and packaged sales. Different rates are often involved for different categories, and in many states, distributors pay state taxes. Don't think for a moment that that little item will increase your profit margin—you also typically are paid a substantially lower price by a distributor than if you were to self-distribute your beer. Generally speaking, however, state taxes are tied to sales, where federal taxes are tied to production. The two are no doubt related, but not directly. Remember also that you are responsible for the filing and payment of taxes in every state in which you distribute. You are probably more likely to see a state auditor regularly than you are a federal one, and if everything is in order there is no reason to fear this any more than you would the maintenance of other business relationships.

As cities and counties here and there prohibit the sale of alcoholic beverages altogether, there are those that tax its production beyond what state and federal agencies require. There are local beer taxes, in fact, in specific parts of Georgia, Illinois, Louisiana, Maryland, New York and Ohio. These can involve straight-up production taxes, on-premise taxes, wholesale taxes and private club taxes. Where does it all end, you ask? Neighborhood tax? Kitchen tax? Don't ask that. You're just getting started, remember? Oh, and should you, through all of this and your other travails, find that you've made a little money despite everything, you'll probably need to pay income tax as well.

Chapter Highlights

Compliance Hurdles to Clear
- Brewers Notice—describes project, including business structure, location and layout, and security
- Personnel Questionnaire—identifies principals, their legal histories and eligibility
- Environmental Information—describes power types used and solid and liquid waste
- Brewers Bond—an amount pegged to production, from $1,000 to $500,000, filed to guarantee payment of taxes

- Power of Attorney—assigned to agency filing the Brewers Bond
- State and local licensing and permits—variable
- Label and process approvals
- Brewer's Report of Operations
- Excise tax payment—federal, state, and sometimes local
- Business Income Tax filing

BUSINESS STRUCTURE
It Isn't Easy Being Us

13

It isn't easy being us. On the one hand we love the illicitness of it all, making beer under the radar in our homes and garages, smugly exceeding the legal maximum gallonage as a badge of bad-boy (and -girl!) honor. It binds us to a rollicking rebel past of moonshiners, bootleggers and speakeasies familiarly chronicled in Marx Brothers movies. Younger practitioners speak in hushed, reverent tones when in the presence of one of our venerable and invariably bearded fossils: those who can claim to be homebrewers since before 1976, when it first became legal in this country to do so (though still not in Mississippi and Alabama!). It'll also pass to have been doing the deed since, say, age fourteen.

But we want to be legit, too—to be legally recognized as professional brewers, with licenses and permits to hang on the wall, big-girl (and -boy!) brows to furrow, the concerns of commerce to be borne stoically, inevitably as we ply not just our hobby but our trade. Our movement, after all, would not be complete without the zeal of the recently converted, first as we learn our diastatic enzymes and later as we extend our necks ox-like to accept the yoke of incorporation.

For incorporate we must, or at least probably should, in order to protect ourselves from the kind of legal stuff that can really wreck any brewer's day. Bankruptcy, scandal, and prison—all those things perhaps unwittingly brought upon us by some unincorporated Uncle Billy or the turn of some other worm of happenstance. I feel like a bit of a sell-out to say it, but we need to get serious for a moment and examine our options where submitting to the Man is concerned. And while we're at it, let's take a look at how to protect ourselves from each other as we form these constructs. Partnerships, shareholders, S- and C-corporations, bylaws—who knew we'd be so grown-up when we floated our first hydrometer? But here we are.

Cheese Stands Alone Brewing Co.— Sole Proprietorships

Take heart, lone wolves. The necessities of commerce notwithstanding, it's still possible to go it more or less alone, to have your cake and reap its profits, too. The downside is that you're also responsible for debts and losses. It's yours, all yours, if you desire to so structure it, even if you take on investors and have employees; even, in fact, if you have partners (but more on that later). Why would anyone invest in something somebody else owns and controls, you may ask. Well, you'll hear this a lot, in this chapter and in this book: it's up to you. If you can make it happen, it will happen. Maybe you agree to pay your investors off in fairly short—or even longer—order. Perhaps there's some other way you've managed to put it all together. Maybe you don't have investors beyond yourself, but still want the protections that can come with organization outside of incorporation.

Admittedly, these protections are spare in a sole proprietorship, extending to officers, should you have them, and employees, but not to yourself. For in a sole proprietorship there is no distinction between the company and its owner. What this means is that it's all on you—profits and losses, the personal responsibilities of taxation, including those subsidizing Social Security and whatever other programs arise. About the only distinction there might be between you and your business is in the name, and even then there could be a legal requirement stating that you yourself are "doing business as" whatever the name of your company happens to be.

The advantage to sole proprietorship? Simplicity. As one useful website put it, you might even have a sole proprietorship already, without knowing it, as any solo business activity incurring either profit or loss—creative, mercantile, or whatever—is just that. No registry is required, so there are no legal restrictions beyond those involving taxes and debts. Should things go wrong, however, you are on the hook; everything you own as sole proprietor, including the business itself, is subject to seizure under the appropriately unhappy circumstances.

S, C and LLC—the Alphabet Soup of Incorporation (or Not)

To some, the sole proprietorship might seem the least knee-bending way to go. But there's no legal escape from the harsh glare of attention and direct demand. In most cases, some type of incorporation is desirable, establishing a so-called veil between the activities and responsibilities of a company and its proprietorship, as well as providing some structure for operation and accountability. There is also something of a middle ground: the LLC, or limited liability company, which does require an operating agreement, but falls short of actual incorporation and some of its requirements, and still provides legal protection from liability for its operators. The LLC passes tax responsibility for profits (as well as the declaration of losses) on to the individual shareholder, thereby absolving the LLC from direct income taxation. It can, for tax purposes, choose to manage itself as another type of corporation. No

organizational charter, operating agreement or board of directors is required.

To some, this simple approach might seem like the best of both worlds: protection from personal liability without onerous submission to the Man. To some it might actually be all this. There are potential difficulties, however, such as the effect such an apparent lack of legal and conceptual structure could have on the willingness of potential investors. In addition, should there be more than a single person operating the essence of the company, the pathways to formalized problem-solving, shall we say, might be limited. Without a charter or board of directors, without in fact any recourse to agreed-upon structure, things could turn ugly in a hurry.

The S-corporation shares with the LLC the tax advantage (should you see it that way, and why shouldn't you?) of passing responsibility on to individual shareholders. By contrast, the scenario of the C-corporation taxes dividends twice: once on the corporate level, and after dispersal, once on the personal returns of shareholders. How? Why? What? Yes, indeed, but there's more to the distinction than merely that. The C-corporation carries no restrictions where ownership is concerned, neither to number nor citizenship. It may also have different classes of stock, such as non-voting shares offered as an incentive to valued staff in addition to the more powerful shares tied to initial investment. By contrast, the S-corporation may have a maximum of 100 shareholders, and all must be US citizens. This is the tax rub for the C-corp, in order to ensure that all profits be taxed at some point, on-shore. Both S- and C-corporations provide limited freedom from liability for operators, shareholders and officers; both require boards of directors, bylaws, filing with the state and codified corporate procedures.

Simple, right? Of course there's so much more to it than that; this is just the barest sketch of distinctions and similarities, merely to give you an idea of where to turn your research and what to rule out knowing what you do about the potential structure of your fledgling business. I'd also recommend sitting down with a general attorney, tax attorney or CPA just to make sure you understand all the options and haven't overlooked something. Also, never forget that state requirements and allowances vary; these folks are certainly going to be more aware of specific local requirements than you are. My coast-to-coast characterizations are a fairly homogenized look at the options out there. Handfuls of legislative entities require this or that, others forbid the same things, and require others. Not all possibilities exist everywhere. Does any of this surprise you?

Dotting I's, Crossing T's and Taking Names

It can all seem kind of funny when, hammers and wrecking bars in hand, you decide who among you and your partners wants to be president of the company and who secretary. Usually it's because some papers need to be signed, and whichever bank or agency or other necessary entity insists on specific designation before they can proceed. It can give you pause, if only because it may be the first time you've had to address how the outside world sees your divisional organization. President of a company? Me? Well, yes. Or vice-president, or secretary, or Chief Financial Officer. For there will be lots of papers to sign, from things required by lenders, vendors and other administrative and mercantile types to those necessary for convincing governmental agencies such as the IRS and TTB that you mean what you say and that simply put, you are for real. You won't wake up seeing the world a different way for having taken on these titles, but you will continue in that role—or at least sign your name to it—until such time as your Board of Directors deems otherwise.

Perhaps that's where we should start. Though not required for either a Sole Proprietorship or an LLC, a Board of Directors is required for the formation and operation of any legally recognized corporation. The number of members of the Board is not in any way set in stone. Many small companies have as few as three Board members; some non-profits and larger corporations may have dozens. Prevailing wisdom holds that however many Board members there may be, that number should be odd, in order to avoid potential deadlock, and that some of the members should be from outside the company's employ, to retain some degree of impartiality.

The Board of Directors constitutes the supreme authority in any corporation. It guides policy and strategy, has the power to hire and fire the company's chief executive, set salaries and budgets, determine dividends, and is required to meet regularly and communicate with the shareholders on matters fundamental to the maintenance of their investment and ownership. It is typically not involved in decisions regarding day-to-day operation, but is generally made aware of the function and effectiveness of those operations via reports from department heads. The Board is elected by the shareholders. Within the Board, there must be a Chairman and a Secretary, and there may be other titled officers.

The Company can be organized in as much or little complexity as seems appropriate, though a Chief Executive must be designated, even if this role is shared. There will likely be a Chief of Operations and Chief Financial Officer, and Chiefs of other departments as designated, such as Brewing, Restaurant Operations, Human Resources, Sales, Marketing, Information or Sustainability.

It is important to maintain continuity on both of these levels—Board and Operational Organization—when signing documents, or when licensing and other governmental interface comes into play. A change in role or title will often require re-filing of appropriate forms.

Papers, Please—Bylaws and Other Legal Niceties

In order to ensure continuity, consistency and recourse between shareholders and the operating entities of the company, a set of bylaws must be drawn up and unanimously approved by the shareholders. This is typically assembled by lawyers, and consists of customized boilerplate covering appropriate legal requirements of the company's home state. It specifies such things as the procedures for the nomination and election of Board officers, the frequency and timing of general meetings, and the processes by which shares in the company can be bought and sold. Often, such a Stock Purchase Agreement is a separate document, and there may be others, tendered at the beginning of investment by shareholders and requiring unanimous approval for alteration.

As with all legal documents, these agreements should actually be read and their language weighed. It's often extremely difficult during a flurry of signing and agreeing—generally undertaken during myriad other concurrent flurries—to anticipate future eventualities. At the very least, the attorneys who draw up the agreements should explain their language. "This is here because of the possibility of…", for example, or "this probably won't happen, but…"—to list a couple. It often isn't easy to get all your shareholders to get back to you with their approvals for change, should such a thing be determined necessary, so the fewer times that "favor" for alteration is invoked, the smoother things will probably run. There's no onus, of course, on deciding that things need to be changed; it's simply more difficult to implement later on.

The Thing with Two (or More) Heads—Partnerships

There was a time when educated people embodied all the knowledge of their age, from the social arts to the sciences, the humanities and mechanical masteries, foreign languages on back to Latin and Greek, with an ability to passably sing and play the piano thrown in for good measure. Blame it on whatever you want—the Industrial Revolution, the Atomic Age or dissolute youth—but the polite way these days to describe a typical individual's breadth of knowledge is "specialized." Expensive liberal arts educations notwithstanding, the societal push is in the direction of focus, grasp and niche occupation. Throw in the fact that relatively few of us are actual experts at all aspects of what, by reading this book, we plan to embark upon, and the desirability of partnership pretty readily suggests itself.

For the sake of both diplomacy and discretion, I'm going to try to steer away from specificity where my own business partnership is concerned. I will say, however, that our division into the areas of sales, finance and brewing is a pretty common triumvirate. For a cuisine-heavy concept, it's also typical to have a kitchen person thrown in.

You've no doubt heard the old chestnut that a partnership is like a marriage, or perhaps acknowledging that we're actual people and not shadows on a cave wall, that it actually is a marriage. Both are true, and in pretty much all ways: richer, poorer, in sickness and in health, as well as the fact that no one outside the marriage has any idea what goes on within it. Sometimes it's actually an agreement between people who are legally married to each other. Like a marriage, it can be broken, with consequences according to the cooperation of all parties pursuant to their original agreement. Like many marriages it can work beautifully, with the talents and strengths of its principals working in harmony; and sadly, like many other marriages, it can drag dismally on for years. In the experience of my awareness it can be both, with ups and downs, periods of great meshing and effectiveness and other spans during which nothing seems to work. In short, it's an extremely common way to go.

Two partners? Three partners. Four? Six? You don't need me to map out the potential dynamics of every geometric configuration. Just get it in writing, for the sake of everyone.

Organization as Chameleon— the Kind with the Independent Eyes

Companies and corporations can often begin one way and end up another. Simply put, sometimes somebody gets pissed off and leaves. With partnerships that included brewers, it was usually the brewer who left, airily having taken offense at over-pragmatism or some artistic constraint. That may simply be my own guardedness talking, or self-loathing. It may also have been because in a consortium of people bringing money to the table, the brewer often has to borrow from his or her friends. These days, more enlightened business plans bring the brewer in as more than just a poor relation. (Of course I would say that.) The point remains that in order to maintain continuity and loyalty, the incentive for ownership should be part of the picture for all key participants.

Sometimes circumstances change due to market factors such as an alteration of law or perhaps a stock shuffle. Tax structures change occasionally, and new advantages to the path not taken can be spied over there in the receding distance. This kind of reinvention can be prudent at times, but it is a fair amount of work, as all participants must be signed on once more.

Fortunately it doesn't mean the previous entity must be dissolved prior to re-formation. You aren't back to square one, exactly; you just need to get everyone to agree to the change.

And not all changes make sense. The circumstances of growth and success can make untenable a change which on other levels might seem right. Say you're operating a C-corporation which with its other restrictions requires that dividends be taxed twice (by the corporation and then again personally, by individual shareholders). Wouldn't it be nice, given this or that bit of organizational happenstance, to re-form as an S-corp, where it's every man for himself, tax-wise, with no corporate filing necessary? Well, it would be, if it were that simple. The C-corp, you see, keeps all assets within the company as it goes along, including equipment, buildings and anything else that might be lying around. The S-corp passes this ownership on to its shareholders as it acquires them, requiring them each year to render a comprehensive statement regarding their little piece of the company and its attendant profits or losses. To change designation from C to S would, overnight, transfer appropriate percentages of ownership of every piece of whatever the company itself possesses to its shareholders, thereby requiring them to declare income on the apparent windfall. That's a tough one to swallow, even if it might eventually be neater. It can certainly be managed, usually by the company taking charge where taxations are concerned, but even this involvement would need to be reflected in individual tax filings.

If "The Big Sleep" is noir-speak for death, perhaps bankruptcy could be similarly termed "The Big Bye-Bye." But you aren't, I presume, reading this book to figure out how to close your brewery. Just bringing that up gives me the shivers. There are, however, other "Big Reorganizations" involving the sale and merger of companies. Entirely unrelated companies can find themselves in sudden cosmic alignment owing to independently fortuitous (or perhaps less felicitous) circumstances. A particular corporate entity might think it advantageous to move into a new geographic or conceptual realm by glomming onto something already existing.

The terms for such combination or absorption can also vary widely. Sometimes it's straight-up cash. More often it at least involves the transfer of stock. Sometimes both structures, organizationally, are burned to the ground, with a whole new corporate phoenix rising from the ashes. There are also all sorts of ways of bringing this change about. One thing to keep in mind, should such a thing happen to be a priority for you, is what effect the weather of change will have on your job. Not every company needs two CEOs, for example, or two supremely powerful brewers. Presumably all that stuff will come up in the negotiations. One thing, to me, at least, is certain: the future will surprise us. Lion & Lamb Brewing Company, anyone?

Chapter Highlights

Characteristics of Corporate Structures

Sole Proprietorship
- Linked to a single owner, who owns all assets, is entitled to all profits and liable for all losses and debts
- Protects investors and officers, should there be any, from liability and prosecution
- Minimally regulated, requiring only the filing of "Doing Business As" paperwork
- Dissolves on the death of the sole proprietor

Limited Liability Corporation
- Does not require incorporation
- Protects investors and operators from personal debt and liability
- Passes tax responsibility to individual investors, but can be operated as another type of corporation (e.g. C- or S-corp.) for tax purposes
- Provides no structure for dispute within the company

S-Corporation
- Requires incorporation and all that goes with it—a board of directors, bylaws, regular meetings, etc.
- Protects investors, officers and operators

- Passes tax responsibility on to investors
- Requires US citizenship for investment
- No more than 100 investors
- May only have one class of stock

C-Corporation

- Requires incorporation
- Protects investors, officers and operators
- Dividends effectively taxed twice, as income by the company and by individual investors
- Does not require US citizenship for investment
- May issue different classes of stock

COMPLIANCE
Other Legal and Ethical Issues

14

For all our frame breaking and iconoclasm, we are in most ways a pretty law-abiding bunch. We have to be. With all the revenues to be gained from what we do by federal, state and local regulating entities, we are definitely worth the trouble of noticing (and perhaps occasionally nudging). Still affected by the legacies of Prohibition, ours is a volatile and attentive industry for oversight. We're all required to pay taxes, we know, but there's a huge, wondrous and amorphous body of permitting and compliance with which we are also expected to be familiar. Beyond that there are areas even less certain, involving behaviors, ethics and codes of conduct that can affect the way we all do business and coexist in the market.

Of course laws themselves can be changed. Many pioneers of the craft brewing movement had to petition their legislators and generally make a nuisance of themselves to pursue their visions of doing business. Where the differences of interpretation of alcoholic beverage law by the states are concerned, some had merely never considered the possibility of tiny and entrepreneurial breweries choosing to enter the game, while others were patently resistant to the idea. Even today this ambivalence exists. Homebrewing itself was forbidden throughout the land until 1976, and while today most of us consider this our Magna Carta, two states (Alabama and Mississippi) still manage pretty steadfastly to

hold out. As with any other attempt at legislative change, it is possible to enlist the support of individual or groups of legislators to alter the interpretation or wording of previously-held law. Happily, the creation of jobs and tax revenues by a successful line of business in a difficult economy is nearly always looked upon favorably. Legislators are happy to help on many levels, but politics is complicated. State or local brewers guilds too are an important tool in effecting legislative change. In addition to providing brewers of all experience and command a community in which to move and interact, guilds tend to recognize the common good in pursuing changes that will benefit individual members (though there are contentious exceptions). A campaign for legislative change is far more effective when conducted in numbers, and especially with the endorsement of a recognized trade organization.

But say your first order of business isn't hastening the Revolution. As a hobbyist in transition or perhaps a business-savvy person looking to develop a concept, your idea of changing the world probably has more to do with conviviality than out-and-out iconoclasm. You just want to make and sell beer, and perhaps eventually make a little money. But in your position of craftsperson, of artisan, of generally benign owner of a small business, dilemmas involving action and responsibility will eventually cross your path.

Grey and Greyer—the Skull and Bones of It All

We'd all like to believe that everyone in our industry is honest and above-board, and that shady dealings, kick-backs and bribes couldn't possibly stand between the artisan brewer and the loyal craft beer consumer. Unfortunately, that's not always the case.

So when someone intimates that you might be able to get your beer on in their tavern or store if you somehow sweeten the pot, it may or may not come as a surprise to you. We figure that on our small scale of operation, costs and margins are so narrowly realized that such a suggestion would be unseemly at the very least. And yet they are tendered, as though the very word beer carries the assumption of royalty along with it. It's rare that an actual cash payment is demanded (though one does hear of this happening, in an unsubstantiated way); more common is the free keg for every however many purchased. Occasionally a new name will be given to the same old beer, and offered exclusively—and at a lower price—to a particular retailer. Or you'll be asked to provide menus or other operational matter. There are lots of sneaky ideas. The fact that many of these scenarios are legal in some states makes it that much more difficult to deal with them in others.

We aren't collectively allowed to discuss specifics of price where our products are concerned. To do so even conversationally would amount to collusion, a violation of anti-trust laws. But to enter into grey-market agreements with retailers and others where free kegs and cases are slid in set ratio to those actually paid for is no less nefarious, and does none of us any good. Straight-up cash for placement is legal in the worlds of food and other commodities, where they are called "slotting fees" or "incentives"; in ours it generally isn't. Rumors abound, of course, of dirty breweries that make a practice of such things, careening around markets enacting what might be called brand-cleansing, targeting specific competition and perhaps shutting smaller producers out entirely. Like most rumors, there's some truth to them.

Not only can a company the size of yours and mine not afford such strategy, it's wrong at any size, and undermines the integrity of what we do and believe in. It suggests that we make beer for nothing and take in money hand over fist as a matter of course, that somehow it is we who take unfair advantage by the free and easy lifestyle afforded by our profits. Get to the point at which perhaps you can hire a salesperson to work even your home market, and the subject will come up (if it hasn't before). Laws exist, as I've said, to specifically prohibit cash payments and discounts not offered to all. Laws also exist in varying form, state to state, to enjoin the gifting of expensive free stuff and services accruing to the benefit of the wholesale customer without appearing on an invoice. Admittedly this can sometimes be taken to an extreme, such as forbidding the provision of coasters or trinkets such as bottle openers. In Oregon, for example, it is illegal to use Internet social media to advertise an event. But the spirit of such laws is intended to protect us, and to keep our world from tipping back into Prohibition-era abuses. Often enough it is policies formed in the 1930s and 40s which constrain us.

Other parts of the world see things differently. In Southeast Asia, for example, not only is it routine for breweries to provide all draft equipment—lines, taps and refrigerators—but an incentive system exists for actual payment back to accounts for numbers of kegs sold. It's essentially a restructuring of the free-kegs-in-ratio deal, but the more beer sold, the better the terms. In the UK, of course, most bars are owned by breweries, providing ready retail outlet—and cash—for the particular products of the allied brewer. The system isn't nefarious in itself, merely a different business model, but like the Asian example cited above it presents a game beyond the means of the small producer. Small wonder that in such markets it's taken a bit longer to foster enthusiasm for the craft beer movement. It is happening, however, even there.

The gentlemanly side of competition pretends that it doesn't exist, or at least that it isn't some microcosmic statement of general worth and the tooth and claw nature of the world. We are all competitors, to be sure, vying for a finite amount of commercial space within myriad arenas of geography and market. But we are also undeclared co-conspirators, united in our devotion to our craft and its production of great beer. We also tend to enjoy each other's company, and don't particularly enjoy being enemies. When do the gloves come off, you might ask. Aren't there times when the stakes might seem high enough to set all that aside and just go for it, no holds barred?

Oh, there are squabbles, and particularly on the level of growing regional breweries (of which there are more each year), very real stakes. And unsurprisingly, it's easier for brewers to set aside commercial rivalries than it is for salespeople. But the road most of us choose to take when it comes to prevailing—or at least succeeding—in a market is to do what we do the best we possibly can, whether it's brewing, creating great labels and affecting brand campaigns, or putting together a cozy little pub that people want to come to. The general positivity of our movement is one of its strengths, even if on some levels it's a bit of an illusion. Which is why, if at all possible or unless attacked, we should avoid fighting among ourselves, and employing tactics in the market which would amount to as much.

It's bad form to gun for specific others in the marketplace even if what you want is to be the best selling beer in America. Just put your head down and do your work, without begrudging the success of those who have come before you. Similarly, it's indecent on the surface to poach brewers, salespeople and others from colleagues. It's possible to make it generally known that you're looking, to send the message without actively plucking, and it's best, if you get what you want, to avoid crowing about it. Do I really need to go into this? I know it invites judgments of naiveté and attempts to recreate a lost Eden, but it's something close enough to what we've already accomplished in that direction to be sustainable, or at least worth the attempt. If nothing else, it confounds the big brewers.

A Beer By Any Other Name—Trademarks

One of the issues with which our gang will increasingly come in contact is trademark. I once wrote a column, a sort of beer name-related parody of the Arthur C. Clarke story "The Nine Billion Names of God," in which, in both cases, the end of the universe is triggered by the very last respective name having been tabulated. The fact is that there are lots of us looking at the same oceans and vistas, watching the same movies and listening to the same music, sharing a similarly tilted time on Earth and in America. The same and similar names for our beers are liable to pop up somewhere between Arcata and Acadia, and as we all grow, to begin to occupy contiguous and overlapping commercial space. By all means, protect your names and brands by trademarks, but when such overlap inevitably occurs, at least try to pull in your claws and avoid digging in your heels. If we can't self-police, allowing for a little deference and sense of humor, there are plenty of surrogate enforcers out there, eager to take our money and by their efforts incidentally satisfy the larger brewers eager for a discordant stumble in our march toward increased market share. Don't forget to cast an eye to trademarked names amid our brethren in the wine and spirits world.

Two brewers who also happened to be friends found an elegant solution in keeping with the spirit of our movement when they discovered that each of them brewed a beer with the same name. Instead of fighting over the fact that both had a beer in their portfolios called Salvation, Adam Avery of Avery Brewing in Boulder, Colorado and Vinnie Cilurzo of Russian River Brewing in Santa Rosa, California decided to brew a beer together called Collaboration Not Litigation. What happened to the original beer of potential contention, you may ask. They both continued brewing their own versions of it, having already called attention to them, and their difference—and of course incidentally advertising for them both along the way.

Of course there are those among us bent on enacting, in miniature, the dramas of bluster and conflict more familiar to big business. Figurative shots are fired not only in an effort to diminish the sales of a competitor, but sometimes merely to criticize ways of doing business and relating to the world. We occasionally draw lines which are difficult to undraw, even after decades, and which can create enough stir for those outside our industry to take notice. Such enmity no doubt brings a smile to those waiting to see how it—everything we have all created together—will all end; news-hungry business pages are particularly interested in such stories of proto-demise. I urge us all to forget petty squabbles and remember our collective stakes. Self-definition, whether through beer quality, branding, or styles of doing business, need not involve actively opposing or detracting from others. No one among us could have achieved what we all have done together. Better to move into our futures back to back than to duplicate the gamesmanship and conflict that once nearly consolidated American brewing out of existence.

Chapter Highlights

Slippery Slopes: Four Ethical Issues to Avoid
- Refusing to pay—Always compensate services or labor with cash, discounts or excessive stuff.
- Targeting specific competitors
- Poaching staff
- Suing each other unless absolutely necessary

SECTION IV

BRANDING/ MARKETING/SALES

BRAND IDENTITY
Marking It with Your Brand

15

Britain's first trademark was for a beer, Bass Ale, its simple triangle device so recognizable as to cry out even now from Manet's 1882 painting of the bar at the Folies-Bergère. That's Bass Ale, remarks the modern enthusiast. The mark at that point was only several years old, but it was over 130 years ago. Similarly, and at around the same time, I suppose, ranchers in the American West were literally branding their cattle with devices geometric, pictographic and alphanumeric. These brands served to separate the property, or products, of one ranch from another, for without the lazy 8 or the rocking R it was impossible to tell one group of cows from another.

Of course there are cynics among us who might say that branding (and its subsequent marketing) is all that separates one beer from another. Craft cynics might reserve this generalization for the big brewers; some among the big brewers might say the opposite. Both positions come from a willful ignorance, as does a third, that the beer in the bottle should be able to sell itself; that branding is merely a game enacted by marketers who never made a drop of beer in their lives.

I love brewers. I am a brewer. As a brewer I should probably not complain too loudly about the cult of personality that has arisen surrounding craft brewers themselves, and some of them in particular. In some cases these anointed individuals, the actual (or once-actual) brewers of the beer beloved by fans, have literally become the brand of their breweries, recognizable everywhere they go within the bounds of our own little world, sought after by the cognoscenti. Some, like Sam Calagione of Dogfish Head, revel in this, riding it to wider fame and recognition. Others, like John Maier of Rogue Ales, are more self-effacing but no less revered, surrounded by a coterie of generally quieter fans. That other stuff—the books and TV shows and dinners and lines of adoring fans, well, that's just Sam. And maybe Garrett Oliver of Brooklyn Brewing. And as odd as it is, it does us all good.

But most of the rest of us should probably just get over ourselves. What we do is important, of course. Not to do it well or creatively is to consign ourselves and our brands to obscurity. But to think it's the only thing that matters is to make another mistake, the mistake of pride and egotism. And I know plenty of excellent brewers, by the way, who have either lost their jobs or settled into an enduring state of discontent because they favor their egos over their brands and their jobs. Alan Newman, the founder of Magic Hat, has been quoted as saying that Magic Hat is a marketing company that simply happens to make beer. This is no doubt dissembling, given the loyalty to its products—and not simply its campaigns—that customers have displayed over the years. Taken seriously it might show a different kind of egotism.

A successful brand is a team effort. It's about great beer, sure, and the people who make it with pride (the good kind of pride, not that other kind), but it's also about where it fits in the landscape, who it's aimed at, what it looks like and what it says. It's about personality, for sure, but it's more collective than just a person. It's the combined creative energies of brewers, graphic artists and copywriters, as well as the no-less-creative energies of the people who run the company, make the decisions, place the products and sponsor the events. In the case of the smallest breweries these may all be combined in one or two people, but that doesn't make it any less an alliance of expertise.

It can cost a lot of money to create and maintain a brand, and it can be money well spent if it's part of your plan to create a splash with a professionally-generated campaign and set of images. Expect to spend twenty or thirty thousand dollars to have someone else—someone who does it for a living, and not a relative—take your concepts and breathe life into them, make ads with them and get the word out. During the boom times of our movement there have been plenty of companies who started this way. Their thinking was that a more polished image was required to bring craft beer to a crowded specialty market poised to move more into the mainstream. Many of these projects were cynically conceived, placing far more importance on the quality of the campaign than on the quality of the product. I can imagine that from a certain perspective of sophistication and general market awareness it's tempting to think that all a fledgling and artisanal movement needs to really succeed is the touch of an adult hand.

Take a look at the list of the top fifty American craft breweries as ranked by the Brewers Association or tracked by the statisticians of any other trade entity. Truly, there are some sophisticated organizations among them. But even those we might consider most successful began their brand lives with simple and essentially homemade identities and imagery. Even the biggest American beer brands, those with origins dim in the mists of the nineteenth century, probably did not begin with branding much more sophisticated than those cowboys with their hot irons. In both cases those were simpler times. In neither would it have

seemed appropriate for a new beer brand to appear between the slick covers of a well-regarded public relations or advertising firm: in one case because it would have been a violation of the ethos of the time and the tenor of the movement; in the other mainly because such treatments hadn't yet been invented. They pay for their branding now. You know they do. But whether you do at the outset of your endeavor should be a well-considered decision based on your assessment of balance in the landscape you're about to become a part of.

There's a lot you can do without dropping a lot of cash. These are the cold winter night projects, in fact, the stuff of momentary inspiration and the hours-long brainstorming session. Beer may be involved. The earliest American brewers may just have wanted to get their factories up and running, their beer into the market any way they could, incidentally, unthinkingly branding them with a family name. But these days we think in brands. We can't help ourselves. Part of the reason is that it's narcissistic fun to collectivize ourselves and create a larger image of what makes us and our prospective brand special. Another part is that it works. When well conceived and well executed, other people will get it too.

Greg Owsley, the man behind many of the successful brands and campaigns of New Belgium's last fifteen years, once sent me and my company an interesting exercise. "Who is Elysian?" he asked. Not who drinks it and buys it—though that's no doubt part of it—but who is this person embodied in the company's brand and image? What does he or she look like? What is this person into? What does he do with his time? What does she believe? Off the bat it might seem that I'm having a hard time deciding whether Elysian is a boy or a girl, but I think you get the line of inquiry. To create or corroborate a personality embodied by your brand can be helpful when making a judgment on what's appropriate to it.

Who is the person embodied by your brand? Do they live in the country or in town? Are they outdoorsy, cynical, working class, wise? Do they go to galleries or work on cars? What kind of food do they eat? Do they make it themselves? Sure, it's a bit of a filter, this game, combining aspiration and demography. But it's something you can do yourself, with no money, to help you decide what works for you, what feels right and different and unique about what you're about to put out there in the market and in the wider world. Try it. It don't cost nothin'.

Another inexpensive brand inquiry involves asking people directly for their help in defining or giving some impression of what they consider your brand to be. It can cost as little as a couple of beers and some old magazines, or drawing and writing materials, for people to take a few minutes or a half-hour to create a visual or written representation of what they associate with a particular beer, or with your whole, collective image. At the very least you'll learn something; you certainly aren't bound by what they present to you. You are the boss, right? It's important along these lines to remember not to be a slave to your brand. Themes can be flogged: too many mountains, too many mythological figures (ouch!), too many modes of alternative transportation, too much (or too little) whimsy. And at times it makes sense to rethink it all, to change it up completely or at least to reinterpret some of what you've already created. One of the most successful updates of a brand I can think of is the one implemented several years ago by Mountain Dew®. Once centered on making fun of hillbillies, the new ads made use of the snowboarding craze and other extreme sports.

You'll find that variations of this kind of self-examination will resonate in other inquiry, and influence decisions that might on the surface seem unrelated to brand building and identity. Is that couch right? Should you serve lobster tails? Does it make sense to have games behind the bar to loan out to customers? Will the display of a little bravado in your brand be off-putting, or hilarious and compelling? You may fall into some of this stuff along the way, putting details together that seem at the time like things everybody does, but at some point you're going to have to think about what it all means for who you want to be in your market, and to your patron and consumer.

Branding Informs Marketing—or is it the other way around?

At some indeterminate point the crafting of your brand will become marketing, which in turn will build

on what you've created. You'll come up with ideas, for beers, for events, for sponsorships and collaborations that will both cement elements of your brand and serve to sell it. For that is what you're trying to do, right, sell beer? Once again, you can choose to spend a lot of money on this, bringing in outside help. At some point in the life of your business, such an approach might make sense. But when you're just getting started, the more you can come up with yourself, the better.

One of the buzz-terms of recent years is guerrilla marketing, referring to the idea of making something—a poster, an event, a whole campaign—out of practically nothing. Many fledgling movements have taken off in this way, making a part of their look and feel this kind of low-overhead creativity. Think of the cut-and-paste cover of the Sex Pistols' album (and no end of punk rock posters), but then remember that their manager, Malcolm MacLaren, was one of the shrewdest dissemblers of modern marketing. That's the idea, though, taking found objects and other opportunities of happenstance to get the message out. It doesn't mean literally that your marketing materials should look like a ransom note. It does mean that a lot of decisions and actions can be determined by an awareness, even a celebration of your limitations.

The earliest craft breweries were such a novelty in the commercial landscape that they drew attention to themselves without having to do anything. Making your own beer in quantities small enough to be apprehended by the average person was so new and alien, so interesting, that there was almost a compulsion among the curious to check it all out. This is still part of our collective brand, rolling together the honesty of our processes, the fact that we all did it in the face of near-monolithic control of the industry by the big brewers, and that what we produce is flavorful and interesting. So unlike other, less populist pursuits, we begin our efforts out in front, up two balls in the count and looking for a fastball. We aren't at all assured of commercial success, but we can—and need to be—selective in how we choose to proceed. Our movement is maturing, and bringing sophistication and awareness to how we make and sell beer. We may not be as cute as we used to be, but a certain amount of whimsy and improvisation is allowed us, especially when we are starting out. Like the exercises that help an actor find his character and help build the confidence to successfully execute, the niches and opportunities created and presented in our earliest days of business can inform the direction of years of identity.

There's a paradox in all this. On one hand we are, as a movement, growing up. We're required to be shrewd and knowing about what we do in the market. We're no longer under the radar where the big brewers are concerned, and we have to be vigilant of their attentions. But we also have to be aware of who's coming up behind us, not so that we can keep them from succeeding—that would be antithetical to our origins, and cynical, to boot—but in order to maintain nimbleness and honesty in what we do with our brands and our businesses. "There's always a bigger fish," observes the elder Jedi played by Liam Neeson in the first of the lamentable *Star Wars* prequels, a supposed lesson in humility. For us this is true as well. But no less true is that there's always another, smaller one too—lots of them, in fact. This thing we've created isn't evolving exactly like other collective models. In a way it's the conscience imparted by our pasts that prefigures our collective future. This truly isn't your grandfather's brewing industry. We may need, in fact, to look a generation or so farther back as we move forward. The Bass triangle is as good a place as any to start.

Chapter Highlights

Brand Mantras
- You are your brand, but keep things in perspective.
- What person (and personality) is embodied in your brand?
- Every decision you make reflects on your brand.

PROMOTION
Promoting an Artisanal Movement—a Paradox?

16

Actively promoting an artisanal movement can be a tough line to walk. The products, after all—bread, beer, coffee, cheese—are so authentic and interesting that not only should their merits be self-evident, but to trumpet them beyond the effort-driven reach of the supporting cognoscenti might in some ways seem distasteful and antithetical to the passion of creation and loving nurture. Or so goes a line of reasoning based more on snobbery and protectiveness—and fear—than on sales. It's a common conceit among producers and consumers of products for which demand far exceeds supply. But then comes expansion, or the next big thing, and with rare exception those passionate producers find themselves needing to get the word out in some way. Either that or retreat, beautifully and tastefully—and who knows, perhaps with a considerate amount of success and profit—into commercial obscurity. It is possible, however, to be both legendary and successful.

Part of this artisanal ethos lies in the notion that such operations are financed on a shoestring, that all monetary muscle is necessarily exerted toward production, and that to divert even a little of it would imply some Faustian compromise of quality. Creative power is currency too, however. You may have what it takes to produce top-quality beer; you may also write good copy, craft compelling images and interact well with the media and the public.

I don't hate you because you're beautiful. However, those same talents and sensibilities you and your business partners possess can serve to oversee outside help as you get too busy to do everything yourself. Barter can also be a good early way to swing it; I've learned you can trade beer for practically anything. If it still bothers you to bring outsiders into your creative process, I suppose you can always put them on the payroll.

One thing that comes as standard equipment for our movement is the fact that it continues to be a good story. To make a quality product with the best ingredients available on a small scale, that's something that just resonates with people as more and more of them rebel against an overly packaged, overly processed world. We've come a long way though. So you do need to recognize that you aren't the first one to pull it off, but a certain amount of artisanal, DIY bravado is allowed. Concentrate on the best parts of what you're doing, rather than how much better it is than everything else out there. And recognize that people enjoy a little nuttiness along with all that integrity.

Hitch Your Wagon to the Internet

There have always been multiple ways to skin a cat. In terms of promotion, those ways don't have to cost a lot of money. It's possible today, especially, to create a great deal of buzz about your brewery without even leaving your desktop, as there seems to be an endless vicarious thirst via electronic media for the interesting things we do. The new social media may in some ways just be snappier versions of the old: press releases, calendars of things to do this weekend, etc. But now they are accessible on a variety of ubiquitous electronic devices, endlessly updated and updatable, so don't neglect their marketing potential. Things arise and change so quickly in this arena that I hesitate to get very specific about the different platforms available, but we should at least take a look at a couple that in our era anyway have proved tried and true. It's likely as well that inevitable improvement and innovation will merely provide more detailed and adaptable versions of what already exists.

These days, having a Facebook page for your business is simply table stakes. Even if you don't spend hours a day updating your posts and providing linkable photo and video material touching on all the incredible things going on at your brewery or pub, merely collecting "friends" and "likes" is to be part of the blurrily defined world in which personal outreach coexists with professional promotion. You may at times wonder at the desire of people to be a part of your little network, but the fact is that they enjoy it, and will spend more time than you think reading and reacting to things that you put up. All this will serve to add to your business identity and make it unique. You may have more or less penchant than most for attention to and maintenance of your Facebook interactions, but you'll find a surprising and frankly gratifying return on your investment of time and effort. Post something new, odd, and hilarious and it will take on a life of its own, prompting comments, "likes" and threads of reaction beyond what you might have done on your own.

Of course like many things involving nearly instant gratification, Facebook and its progeny can be taken too far. This is another of those lines you'll need to walk. You will no doubt develop a sense of discretion, a recognition of what's appropriate, and an eventual saturation. Two and three posts a day from a single sender cluttering my email inboxes seems excessive to me, but I am fairly old (and filters offer recourse). For those finding themselves in need of this kind of

immediacy there's Twitter, and other similarly lightning-fast engines of outreach. This is after all an age of transition, with different tastes and aptitudes for electronic connection. The best way to develop a sense of the different tiers of engagement where the new social media are concerned is to use them.

Twitter can be both useful and obnoxious. There are those among us with a following interested enough to receive hour-by-hour news of whereabouts and engagements. Particularly when a special project is involved—developing a new beer involving a rarified ingredient that needs to be hunted down, or simply going to Yakima for hop selection—Twitter can be a good way to carry your public on your shoulder. But let's not forget that you also exist in the physical world. Choosing constant e-posts over interaction with real people can indicate excessive narcissism. But Twitter definitely has its function, and simply enabling it allows access to its instantaneous brand of news (and non-news).

YouTube is a more unqualified boon, as a potential viewer can take it or leave it. To post video "footage" of your events and occasions is to invite your fans to get a feel for having been there even if they weren't, and documents events at your brewery for public access. It's surprising how much material is available on all of us and our breweries, to say nothing of other aspects of our lives. It may no longer be necessary to remind people of this—though once more I'm continually surprised—but it's wise at all times to recall that with smart phones in nearly everyone's pockets and purses the cameras are always rolling. Your personality is one of the most important parts of your brewery's identity, but unbridled and perhaps over-served it can also be one of its touchiest liabilities. Of course you do have recourse to unflattering characterization. All the more reason to be aware of both sides of the blade.

I hate to say it, but you might as well blog. A posting as often as you can manage on your website keeps people informed and engaged with whatever fascinating things you're up to. I may sound disdainful, and while perspective can sometimes foster disdain, the fact is that we all do a hundred fascinating things a week. A meeting about a new beer with your co-workers, a trip to Europe or to another brewpub, an R&D rove through the produce aisle at your local Asian or Latin grocery or a thought about brewing that you had while watching the latest Transformers movie; if you can put a spin on anything in your life as a brewer and a person who thinks about beer, you can briefly and periodically connect with your public and make them feel at one with you and your brewery. Did you ever keep a journal? This is a lot easier. You'll be surprised at how quickly you rack up the verbiage. Next thing you know you'll be thinking about writing articles, and books.

Even if you don't have your own personal platform for your vision of the new world order of beer and brewing, there are plenty of those who do, and these are the people who can help to get your message out. Bloggers are usually self-appointed and sometimes self-important, but they're willing to do the work, and therefore should be acknowledged if not perhaps literally embraced. It doesn't take that much effort to stay in touch with those you keep running into at events. They are generally in love with new breweries that no one has heard of (like yours), will repeat anything you tell them, and are surprisingly influential with a public thirsty for both beer and information, and particularly in developing beer scenes (like all of them).

It also warrants mentioning that should you wisely decide to join the Brewers Association, our movement's increasingly effective trade organization, there is a handful of well-crafted websites you can use to your advantage. Tiered in such a way as to be appeal to different levels of brewing enthusiasm: home-brewer, professional packaging brewery, brewpub, or simply interested member of the public, craftbeer.com is the recognized organ of the fabric that unites us. Your vital statistics, video footage, event listings, and should you be so inclined, your actual words can all be uploaded here.

Speaking of cyber-stakes so old school as to seem downright analog, isn't it time you updated your website? I say that because I assume that you already have one, no matter how early in this process you are. Not only are our ranks thickly peopled with the computer-literate (and particularly in my area, the computer-employed, many of whom seem to want to open breweries), to have a website is in many cases an early step toward getting a new business off the ground. You know as well as I do that a brewery website in no way implies connection with an actual brewery. At least not yet. It's a way, once more, to reach people, and to have a go at crafting your brand and your message, even to invite reaction and engagement. Unless you have ones and zeroes tattooed across your knuckles, website design and development can be expensive, of course. Just don't spend it all in one place; you've still got to shop for brewing equipment.

Slow Down, Take It Easy—Ye Olde Media

Let's go back, way back, to a time when the things people read were printed on paper, when a little bit of foresight was involved in even getting material entered, processed and posted—whoops! I guess I mean written, edited and printed. I'm talking newspapers and magazines. While these days such media are often read online, they are still something worth tapping and cultivating when it comes to getting your tale told. There's something quaint and legitimate and, well, permanent-seeming about seeing your name or picture in actual print, to be part of a story either about just you and your brewery or about the gang of new ones in your area. As institutions, the print publications may be on the ropes, but all the more reason for them to be interested in hot new stories like you. They have bloggers too, you know.

Television is another great way to get your story out there. One benefit of this medium is that it requires and generally desires one's involvement in its content, especially on a slow news day. Keep your local television entities apprised of your events and activities by including them on your list for press releases and announcements. It's surprising how often they're willing to show up, cameras ready to roll. And when the big shows come to town, if you're one of the local breweries recognized as media-friendly, you're likely to be a part of their pastiche. I once appeared in a brief segment for "Today," and because it was on so early, I didn't actually see the spot until it was part of the in-flight news show on a plane I was taking to Denver for the GABF®. The lady sitting next to me was probably more surprised than I was.

Nor is radio to be scoffed at as obsolete. Beer diversity in this country came close to obsolescence in the seventies, after all. Talk radio needs something to talk about, and all that chatter makes throats dry. Make sure you're one of the ones who steps up and volunteers to be interviewed before an upcoming festival.

Mad Men and Brewers— Advertising and Sponsorship

We all know what advertising essentially is; it could be argued that to contemplate using it is merely to be negotiating the price. The trouble with it, no matter the medium, is that it's difficult to track. Who and how many is it reaching? It also happens that once you've started using it, it's like an addiction in reverse. The entities with whom you advertise get so used to having you on board that they're continually trying to sell you more, and more often.

It may, once again, seem incongruous and disingenuous for a small craft brewery to advertise at all. The apparent money-to-burn aspect of putting the image of quality craft beer on buses and billboards, glossy pages and prime time TV spots somehow just doesn't always seem to work. For pubs it might make sense to work the restaurant side of advertising in the mainstream media, and of course anything goes within the cozy confines of the specialty beer press. It's important in all cases to pick the time and the place, and to consider what is appropriate and what we can afford. Spots aired between innings of minor league baseball broadcasts seems more our style; you can even take it up to the majors if you're a regional brewery of sufficient heft. But our movement is growing up; the homespun humility so long taken for granted, which has kept us out of arenas like high-dollar advertising and other overt self-promotion, is slowly giving way to a confident stepping into the mainstream. We can do it if we feel like it (and can afford it). It no longer seems odd to see Jim and his Carhartt-clad boys hawking Sam Adams on TV. You likely won't have the resources or profile of Boston Beer for some time, but as Mr. Koch's earliest efforts helped pave the way for many of the rest of us, so his decisions on where to plant his message can once more provide example.

Like the collaborative efforts these days undertaken by more and more pairs and groups of breweries, sponsorship offers the opportunity to align your brand with like-minded or otherwise worthy brands and organizations. At least that's how you'll find yourself weighing the many requests you'll get to donate, subsidize or otherwise pay for participation in programs, entities and events. Many are worthy, of course, but resources are limited; you'll need to pick and choose. It can be a very good thing to tie your name and image to the efforts of schools, foundations and athletic events and programs, and to show people that you believe in helping support a community. There's a centuries-long tradition of philanthropy in the brewing industry, a tradition of public belief that we all want to donate money and give away our products. As in so many other things, the trick is to strike a balance of appropriate scale.

One good thing for us is that cash isn't our only currency. Our closeness to community makes it more appropriate for us than for our industrial brethren to donate or discount actual beer in lieu of monetary event sponsorship. Auctions for non-profit and charitable organizations often need a socially loosening aspect to their proceedings. A glass of beer or wine and some conversation with the other parents or neighbors associated with the cause, and let the bidding begin. It's important to be sure that state and local law allow such donation and discounting, and that the organization concerned qualifies for your support. A certain amount of due diligence on your part will make sure that not only is your participation worthy of the group, but that you won't be cited or fined.

Ducks need particularly to be all in a row where beer festivals are concerned. You'll find yourself being invited to participate in all kinds of them, from the hard-bitten to the altruistic, and it's up to you and legal authority as to whether your participation is advisable. Even those sponsored by brewers' guilds cannot be assumed to have things all buttoned up, particularly where liability is concerned. You may need to take charge of some of this yourself. Some festivals very clearly raise money for a cause, inviting small-scale, craft-beer-appreciating philanthropists to donate by attendance. Others may have a titular cause receiving a nominal donation while the lion's share of profits goes into the pockets of organizing entities or individuals. Some make no bones about it—they're there to make money. The degree of participation by brewers is also a sliding scale, encompassing beer donation or purchase (and the terms of the same), booth fees and staffing—do you need to provide people to pour or are there volunteers? Festivals are a great way to get your name and products out there and to show by association that you're not just new; you're legitimate and a part of the brewing community. Long lines at your festival booth are a great endorsement. But you'll get enough requests to fill every weekend of your life for the foreseeable future, and to set you crisscrossing your region like a child's crayon on paper. You have the right to decide which are the ones for you. Also make sure that when sending beer to an out-of-state festival managed by a distributor that simply doing so doesn't establish any kind of binding relationship.

Guerrilla Marketing—Taking it to the Streets (or is it the Stage?)

Some words just sound good together. Nut Brown Ale. Honeymoon Suite. Free Bird Seed. Sometimes, in fact, they sound better than they are. Sometimes they are truly descriptive and exciting. Some are vague enough to be either, depending on what you make of them.

Guerrilla marketing is another such pair of words, sounding exciting and warlike in an on-the-ground kind of way. Stunts and pranks in place of ads that cost money often seem appropriate and emblematic of the Craft philosophy. Even when we can afford more, in fact, it's often our style to downplay professionalism and make it all look like something we just threw together for the sake of hilarity. Shrewd marketing or merely dissembling? Often there's little or no difference.

A good event centered on something unique about your brewery can attract attention, as well as the admiration of your peers. If it's a success, you can bring it back for years to come. If it isn't, well, you can always laugh about it later. Sometimes you can do both.

Even brewing a second style of pumpkin beer was a joke for us. With a small pilot system, you can brew pretty much whatever you want with virtually no stakes, and the great thing is that the mere existence of something is often more important than actually being able to get it. To brew an Imperial Pumpkin Ale seemed to me a hilarious departure, a chance to twit the seriousness of a venerable style—Imperial Stout—and the over-seriousness of the big IPAs that were beginning to lumber into vogue. But I didn't hit my target gravity, and—joke or no joke—I couldn't release a mid-weight beer and call it Imperial. Next time out I managed to make a monster, and not a bad one, either. That made three pumpkin beers; a few more and we could be even sillier. So I made a stout, a pilsner and a wheat beer, all with pumpkin, and we invited some of our local friends to join in, as well as ordering in some of the pumpkin beers available from out of town. We conditioned beer in a pumpkin. We threw a one-day festival, with pumpkin carving and pumpkin-themed food, and wondered if anyone would show. We had a line out the door for ten hours, and haven't looked back.

Lots of breweries have their own events, often having begun with a single, definitive idea. It can center on a particular beer, or spring from a real, unheralded or downright imaginary holiday. Eccentric Day, foisted by Bell's Beer on the citizens of Kalamazoo, is one of the latter; Dark Lord Day, held yearly, mainly in the parking lot of Three Floyds, in Munster, Indiana, is of the former, beer-centered variety. Tour de Fat, the traveling circus/environmental message/ promotional event put on extravagantly by New Belgium Brewing in several cities throughout the summer and fall is practically its own industry. You too can stake your claim.

Just because a stunt you've orchestrated doesn't turn out to be an entity unto itself doesn't mean that it hasn't succeeded. Several years ago the BA urged a free-form, collective commemoration of the repeal of Prohibition. Our version involved renting a claw foot bathtub and fermenting fifty or so gallons of our flagship IPA in the middle of the pub. Having informed the crack BA staff of what we were planning, contacts were made and a news crew showed up to document it all. No big deal, but good for a photo and article. In 2012 we at Elysian celebrated the approach of the end of all time (according to the Mayan calendar) by releasing a new beer each month and holding a sardonic (and hilarious) celebration in one of our pubs. While such preparation isn't free, the return on investment through sales both retail and wholesale, as well as the attention garnered along the way, has been substantial. All this, of course, grew out of a mere idea. Depending on the veracity of modern interpretation of the calendar, you may or may not ever read these words.

The craft brewing movement is something of a cult of personality. Some brewers are so much bigger than brands that they represent our whole movement. They are to be credited for the heavy lifting. Others are so in love with themselves that they really don't care about a brand message beyond their own. If they promote specific brands, so much the better; call it collateral benefit. But what matters most is that awe is garnered. Sometimes a clever ad or promotion is just a clever ad or promotion, passing without a ripple of residual branding. We dive in bravado-first, thumbs hooked and swaggering. Look at me! Look at my brand! Much so-called guerrilla marketing, however, never gets past the "look at me" stage. Events can be like that, too, splashing and exploding and perhaps selling beer, but not leaving much else of apparent value behind. Be aware, however, that whether your customers are able to put these things into words or not, they now have a better feel for the image you're projecting, for the person and the business that you are. And in the larger scheme of things, that can be a powerful benefit.

Chapter Highlights

Six Inexpensive Ways to Promote Your Brewery
- Electronic social media: Facebook, Twitter, YouTube and the rest
- Blogs
- Contribute to BA and other websites
- Press releases
- Guerrilla marketing
- Stunts and events

DISTRIBUTION
Bringing it to Market

17

Every brewery begins with a plan of controlling its own sales and profits as much as possible. The simplest plan of attack is that of the pub, in which every drop sold is at a retail price point that pencils out to the greatest profitability, even considering such things as overhead and staffing costs. For distribution breweries, which offer their products at a wholesale price to other stores, restaurants and bars which in turn offer them for retail sale, self-distribution is the most common early course. In either of these models, direct-to-customer retail keg and package sales may offer a middle ground somewhat more profitable than wholesale but still not as much as pushing it across the bar to the on-premise drinker.

Any discussion of even the simplest distribution arrangement needs to begin with a consideration of law. Some states, for example, prohibit any direct sale by a brewery to the consumer. Some allow self-distribution to a retailer (often with a ceiling on annual barrelage), while several others forbid it, requiring an arrangement with a licensed distributor. Localities also restrict and monitor the sale of alcoholic beverages in myriad ways. Hence, an awareness of all pertinent law is essential before proceeding with your plan. And depending on the complexities involved, you may find it necessary to foster an ongoing relationship, or perhaps just initiate a conversation with a lawyer specifically experienced in the laws governing the sale of alcohol in your area. Remember above all that law trumps the language of any contract.

Individual states also govern the legal relationships between brewers and distributors. As in other regulated industries, this is what is known as franchise law. Perhaps more than in other industries, however, it varies from state to state. It was originally intended to protect small, independent distributors from big brewers, but now that those big brewers have taken over—or at least taken an interest in—many of the distributors, the shoe is on the other foot, especially with the plethora of small brewers these days, themselves sometimes needing protections. In its most altruistic form it is intended to protect both sides in a business relationship that can change based on many factors. Take, for example, the growth of a brand. A brewer has undertaken an agreement with a distributor, but has succeeded beyond its wildest dreams and no longer feels adequately served. It wants to sever the relationship with the present distributor and move to another which it feels is better poised to accommodate its growth. In some states it is as simple as that; the brewery can move to another house at will. This is weak franchise law. In others, the move can be accomplished with a cash consideration usually based on fair market value of the brand, generally figured in a multiple of annual sales. Or there is a negotiation. In its basic form, this is the most common construct, and is often pursued even in states with weak franchise law, mainly in the interest of good faith and the avoidance of litigation. It's important to acknowledge the effort and investment on the part of distributors, after all, and to recognize that a lost brand results in lost sales.

Where strong franchise law is concerned, it's a whole different story. For unsuspecting brewers, that is. A good rule-of-thumb reference is the section put together by Marc Sorini of McDermott, Will & Emery for the Brewers Association's *Brewers' Resource Directory.* In it he runs down, state by state, the laws governing distribution agreements.

In some states, a brewer and its brands are regarded as inalienable property once it makes an agreement with a distributor. This means that the distributor can do what it will with a brand, with little recourse for the brewer who created it. It can run with it if it thinks it's worthwhile, increasing sales and market presence in a way that is beneficial and profitable to everyone involved in the collective deal, from the brewer to the retailer, as well as the distributor who is making use of its network of contacts, delivery drivers and salespeople to implement the program. But it usually isn't that simple.

Sometimes an agreement with a broker of brands can be advantageous to the small brewer. In this case, the brewer pays a person or group to advocate for its brands with both retailers and distributors, thereby providing support essentially on a per-product basis. As with a potential distributor, it's important to research the quality and reputation of the broker who will represent your brand in other markets, as well as the other brands they will represent alongside yours. Such an arrangement can be a good fit for small brewers with limited resources.

Many distributors—and, for that matter, brokers—can become overburdened. Consolidation in the distribution industry has caused some entities to become so inflated, they barely seem aware of the multitude of brands in their inventories. On the other side, to be fair, a proliferation of brands and individual products has stuffed even sophisticated computerized distribution systems to the bursting point. Barring the

(often fleeting) pay dirt of being the new hot brand, it's therefore unrealistic to expect disproportionate attention from distributors; after all, they are usually dependent on a core cluster of brands to sustain the demands of an often-fickle public. For some distributors, having a brand is as much or more about keeping it away from another distributor as it is about actually selling it. One can only hope, of course, that that exclusivity is recognized and will work in your brand's favor, but the fact remains that in states with ironclad franchise law it is difficult to prove inattention on the part of a distributor. Without this proof you're stuck.

On your side of the agreement, even if luck is with you, you've got to have the beer. Intermittent and unpredictable supply is the surest way to lose the attention of a busy, often disinterested distributor sales force. For though you may hope they are out there talking up your beer, in reality much of that responsibility falls to you. Who else, after all, can better represent your brand? Distributors by definition primarily deliver beer. If it is worth their while to bring up yours and other craft brands on the routine sales calls keeping core big brands in steady supply—getting them in the door, for example, in establishments with an interest in Craft which might otherwise only deal with specialty distributors—then you may get some play. If they don't see some value in having your brands around, then it is entirely up to you to get them—and your customers—to see the light.

But no matter whose fault it is, if your brands are not adequately served, you've still got an agreement with every distributor you've taken on. In some states it is possible to simply come to the conclusion that it isn't working and move on. In others, it's the distributor who holds the cards. An underperforming brand can sit neglected and trapped, not selling much but at the mercy of the distributor who holds the contract, often even if no actual contract has been signed. That's because in many states, simply employing the services of a distributor implies a sort of common law agreement.

Even in states with strong franchise law though, the rights of distributors are not unlimited. Insolvency by a distributor, or the commission of serious illegal acts, is grounds for the dissolution of an agreement.

But define serious, or insolvency. And when it comes to proving lack of attention or incompetence with a brand, the burden is definitely on you, the supplier. In some states a hearing is required with the appropriate state agency in order to end any distributor agreement.

Of course there are horror stories: distributors who take on brands they have no intention of supporting simply to keep them out of the hands of their rivals; or who buy and sell brands among other distributors without even needing the permission of the brewer. In some states a single shipment to a distributor signifies the establishment of a relationship; so beware of requests for a single pallet, "just to test the waters." I bring these examples up not simply to terrify, but to illustrate the wisdom of doing a little research on your local state laws, including those governing beer festivals, and to make a wise rather than hasty decision. Like any partnership it's got to feel right, even recognizing that business is business.

The success of larger brewers, craft or not, literally depends on the tireless maintenance of their distribution networks. From evaluating effectiveness to offering incentives to the provision of point of sale materials, effort and expense are required to keep a distributor arrangement functional and effective. This is no less true for the small or even startup brewer. Don't expect to simply hand off the ball and move on to the next thing (or more likely back to the thing you've neglected). You've got to at least watch the play unfold to know what you'll have to do next.

Nearly all brewers feel neglected by their distributors, or at least that insufficient attention is being devoted to their brand in order for it to sell as well as it can. Nearly all distributors feel beleaguered by their supplying breweries. It's important for both sides to have some perspective. This is what sales projections and regular meetings are for. This is the balance essential to a successful brewer/distributor relationship: to establish reasonable and realistic expectations of both supply and execution of goals, pegged to a reliable schedule and with prices that make sense to everyone. A small brewer who brays about missed opportunities at the same time they short orders, or provides seasonal products weeks later than promised is not holding their end up. A small

brewer who doesn't provide brand-specific sales help to a specialty distributor knee deep in brands isn't one that should expect their beer to sell better than that of brewers who do provide such help and guidance. Conversely, a distributor that collects brands without the rudiments of a strategy for each one is probably devoted more to window dressing than small-brand sales, or to seeing what sticks and letting all others fall away without actually letting them go. It takes dialogue and maintenance on both sides to keep all these things from happening.

It sounds silly and obvious, but aside from actual beer production, an effective director of sales is perhaps the most important thing a brewery can have. The person whose primary purpose is coordinating the interface between production and distribution is the one who keeps things running smoothly, accommodating and tendering deviations in schedule and expectation, encouraging and rewarding performance, and planning far enough ahead so that everyone involved feels gratified by successful execution. Many breweries throw sales onto a list headed by other things, as though sales happen on their own without specific attention, or as though selling beer is somehow less dignified and vital than making it. In an age of widespread expansion, many breweries appear to get away with this, mainly by continually growing territories and making simultaneous honeymoon periods look like ongoing success. The ones who truly succeed, who build structures that last beyond initial shipments and the buzz of the new, are the breweries who have devoted the manpower and resources to analyze and understand the market.

Over-extension of territory is one of the easiest mistakes for a brewery to make. There are brands hot enough to sell wherever they go, but even unlimited willingness and acceptance doesn't necessarily provide adequate supply or cogent brand support. Other breweries have brands so popular, they seem to open territory after territory in a kind of Ponzi scheme of expansion—as long as there are new states or even countries to initiate shipments into, the line continues to move upward. But once the dust settles and the work of actually having to sell beer presents itself, the worth of the brand and its supporting systems will make or break it. Recall that one of the mantras of our movement is to "drink local." It isn't always easy to take that one on the road, especially without a sales force to at least attach a local personality to an out-of-town brand.

You'll likely hear a lot of flattery where your brand is concerned, from distributors and retail chains specializing in new, high-quality brands in Texas, Arizona, Michigan, Florida or wherever. In Sweden and Japan, too. They'll make it sound easy to at least get started, and you will be tempted to say yes to all of them. After the struggle of getting started and all that involves, it will seem like a just reward. But take a deep breath. It's a lazy game, in the short run, to ship pallets to splashy markets eager to sell your beer. It's an ego boost to see your beer on tap in Daniel Boulod's new restaurant, or to know that it's knocking people dead at the White Horse in Parson's Green. It is far more labor-intensive to build a grassroots network one bar, store or chain at a time in your local market. It may occasionally turn your smile upside-down to be out there working it in more familiar provinces when the lights of Broadway beckon. But that's where meaning and success reside. It's okay to dabble and take advantage of marquee opportunities, but don't lose sight of your center: home markets. When the time comes and you can adequately manage it, then you move carefully outward.

Plans can change, to be sure, but they must be laid first. Simply belching beer into a market, even one eager to receive it, is not the same thing as controlling or understanding what you're doing. Handing it off to a distributor without providing guidance and limitation is to enter the world of sales with your eyes closed. Not only is the amount of your beer limited by the equipment and manpower you have to produce it, but the number of brands you, your salespeople and your distributors can adequately maintain should also be kept to a harmonious core. You'll likely be able to make placements of a brand or two in the appropriate specialty outlets—perhaps even right off the bat—but to expect and demand blanket attention to everything you put out there can be unrealistic and wearying. It may not all work out as originally envisioned. It may also not completely make sense as the sales data rolls

in. But paying attention is maintaining control, and then you'll be ready for the next step.

Somewhat along these lines is a mistake common even to attentive small producers: expecting, without initial proof of worth, disproportionate bandwidth by distributors and other outside salespeople. To barrage distributors with constant "never give up" pep talks, make fervent mention of your brand at every opportunity no matter how unlikely, or compare it incessantly with proven and established brands because you have a relationship, dammit, will wear people out and probably discourage them to help your brand succeed. You'll probably achieve better cooperation by being nice to the people selling and delivering your beer than by constantly riding herd on them. Assuming their lack of support and attention can be as damaging as not being aware at all.

Support for distributors can come in many forms and with many price tags. It's important to remember that such an agreement is a partnership, and that it will take input and attention from both sides to make it work. Incentive programs for salespeople don't have to be hugely expensive ski vacations or Broadway show packages; sometimes dinner out or some modest material reward can be enough to make them feel appreciated and compensated on a scale that makes sense for your size and sales. Point of sale materials can be modest as well, and in many cases can be co-sponsored with distributors. To offer these and many other things is an indication of willingness to work together, to put some skin in the game in an effort to sell beer and make a little money for everyone.

There's much said about the adversarial relationship between brewers and distributors, and especially on the largest scale, between their trade organizations and within legislatures. As in many negotiations between self-interested entities, molehills can rapidly become mountains. As with brand strategy, plans and circumstances can change. The startup brewer today enters a market far more mature than it was only decades ago, and can leverage a collective power far greater than the days when small brewers were compelling only because of their novelty. Remember those who have gone before you and maintained dialogues that have already, even as you prepare to brew your first batch, benefited you and opened options for your success that didn't always exist. As things are and as things have developed, we may individually have ambitions for our brands and ourselves, but we are all in this together.

Chapter Highlights

Things to be Aware of When Considering a Distributor Agreement

- What are the franchise laws in your state?
- Are you a good fit, size-wise and personality-wise?
- What other craft brands do they carry, and will you get the focus you need?
- Do you have the resources—manpower, money, and a steady supply of beer—to make the partnership work?
- A distributor is primarily a deliverer of beer.

Common Misperceptions Regarding Distribution

- My beer is so good that it will sell itself.
- My distributor's sales force will sell my beer.
- I should say yes to all the distributors in other states who want to sell my beer.
- The best way to get results from my distributor is to ride him unmercifully.
- Distributors are my friends.
- Distributors are the enemy.

EQUIPMENT/
TECHNICAL

EQUIPMENT OPTIONS
Building a Functional Mousetrap

18

It's easy to want it all when conceiving and prioritizing one's first commercial brewing system, to convince one's self of the rightness of nailing it the first time. This is especially true given the mindset of tinkering and continual improvement inherent to homebrewers. But markets and fortunes intervene, imposing an unforeseen intelligence on the function of nearly every system and plan. It's best to build in some flexibility, the ability to move in this or that direction as fate and opportunity decree without necessarily having it all to begin with. Or, given the extremely high incidence of expansion in our movement, there's no sin in flattering yourself that you'll get every detail right the next time. At this startup stage of the game, you probably want to get brewing as quickly as you can, with the best basic resources you can muster.

What we're going to assume, in short, is that you've never done this before. You almost certainly have some homebrewing experience. So you have probably come in contact with some of the ludicrously sophisticated equipment out there manufactured and otherwise rigged for the purpose of making small amounts of beer for either immoderate personal use or the incipient opening of a licensed brewery. You know the basic principles of brewing, through some mix of study and experience, and you have a sensibility. Yes, you do. This sensibility is what serves you each time you prepare

to make a decision, whether it's what color you want your beer to be, how long you plan to run off, or where you hang your spoon. There are certainly wrong ways to establish an equipment setup, but guided by this sensibility, combining available options with the wherewithal at your disposal and the time you're willing to put in, you will devise a functional brew system. Let's take it from the top. Maestro?

Gentlemen, Start Your Engines—Grain Handling and Milling

Grain storage is not an active process, but given that you'll likely be receiving enough malt at a time to brew multiple batches of beer, you'll need a secure place to keep it between brews. The smallest breweries typically receive their malt in bags, either of 50- or 55 (25 kg)-pound size, depending on the country of origin. Larger "supersacks" or "totes" are also available in sizes up to around a ton. A dry room or area, sufficiently remote from the fermentation area to avoid dust contamination, and you've got the most important thing covered. Bin or tie off partially used bags between brews and Bob's your uncle, without rats.

Larger breweries, and small breweries with foresight (and space) will often have silos, or bins that serve as such, connected to the milling area by some kind of grain moving device. These devices vary, but are typically some version of the basic screw or auger, which moves whole malt up inclines, around bends and along straight stretches to fall, essentially unmolested, into the hopper above the mill. Another, somewhat more sophisticated—and substantially more expensive—system is the cable conveyer, which operates by means of inclined discs attached to a cable drawing the malt along an enclosing tube. This system is generally recommended for longer runs and more complicated journeys which might otherwise beat up the malt more than desired. Generally recommended does not mean that you have to do it; simple and inexpensive augers will serve surprisingly often, and are cheaper to repair and replace when they break, which they do far less often than cable conveyers. When up is essentially the only direction your malt needs to travel, consider using a bucket elevator. This is basically an ovoid Ferris wheel, which instead of amusing its cargo of a summer night, dumps it into the milling hopper.

Time was, malting companies would finance grain silos, providing upfront costs for their purchase and charging the higher price—ten or twelve cents a pound higher—for bulk-delivered malt until the whole thing was paid off. Alas, like tuition benefits for the children of college professors (thanks, Pop), this is an industry benefit now gone the way of the dinosaur. Just the same, the theory is sound. The return on investment of a grain silo as opposed to receiving malt in bags is surprisingly short; often less than a year in even a moderately active small brewery.

Malt mills vary in sophistication and effectiveness, but their essential design and function is the same. Rollers crush whole kernel malt to expose its starchy core, while still leaving sufficient husk integrity to aid lautering. The simplest and least expensive is the two-roller mill, which requires exacting calibration and ongoing attention to minimize whole, uncrushed grains without pulverizing the malt. Four- and six-roller mills are configured to allow the diversion of smaller, uncrushed grains and properly milled materials along different pathways, resulting in greater uniformity of grist without overmilling. In addition, they can generally accommodate multiple mill settings, for the additional effective crushing of wheat, for

example, or more brittle specialty grains. Once again, greater versatility of choice means more control over uniformity of grist and improved extract. In the course of your researches you'll no doubt hear mention of wet mills. In a larger brewery setting these are deemed most effective, employing steeping tanks which soften the malt and lessen the trauma of crushing in order to maximize extract-producing material and leave husks beautifully configured for runoff. As a first-time startup your mill will almost certainly be dry.

I've worked in breweries that milled directly into the mash tun, receiving imperfect hydration along the way. I've also worked in breweries that hand-dumped grist into the mashtun after or as it was filled. All of the above require stirring in order to ensure mash uniformity and the breakup of lumps and dry spots. Dumping into an accumulated volume of hot water also risks enzyme fry, as malt is inconsistently brought into contact with water necessarily hotter than the desired mash-in temperature. A grist case either suspended above the mashing vessel or a short auger run away will allow both for prior milling and the controlled introduction of grist to the first stages of the brewing process, whether by gravity or mechanism. Some kind of hydration collar is probably most common in the wetting of grist on its way into the mashing vessel, perforated on its inner surface to wet grist more or less uniformly as it enters. Others are designed to direct the grist against a concentrated stream, forcing an instant's additional contact with water on the way downward. One of the most effective hydration devices out there is the Steele's masher, a device employing a short horizontal auger which introduces water along the way to yield a consistently and un-traumatically hydrated mash requiring minimal stirring once deposited in the mashing vessel. In any case, some kind of pre-hydration is desirable in any mash setup.

To Infinity and Beyond—the Philosophy of 2-, 3-, 4- and However-many Vessel Brewhouse Systems

Space is at a premium in any production setting, of course, especially in a pub. The presence of each vessel, whether used for mashing, boiling, fermenting or conditioning, needs to be justified in order to offset the otherwise profitable use of the space it occupies—like seating. The most common brewhouse configuration, therefore, employs two vessels: an insulated mash/lauter tun in which both mash and runoff are conducted; and a kettle/whirlpool, often also used for heating brewing liquor (water). Sometimes you can also save space by combining a hot liquor tank beneath the mash/lauter tun, consolidating the footprint to a single, compartmentalized vessel which also makes use of gravity for runoff. It's surprising how small a room can accommodate a system of this configuration. It's also striking how many dislike this compromise of function.

While the simple two-vessel system is most common, it does present a couple of restrictions. First, generally without the ability to apply heat to the mashing vessel or make use of the kettle for this purpose, single-temperature mashing is the only feasible possibility. Second, boiling and whirlpooling in one kettle means only pelletized hops can be used—whole hops tend to foul the pump. Neither path is necessarily a handicap to versatility or innovation, but it's best to recognize their inherent limitations.

The third vessel to be added to brewhouse configuration is most commonly a separate whirlpool. This allows the system to stretch out and control its own destiny, since each vessel can perform a more specialized function. Not only do you enhance wort quality by using a specifically designed vessel to separate solids, you also free up your kettle space for a subsequent brew. The separate whirlpool, therefore, can dramatically enhance production capacity. A whirlpooling kettle does the best it can, with a nominally conical bottom (which can waste wort) and some kind of dam or wall near the outlet to retain trub and hop material. Some breweries even mash in the kettle, then transfer to the lauter tun, which can itself be designed with a single, more effective function in mind. A specifically-designed whirlpool will generally have a flat bottom to settle solids as the circular motion of transfer slows, and a drawoff point somewhere along the side, often from a lower level runoff ring. What might at first seem a luxury of both space and direct expense can soon turn out to justify

itself by allowing the system to produce better beer more quickly.

At first thought the addition of vessels to a brewhouse system might not in itself seem to enhance effectiveness and productivity. Think of each vessel as capable of simultaneously holding a single brew, however, and the wisdom becomes clear. A two-vessel system is capable of producing multiple batches in a day, to be sure, but also demands a fair amount of dead time as the brewer waits for the boil and then knockout. Two consecutive brews with this restriction makes for a long day. The addition of a separate whirlpool allows for a subsequent runoff to be commenced at least half an hour sooner, making a two- or even three-brew day a viable possibility.

The same can be said in connection with the addition of a dedicated mashing kettle. Following perhaps a half-hour rest, the mash can be moved along to the lauter tun where wort recirculation and runoff can commence while you conduct a second mash. With each downstream vessel holding its contents for a theoretical ninety minutes or so (runoff, boil and settling/knockout), a new brew can comfortably be introduced every couple of hours. Next up might be the addition of a second boiling kettle, or more likely (and certainly more economically) a heated or simply insulated pre-run vessel to hold a runoff's worth of hot wort. As soon you finish your last boil, you're ready for the next. Extra vessels increase the number of brews possible in a single day. It's all a matter of identifying time spans in the wort production process that can be filled effectively, cutting into crossword puzzle time, to be sure, but ultimately producing more beer through equipment—and human—multitasking.

Bells and Whistles

The more specific the function of each brewhouse vessel, the better it can be outfitted for high quality wort production and efficiency. It's tempting, in fact, to consider including in an essentially rudimentary system such big-boy features as rakes and agitators, flow-sensors and a proliferation of draw points—the brewhouse equivalent of a Fisher-Price steering wheel with its mock instruments, ineffective little shifter and horn. Oh, sure, it's fun to operate all this stuff, and it shows a certain awareness of how things are supposed to work; but you need to ask yourself if, given the system's size and actual function, the additional expense results in better wort and greater efficiency. These additions have their place in most often larger systems engineered in other ways to take advantage of the efficiencies they can provide, but without proper function to back them up, they can be merely a geekishly cosmetic expense. Having said this, there are a few considerations that can make life easier and beer better.

If yours is to be a production brewery primarily focused on packaging, consider a system that minimizes oxygen uptake pre-boil. I can say from shamefaced personal experience that the neophyte is given to parroting half-formed and fashionable terms and concerns, say for example, "hot-side aeration." Another might be "pump cavitation", generally introduced by the neophyte with a sly hesitation in place of a drumroll, as in "say, does that pump ever, uh, cavitate?" The mid-nineties may as well be known as the golden age of hot-side aeration, or at least for its awareness and concern. Every tongue clacked for a few years with the specter of oxygen uptake through excessive splashing and agitation of wort, mainly on its way from lauter tun to kettle, which would result in a theoretically faster product degradation. Never mind that the average pub system (and this is an industry, after all, of mainly average pub systems) cycles through its beer fast enough to avoid all this, or that beers of any color to speak of carry enough melanoidin component to essentially ward off the effect. Did you notice how I slipped "melanoidin" in?

Look at older brewhouse designs, however, and it's not at all uncommon to see columns of wort falling several feet, foaming like Niagara; grants doing essentially the same in their brisk treatment of precious brewing liquid drawn rudely from the grain bed; and whirlpool ports placed above the level of liquid, powered by pumps of a single (high) speed. And while perhaps not all that ruinous in practical effect, once you know something is bad, it's often just as easy to avoid it, n'est-ce pas? I therefore counsel gentle treatment of wort as it flows from one place to another, its introduction into the bottoms rather than the tops of vessels, as well as the judicious and incremental application of pumps in its transfer.

Rakes in the lauter tun are something that everyone seems to want, and that fabricators are extremely eager to sell you. Properly employed they can aid in the distribution of mash and the consistency and effectiveness of runoff, as well as the removal of spent grains. In a small system, however, their worth can be negligible, often amounting to little more than a toy or an aid to visual credibility, kind of like the fins on a rocket ship intended only to pass through the vacuum of space. If the system you're contemplating is too large for hand paddle mixing, and you can afford real rakes (the kind that go up and down, and aren't simply set at a single, undifferentiated level), then by all means consider them. I simply make the point that there are plenty of systems out there in which the rakes perform very little actual function.

Lautering screens generally come in two configurations, either milled plate, in which slots are cut in an advantageous pattern for runoff, or V-wire, which is considered less sophisticated but is functional, and certainly less expensive.

Draw port placement in both lautering and whirlpool vessels can be critical to effective operation and time savings. The central inch-and-a-half charybdis of so many lautering vessels inevitably leaves extract almost literally on the table: not only by its flow beneath the lautering screens but throughout the mash bed. Even spreading it out to accommodate a few, perhaps smaller draw points encourages more effective runoff. Similarly, adding a second, higher draw point to your whirlpool configuration can allow knockout to begin within ten or fifteen minutes of the end of transfer. This can also aid in the retention of aromas essential to the character of many beer styles (as well as the associated economy of hops), as less time is spent simply settling before proceeding to the next stage. Then you merely switch over to the more conventional, lower port partway through knockout.

Without getting too technical about it at this stage, an eye should be cast and some thought devoted to the dimensions of brewhouse vessels. Unthinking fabricators in the past tended to design and manufacture both lautering vessels and whirlpools favoring depth over breadth in a way that decreased footprint at the same time it hampered efficiencies of both extract and yield. It doesn't take a great deal of technical acumen to appreciate the desirability of a shallow mash bed from the standpoint of ease of runoff and extract yield. Nor is it much of a stretch to recognize that the column pressure of wort in a deep whirlpool will compromise function by less than optimal cake formation and degradation during the late stages of knockout. These are certainly considerations for the manufacture of new equipment, as well as the winnowing of options in the used market.

I'll make this one simple by saying that a swept kettle is a beautiful thing. The introduction of a bottom-agitating paddle turning on a central shaft serves as an essential aid for kettle mashing prior to transfer to the lautering vessel. Even better, by turning your wort slowly and continuously as the kettle fills, heat source on, you can reach a boil as much as an hour sooner than with natural convection. Running the agitator during the boil also improves evaporation and the vigor of the boil. This of course requires that the kettle not be used as a whirlpool—that pesky paddle, after all, takes care of that—but bears fruit in the saving of time.

Steam as a kettle heat source versus direct fire by a gas burner is also a short debate: steam is better. Direct fire is the only option in many locations, however. It's certainly the cheapest to start up, but generally turns out in the longer term to be more expensive to run. Steam requires a boiler or steam generator, of course, but is a more nuanced and controllable heat source, usually applied in a couple of independent zones, where direct fire is usually either on or off, roaring or silent, aimed at the side and bottom of the kettle. By its violence gas is more browning, with a greater possibility of wort scorching. Steam also presents a number of options, from heat transfer surface area to the use of internal or external boiling chambers known as calandria, which render the whole process that much more vigorous at the same time it provides greater control. At a certain size of operation, the type of boiler required might make for special requirements—brewer training and certification to run it, for example, or its mandatory separation from

public space. Electricity is the quietest of all, but also the slowest, least efficient and effective (to say nothing of expensive). Elements cannot be fired until covered, and hours can be spent waiting for what passes for a boil to be achieved. There are a lot of small systems out there that have electrically heated kettles, but unless the confines of your brewery space preclude the kind of ventilation needed for either a gas burner or boiler, it's best, both for function and operational cost, to avoid them.

Speaking of steam, whatever your kettle heat source, some accommodation will need to be made for the vast amounts of it generated by boiling wort. Most common is some kind of stack vented either directly upward and/or outward to the atmosphere, often aided by a fan to keep things moving. For various reasons, such as an urban setting or a lower floor in a building of many stories, a simple stack may be less possible (though I did once work in a brewery that vented thirteen stories to the roof). It's also a waste of all that generated heat, even if all it provides is a less-than-frigid workplace. One option in this case is a stack condenser, a column either standing directly above the kettle or bent, still-like, to one side, in which cold water is counter-flowed through a system of many pipes in order to encourage condensation and its outflow either to the floor or a drain. Properly tuned, this can be a remarkably effective, and neighbor-pleasing, solution, especially if the flow water can be reclaimed in a separate vessel for either cleaning or a subsequent brew.

And Since We're Adding Tanks...

Whatever it's called or whatever vessel serves the function, some kind of hot liquor tank is part of every all-grain brewing system. From a pot on the stove to a dedicated, steam-jacketed boiler, hot water needs to be held somewhere for mashing in and sparging. The two-vessel brewhouse will make use of the kettle for heating water and then move the remainder to some other, likely passive station for further use—quite often the day's fermentor. A big step forward is the dedicated hot liquor tank, heatable with steam either by jacketing or heat exchange (or, reluctantly in the interest of full disclosure, by electricity), which can also receive cooling water from the knockout heat exchanger for later reuse. The next option up is a cold liquor tank, an invaluable aid to efficient blending and more effective heat exchange, and coolable by incorporation into a glycol system. Until you have one this will seem a luxury, something once more not likely to be a part of the average startup. The addition of liquor tanks categorically increases efficiencies, and substantially cuts dead times in the brew day.

Since it is technically on the hot side of the brewing process, but isn't what one would properly call a brewing vessel, the hop back is an appropriate segue to cooling and the processes which follow. The hop back acts as both a final opportunity to add hot side hops for aroma, and a final straining step before wort is cooled in the heat exchanger. Hop backs can be simple and small—no more than a few gallons in volume, fitted with a simple strainer—or they can be large, sophisticated and ingeniously configured, sometimes able to hold a couple of barrels of wort. In any case, pump volume needs to be tuned in order to feed the heat exchanger without causing pump, uh, cavitation.

Crossing Over to the Cold Side— Post-boil Brewery Process

Witness the humble heat exchanger, the brewer's first line of defense in preventing infection as wort passes from the rough-and-tumble hot side of the process to the so-called cold. Typically comprised of two alternating sets of very closely spaced plates, one for hot wort and the other for cold water flowing in the opposite direction, the typical small brewery heat exchanger is so cartoonishly cute, it can inspire incredulity as to its actual function (see Fisher-Price reference, above). Recognizing that the wort-cooling systems of big-boy breweries can sometime take the better part of an hour to complete knockout, designers and fabricators have throughout receding history adopted that as a temporal benchmark, cooling four or five barrels with perhaps a dozen wafers of heat transfer surface in about the same length of time. It doesn't take a visit from the Jetsons-era Great Gazoo to point out to the Flintstone brewer the fact that precious and wonderful hop aroma will take flight

in that time, or that there are other benefits to more expeditious cooling: things like more effective protein coagulation and trub settling, say, and the reduction of Dimethyl Sulfide (DMS). Things that separate "You made this beer yourself? That's awesome!" from "Wow! That's a great beer." Ah well, we were stupid then, but now of course we're smart. A practically-sized heat exchanger may not trumpet its need in your plans, but it will bear fruit—and not necessarily fruitiness—in your beer. There is no reason a small system shouldn't chill its wort substantially faster than a larger one. Also keep in mind that as they ferment at different temperatures, ales and lagers should be knocked out at different temperatures as well—typically on the order of a 20-degree differential.

The good thing is that heat exchangers can be easily modified; those bolts that typically extend a foot and more beyond the actual plates can accommodate the addition of quite a few more. A glycol stage is another possibility, with a second, adjacent flow system tapping into the capabilities of an over-arching cooling system. Much depends on the expected temperature of ground water used for cooling—the tropics versus Alaska, say. Breweries of a certain foresight, size and budget will often, as mentioned, have a dedicated cold liquor tank, similarly linked to the chiller system and capable of providing fiendishly cold water mainly for the purpose of cooling wort. This water too can be reclaimed in a hot liquor tank for eventual reuse.

On its way from heat exchanger to fermentor, wort should be oxygenated, either with medical grade oxygen or sterile air, tanks of which are commonly available through whatever local gas source you choose to use. This allows the yeast a healthy leg up on its aerobic phase of fermentation; without it, in fact, a good and complete fermentation becomes a matter of risk. Oxygenation stones are like carbonating stones in miniature, sintered, or porous, installed within sight glasses for visual monitoring; less sophisticated older systems will sometimes call it good with some holes drilled in a stainless tube affixed with an oxygen source. The bubbles from these more rudimentary devices are far larger than those from sintered stones, and far less easily absorbed by wort. Regulators are available which display in liters rather than pressures, making monitoring easier whichever system you employ.

Heat and cold are the matter and anti-matter of brewing, kept separate by remoteness of relative location, tank and walk-in walls, and the narrowest of margins where they most dramatically counteract each other in the passes of a heat exchanger. The universe won't end should they mix infelicitously somewhere along the way, but brewers may lose the next closest thing: decisive and efficient control over the vectors which govern beer quality. If the boiler or burner is the heart of the system, the chiller is its cold, more calculating core, as essential in its temperance as the more dramatic generations of the boil and of fermentation.

Some kind of fermentation temperature control is essential in the crafting of quality beer. Where the homebrewer can take advantage of a range of domestic microclimate, moving the carboy or other fermentation vessel from closet to corner to garage to back porch (I happen to know that the normal outdoor winter temperature in Seattle is ideal for lager fermentation, for example), the professional, presumably larger-scale brewer needs to bring the chill to the fermentor. This is effected by means of a central reservoir of food-grade propylene glycol plumbed to each individually jacketed tank. A system of electronic sensors and thermostats are linked to solenoids, which in turn open or close valves, providing or withholding coolant. More primitive systems may be manually operated, with switches and ball valves. Startup systems are typically undersized, limiting not only the control of temperature but the factors that contribute to quality beer: diacetyl and DMS reduction, yeast flocculation and CO_2 retention.

First, a word about glycols. Propylene (food grade) glycol is a thick and slippery-feeling, generally clear liquid that when thinned to a calibrated degree can provide a chilling medium well below the point of freezing. It is sometimes colored for leak detection. It is expensive, typically in the range of ten dollars a gallon, and the reservoir for even a small (sevenor ten-barrel) system will hold at least a hundred gallons of liquid. It is used in the manufacture of some foods, including inexpensive ice cream, and as such is putatively digestible without harm. Ethylene

glycol, its counterpart intended for heat exchange in automotive radiators, is relatively inexpensive. It is also poison. A cracked or compromised tank jacket can render any amount of beer so much of the same. You'd think that this distinction would be enough to dissuade any brewer from using it, but you hear stories of decommissioned brewery tanks seeping that greenish liquid so dangerous to our dogs. Don't be an idiot. Pay the two dollars. Another, less common but more economical cooling option is brine.

Like steamfitting and surgery, refrigeration is a skill executed best by professionals. Even if you do it yourself it will be an expensive part of your system, both to install and maintain. It's my experience that chillers like to take holidays off, too, especially if you're lucky enough to have a warm Fourth of July. Some basic precautions are therefore in order: a functional awareness of your chilling system, keeping extra fuses on hand, and a backup refrigeration person in case your normal guy or girl is out on another extended call when you need them. Most chillers are outside, after all, on roofs and inside fenced enclosures and hence vulnerable to the elements; providing some kind of shade or shelter can make a big difference in reducing their frequency of failure. And speaking of fencing, consider the copper in your chilling system a precious metal worth protecting from roving bands of the addled and criminally resourceful.

Divine Proportion—Configurations of Fermentation and Conditioning

We've taken a look at the pathways in the brewhouse which determine efficiencies of wort production; of how many batches can be generated in the time of a single day, or a week. But once the wort is produced and chilled, of course, it needs a place to hunker down and ferment, and once that's accomplished, to either further condition or take up residence in its ultimate serving vessel, be it bottle, can, keg or tank. The size and combination of these vessels also determines how much beer can be made, and how quickly, and must correspond to your brewery's idiosyncratic philosophies of production and portfolio.

Perhaps the simplest scenario involves a group of a few fermentors with perhaps an additional tank to receive filtered beer prior to kegging. This was the way it worked at my first brewing job, a medium-sized pub and restaurant with no outside sales. We brewed once to twice a week and served all the beer from kegs. The system was small enough—seven barrels—that we lost a regrettable amount of beer in filtration and transfer, but it was simple and self-contained: in order to brew another beer, we had to empty the tank that would hold it, a flow determined ultimately by sales across the bar.

Other systems depend on a number of downstream tanks for conditioning or serving. End-fermented beer is moved to one of these vessels for the next phase of its life. Once filtered, beer is presumed ready to go, its tank merely a holding vessel before racking or packaging; or perhaps it's diverted to a simpler, single-walled serving tank sitting in a cold room amid the bar fruit and the refrigerated foodstuffs of the kitchen. Other systems can accommodate a period of further conditioning, allowing the disparate flavors of production and fermentation to marry and resolve, especially important in the case of lagers or particularly strong beers. This conditioning phase as well can aid in clarification if filtration has not been undertaken, either by fining or the simple settling afforded by the amount of time deemed adequate to the brewer's, and the customers', satisfaction.

Some breweries employ a battery of fermentors fed to a very small number of bright beer tanks. These are intended for fast turnaround, only holding beer long enough to set up kegging and packaging processes. Others more leisurely turn their fermentors over every week or two to a broader array of tanks devoted to unhurried conditioning and perhaps serving, from which beer can be drawn as appropriate: some put into bottles and kegs; the rest served directly from the bar. The relative size of all these tanks—and of the brewhouse—is critical as well, their ratios determining where and in what combination all that beer needs to go in order both to supply patterns of sale and keep the process pathway active and as steady as it needs to be.

It's easy to second-guess these combinations, to speculate on the schedule of filling and emptying in somebody else's brewery, even as they wonder at your schedule and the relative size of your brewhouse,

fermentors and tanks. For each of us is comfortable and effective making beer in a slightly different way. When putting together these myriad equipment combinations, pencil it all out in a number of different ways then ask the advice, based on what you think you want to do, of people who may have the experience to provide some insight.

Let's say your brewery begins its life with a seven-barrel brewhouse and a gaggle of fermentors of the same size. It's fairly easy to see how that's going to work. With an increase in business or the appearance on the used market of a fourteen-barrel fermentor or two, production can be pretty dramatically increased with the application of extended brewdays and additional labor. It's an interesting side subject that different fermentors behave differently, even when they have essentially the same proportions; but most breweries, sufficiently pressed for production, will learn each tank's quirks and carry on. People generally have the impulse to do things better, more properly as they progress, so it's far more likely that a horizontal dairy tank used as an open-topped fermentor will be replaced by something sleek and cylindroconical than the other way around. Covetousness trends upward, after all. It's therefore probable that changes will be for the better; no one's going to complain about that.

But back to the growth and development of the seven-barrel brewery. Once a fourteen-barrel batch clears fermentation it needs to go to an appropriate-sized vessel for storage until it's sold. It therefore may not make sense to have larger conditioning tanks to receive these larger batches of beer. Especially if those tanks might in other cases receive beer from multiple fermentors. If conditioners are half the size, say of the double-brewhouse-sized fermentors, a batch can be split for different purposes—kegging, maybe, and serving. Or perhaps the larger tank will function as an actual unitank, making it possible for much of that beer to never even see the inside of a conditioner. With this kind of capability, the brewer is less dependent on conditioning in general than before. The whole mix changes. Without getting into every possibility and permutation, I think you probably get the idea, even if you don't yet have the foggiest notion of how you're eventually going to do it yourself.

Clarity of Purpose—Bright Beer or Not

One fundamental way to control the quality and appearance of your beer, and along with it, your market and your brewery's identity, is with beer clarity. Some may object that this is not in fact a choice, that good beer is bright (clear) beer—period. To present classically bright beer is an indication of a certain mastery, to be sure, an allusion to general competence in all things brewing. But bright beer only tells part of the story. A bright beer can also taste bad, and somewhat hazy beer in itself is not necessarily an indication of flawed procedures and skewed priorities. In some markets, in fact, customers perceive hazy beer as something desirable—even preferable—to the factory-polished appearance of beer that in other markets might be just the ticket. It's true that muddy, yeasty beer is something that probably needs a little work, a little settling time, or both. But we are an industry segment of individuals, with individual tastes and often niche markets. Some of us have dreadlocks and bandanas on our heads; others wear lederhosen without irony. For all our differences we have achieved something together, in different ways. Beer clarity is an issue on which I believe we are allowed to diverge, to a point.

Given that general separation of yeast from beer is something to be striven for, it is sometimes therefore desirable to employ some kind of clarification program less invasive and world-rocking than filtration. Fining with gelatin or isinglass can be simple and effective, yielding beer of probably less than perfect but generally tolerable brightness. These animal-based collagens can be easily mixed according to instruction and introduced to a unitank or bright tank either directly or during transfer. Seaweeds and tannins are also an option. A couple of days' settling time and the beer can look pretty darned good.

But there, I said it—animal products. Many of those same enthusiasts in love with the idea of unfiltered beer are vegan, to whom even mention of the exploitation of animal substance is anathema. Never mind that diatoms are animals, too, and that to filter with their kilned teensy skeletons amounts to a similarly brutal act. This is often somehow overlooked, as is the fact that as fungi, the very yeasts that ferment our beer are not definitively fish or fowl, so to speak, in the classification of what's a plant and what's an animal. I've had many, mostly friendly, discussions with people either face-to-face or via email on this specific collection of subjects. Usually it amounts to my telling them the facts about each beer—our dark beers, for example, are generally not fined, nor is much of the cask-conditioned beer—and letting them draw their own ideological lines.

Filtration is the most common and reliable procedure for clarifying beer, either through a plate and frame arrangement using pads of cellulose and perhaps diatomaceous earth (also called Kieselguhr) or a straight DE filter fitted with screens to strip both the filter medium and undesirable yeast and haze-producing particles from the beer as it passes, typically, from fermentor to bright tank. Did I say strip? This can be the knock to zealous filtration; that along with yeast and haze particles, character and flavor can also in some measure be left behind. It certainly stabilizes beer, and can be a good emergency option to retain, if nothing else, when beer absolutely needs to be brightened and other less invasive measures prove ineffective (it happens). The other mechanical method of clarification, and one probably not on the table for the typical startup, is a separator or centrifuge. This device spins beer at extremely high speed, under great pressure, through a heavy bowl fitted with a stack of finned dishes that allow solids to accumulate and be periodically purged. The good thing about a centrifuge is that it can be adjusted from utter clarity to leaving a slight cast behind. It also uses no living things whatsoever in the execution of its function. The challenges to it are expense and maintenance. With the pressures and technologies involved, in fact, neither filter nor centrifuge are projects to take lightly. They have their points and their worth, however, particularly assuming a certain demand for beer clarity.

Another potential point of honor derives from whether all the carbonation in a finished beer is natural or not, the implication being that if anything is added, style points (or something) have been foregone out of deference to the Man. True, the Man likes his beer carbonated, cold and clear, but he's only human, and like many of us prefers (without knowing why) the flavor balance that a consistent level of carbonation imparts in constituting a modern notion of beer. To be able to touch up a beer mainly naturally carbonated is a boon to the brewer trying to sell—if not exactly sell out—his or her beer. Carbonating stones, and the ports that support them, are a comforting option to aid in the finishing of a beer which perhaps should ideally have been bunged in the middle of the night, but because of such prosaic things as sleep has been allowed to chug on past its natural self-carbonation point. Pinpoint carbonators are the next sell-out step along the way to properly carbonated beer, and are most often found in larger production breweries. The expense of a proper CO_2 tester can potentially—quickly—outweigh the return of a few dozen over- or under-carbonated kegs.

Keeping Flexibility In Mind

The earliest days of our movement saw a lot of equipment improvisation. An earlier edition of this book, in fact, had a chapter devoted entirely to using old dairy tanks as brewhouse vessels. Also commonly used in sub-five-barrel-sized systems were steam-jacketed institutional soup kettles. These came back into vogue in later times when brew-on-premise joints had their day. One brewpub which still exists in Portland, Oregon uses a converted Rubbermaid horse trough as a mash/lauter tun. Nor is there any shame in making do. Ingenuity and resourcefulness are not only economical, they are honorable, finding second and third uses for manufactured equipment. Used equipment, whether repurposed or of specific intended function, comes from the boneyard sensibility on which our whole industry was founded.

You can't know everything that will come up in the future of a project or movement, especially in one as essentially self-taught as ours. There are brilliant and well-educated people among us—more all the time, thank the gods—but much of our collective progress where technical and operational expertise is concerned has come as a result of slow dawning. Historically we've done the best we can with the information at hand, or within the reach of telephone or email. There are educational programs available to us, of course, and it's a good thing that an increasing number of entrants to the field have bothered to get a little book learning, but the anticipation of trends and developments is another thing altogether. Prescience is a skill that no institution can teach, not even Hogwart's.

Take the brewhouses of yore, for example, or at least the yore of the late seventies and eighties. At that time, people getting into the crazy business of brewing and selling their own beer were of course unaware of the breadth of style and technique now familiar to the modern brewer and fabricator. Inspiration then mainly arose from a broadly-drawn British tradition of ales of nominal strength and non-aggressive character. Mash/lauter tuns were sized, constructed and employed to produce wort of perhaps 12° Plato/1.048 SG. Within a decade, however, brewers would be heaping these vessels literally to overflowing in an effort to produce higher-gravity beers such as India Pale Ale, Bock and Barley Wine; efficiencies were sacrificed as equipment was essentially hoodwinked into producing worts far stronger than their design should have allowed. Oh well. We learned, and when we got newer, better systems, their vessels were bigger, broader, and more able to accommodate our whims and fashions. Those newer to the industry, the people buying this castoff older equipment, were left wrestling with it the way their immediate forebears had, inefficiently and labor-intensively wringing precious points of gravity from mash beds two and three times as deep as they really should have been. And so it goes.

I bring this up not merely as a matter of interest, but to make the point that if at all possible, it's a good idea to spend some time and mental effort anticipating some of the things you might want to attempt in the future as you set up your brewery today. Many people caught in the vise of the hop crisis of a few years ago, to cite another example, wished their systems could handle more readily-available whole hops, rather than pellets. A lot of improvisation was done then to accommodate the unforeseen. Who knows what might arise in the future? It's best, in short, not to slam too many doors in the choices made along the way.

Chapter Highlights

Equipment-Related Insights

- There's a surprisingly short return on investment in a grain silo.
- A separate whirlpool can help your system make better beer, and more of it.
- If at all possible, wort should be treated gently as it is transferred.
- In small systems, lauter tun rakes can be overrated.
- Dedicated hot- and cold-liquor tanks may be luxuries, but they are nice to have.
- Heat exchangers for wort cooling are very often too small.
- Glycol chillers are also often undersized.
- The faster the throughput of your system, the more heavily weighted your tank ratio will be toward fermentation.
- The best way to speed and increase throughput is by emptying tanks all at once.

FLOORS
Slopes and Surfaces

19

Perhaps the most fetishized and fretted-over aspect of brewery construction is the floor and the drains which serve it. Like clockwork appear the queries in the BA Forum: "I'm interested in finding out everything I can about the right kind of floor to put in my brewery," or something similar, perhaps specifically musing the age-old divergence of the tile and epoxy schools (what a day that was in history!) or staring into the spaces between the stars for the optimal slope ratio so far having eluded thinkers since Avogadro. The brewer who gets it right, it must be assumed, gains eternal bragging rights, and carries the totem of legitimacy forever. The brewer who gets it wrong, well, you want to talk totems? Check out that squeegee in the corner.

For in fact, standing water is a bad thing. It can harbor potential infection, threaten slipperiness and soak into the shoes of visiting enthusiasts. Properly executed, floors and drains are something you never have to think about, running as they do according to the principles of one of the free forces of nature. But they can also dog you like an unidentified rattle in your car. Coatings can peel up, tiles pop out or break, or should passivity and thrift rule your time of decision, bare concrete, however properly sloped, will inevitably disintegrate.

Our floors see a lot of use. We walk them endlessly, of course. We drop things on them all day long. And of course they spend their existences wet, with occasional chemical inundation. Both beer and wort are corrosive as well. It's asking a lot to have them stand up, at least on a budget, and I guess that's what makes the subject so compelling, perennial and philosophical. We all know we can have a great floor if we spend a million dollars on it; what can you get, say, for a few hundred?

Well, you can paint it, and have it look great for the inaugural few hours of your brewery's existence. After that it won't take long to trace the travel pattern made by a size eleven brewers boot with a slightly worn heel. Sadly, this is essentially what many off-the-shelf epoxy coatings are: paint. Their claims are large, but their function is small. It's better, in truth, to do nothing at all and at least keep your options open for later.

There are other inexpensive treatments for hardening and water-sealing floors, but their effectiveness and durability is hardly up to the ongoing demands of an even moderately active brewery. They may also prove incompatible with second thoughts.

Putting Down a Good Base
Some budgets have more to work with, and can actually consider doing things right, beginning with the structure of the floor itself. This is where it all starts. From the moment you walk into your brewery (or envision doing so in the design stage),

you'll be asking yourself some basic structural questions. Will the existing floor be strong enough to keep brewery tanks, once filled, from crashing down to the floor below? What sort of work needs to be done to ensure both structural integrity and proper function specifically as a brewery floor? How much will all that cost? For the answers to many of these questions it's worth consulting a structural engineer. Not only do they presumably know their field, they'll be aware of codes as well. As it's their job to be conservative, they may alarm you with disaster scenarios, but they'll also be able to point out the virtues of various solutions to your concerns.

Many startups—especially these days, it seems—involve the installation of breweries so small that floors barely notice they're there. Bigger and perhaps more ambitious setups require replacement of existing floors with sufficient concrete and other structural material to ensure stability and perhaps anticipate future expansion. The vision of my first self-generated brewery involved a brewhouse fairly large for a pub—20 barrels—as well as multiple brew-sized fermentors. On the advice of our engineer we removed the floor that was there, sank three-inch pipes as far into the ground beneath as resistance would bear (some up to thirty feet), tied all that in with rebar and only then poured more concrete than anyone would have thought possible. The good thing about starting from scratch is that everything is in your control, from plotting the slope to perfectly placing the drains. Conventional wisdom prescribes a slope of ¼ inch to each foot of run, but allows that consistently executed, 1/8 inch is enough. Much more than ¼ inch may result in brewer vertigo, or at least difficulty in the placement, anchoring and leveling of tanks. For in seismically sensitive areas, it's required to "permanently" fix tanks of a certain size to the floor, and this must be inspected and certified.

As with any other building material, there is a great variety in concrete composition and suitability. Others before me have canvassed the subject in great technical detail. Strength, curing time and temperature, thickness and other volumetric measure must all be weighed and considered when putting together the bones of a new floor. Also briefly ponder the quandary once posed by a brewer I know, who asked my advice about a slab that refused to settle and cure owing to the vibration caused by the frequent passing of long freight trains. I really didn't know what to tell her.

It Smells So Bad, It Must Be Good— Epoxy Coatings

Again, many epoxy coatings, even expensive ones applied by a professional, are not much better than paint. I wince, recalling a newly-crafted epoxy floor of utilitarian maroon hue at another brewery in my town, supposedly adequately dried and everything, that came up when it was first walked on. Even if such a thing doesn't happen immediately, the fact that epoxies expand and contract at different rates than the floors beneath them presents one of the innate challenges of the coating, especially with frequent inundation by hot liquids. One of the keys is properly preparing the floor beneath the coating or treatment in advance of its application. This can be done by sand- or shot-blasting the surface. It's messy of course, and like many things should be done long before it occurs to you to do so. Or you can rent a rotary floor buffer/polisher fitted with an emery or garnet disc and amuse your co-workers as you skip it around the room to little constructive effect—and a great deal of danger. With practice these things can actually work, but it certainly takes a little effort. One more aftermarket idea is acid etching, in which a low-pH solution is applied and allowed to minutely erode the surface, allowing the subsequent liquid coating to cling to a fairly consistent stratum of nooks and crannies. Epoxies must be mixed in proper proportion, of course, in manageable batch size, and applied consistently and in reasonable time. They can also be supremely toxic, requiring the use of respirators and some good sense about time spent on the project. By the time you've finished applying your floor coating—stop me if you've heard this one—you've pretty much learned how you should have done it. That's where the pros come in, and while I know there are a lot of things competing for precedence in your budget hierarchy, your brewery floor is probably worth allowing a little upward creep.

All joking aside, the paint type of epoxy is generally too easy to apply, too manageable, and too affordable to be any good at all. Far better to use the kind that cures to a hard and fairly impermeable shell, and incorporates a mineral grit for traction and durability. I once spent a miserable week applying a floor of this type, fortunately in the company of a guy who'd once done this sort of thing for a living, and it has held up remarkably well. (With the exception of the area where, over the years, tens of thousands of spent grain drums had slammed into it.) One incidental fun fact I have to report is that CO_2, say, flowing from an active fermentor, can hamper the even drying of epoxy. Before it dries, it is still a liquid, after all. In fact, this is probably good to bear in mind when applying any coating to an extreme slope.

There, There—Tile

There's something totemic about a well-tiled floor. It may simply be the association of its ritual use in breweries of a certain size and a certain ethnic heritage, but the mere sight of a nicely executed and well-maintained tile floor seems to slow the heart, coax an involuntary smile and whisper "Alles in Ordnung" all at the same time. We can't help it. We like Ordnung. And we like floors that hold together over the years, clean easily and dress the place up a little. Expensive? Properly executed and sourced, you bet it is. But I think you'll find it about the same (or perhaps just a bit more) as a properly applied epoxy coating. Most often, it's sadly true that you get what you pay for. It's hard to financially prioritize something that doesn't directly apply to the processes of making beer, but if you appreciate the fractal sense of putting a place together you'll at least see the wisdom of giving your floor a seat at the table, so to speak.

That said, the decision to go with tile is a bit of a plunge. It takes a certain amount of steely resolve to stay the course and to make decisions about details that keep the whole concept harmonious and of high quality. Blink once and you've consigned yourself to a life of the replacement of cracked tiles and washing disenfranchised grit down the drain. It's like putting a stereo system together—it'll only sound as good as its weakest component.

First off you'll need tile of high quality and a rating that will stand up to the abuses of happenstance—dropped hose ends and tools, kegs that bounce once, twice, three times before finally settling down, the drip and splash of chemical concentration—as well as the endlessly repeated challenges of process—hand trucks and other wheeled offenders, barrels tipped on their angles and rolled, the regular flow of liquids well above and below a neutral pH 7. There is tile that's appropriate for industrial application (which is us) and tile that's better suited for the Sultan's bath. Tell yourself there's beauty in utility as you pick a material and a color better suited to the display of dirt, mold and yeast than something that goes with the curtains.

Nor is base adhesive or the grout that holds it all together to be underestimated. Only epoxy grout will do when it comes to withstanding the kinds of demands placed on the surface itself. Otherwise, erosion is inevitable. That grey grit you can't seem to finish hosing away and down the drain? That's the substandard material holding your floor (temporarily) together. Protect your investment with the good stuff.

My next advice where tile floors are concerned might seem a trifle unfair, a violation of the DIY spirit that drives a great deal of what we do. But unless you've had a previous life as a tile setter or vast experience outside your own bathroom or kitchen, you're almost certainly better off getting a professional to do the job. Surface preparation, consistency of mixture and application, uniformity of slope and level and the appraising eye that knows when the job is done to satisfaction—these are the skills that come with years of experience, not the two days you've assigned yourself in your construction schedule. Pay the two dollars and enjoy what you get, or perhaps, as we managed to do, find a tile guy who likes to drink beer.

Other options exist, of course, such as urethane-based coatings that provide a thick layer not unlike the harder epoxy coating I've recommended. I worked in a small brewery quite a few years ago that had such a coating in part of its cellar. It held up fine to a lot of abuse, but had initially been installed so inexpertly and on such an imperfect surface that stepping in certain places sent jets of water (or whatever) up through holes across the room, like one of those gimmicky fountains triggered by booby-trap flagstones. I hasten to say that this was not primarily the fault of the coating, but rather of its application and installation, and that I have seen such coatings hold up reasonably well when properly integrated and consistently applied. They are, however, extremely expensive.

A Descent into the Maelstrom—Down and in the General Direction of the Drain

The most perfectly executed and expensive floor surface still needs the cooperation of gravity to conduct mainly liquid waste to the actual drain. This of course necessitates some kind of slope, or if such fashioning is not in your budget or plan, at least an awareness of where it all wants to go. There, I've said it. For all my fancy talk of straightening up and affording it all, it has to be acknowledged that for startups, there isn't always the money needed to do a proper job on things like floors when brewing vessels and the raw materials take priority.

When my company got involved in a somewhat odd cooperative project combining a large video arcade with a small brewery, I was assigned a basement room with a flat floor and no ventilation to work my suddenly very earthbound magic. Where drains were concerned, my partner-genie allowed me one wish: I could have a single draw point anywhere I wanted it. Keeping my brewhouse plan more preeminently in mind than I should have, I had it cut where the mess was likely to be the greatest: close to the mash/lauter tun and not far from the kettle. What I should have done, of course, is find out where the liquid wanted to go when chaotically, less predictably loosed. I had assumed a general levelness, which in fact was borne out by the use of an actual level. Again, what I should have done was throw five gallons of water on the floor and see where it went. After that, design would have followed the dictates of the space. It would have violated my uptight left-to-right sensibility, but it also would have saved me hours of damming and squeegeeing. I'm here to tell you that in that case I was stupid, but you can be smart. Damage was minimal in the end. We left that association after five years of squeegeeing and I still had fun making beer there. The next time I was assigned a flat floor and a teensy budget, I filled the bucket and let fly.

Believe it or not I've seen breweries that have no drains at all, in which, presumably, all liquids are to be caught in buckets and flung into the alley. These are generally, somewhat cynically, operations that are put together more for statutory reasons—such as having to do with tied house laws requiring a nominally functioning brewery in order to qualify for an additional license—than anything properly, even briefly, thought through. A sawn-off keg sunk into a hole in the floor, sealed with a bag or two of cement and fitted with a hardware store sump pump fed to a sink is better than the Sorcerer's Apprentice routine.

Two essential types of drain present themselves as options for a floor frequently inundated and highly traveled. The trench drain is widely regarded as the sexiest, as its reach is extensive and liquid is required to flow only a fairly short distance to be through its grating and at least out of sight. The presence of a trench, however—and especially when cut into an existing floor—can compromise structural integrity. One or more focal drains can better preserve the load bearing aspect of a floor. They are cheaper to install, and less invasive and in the way, but the sloping can be trickier, as it often leads to multiple draw points. They are an especially good option when adding a wet-area slab to an existing flat floor of sufficient strength. My company's production brewery is one such setting, and uses drains of this type. The vacated paint warehouse we moved into had floors so flat and so strong that it would have been a crime to cut them. Intermittent circular drains worked into the design of a variously-sloped slab and rigged with pumps to our waste tank has in a way brought us full circle from the flat room and the bucket of water. Volumes (and costs, of course) are larger, but the principle is the same.

Far more than ever before, the site and suitability of brewery spaces vary beyond comprehension and experience, perhaps more with floors and drains than in any other aspect. Slopes, flow, surface treatment, rating, equipment placement and the systems for removal both internal and municipal; these are the variables presented in myriad ways to the startup brewer, sometimes ignored or downplayed, perhaps often squeegeed, but never entirely forgotten.

Chapter Highlights

Types of Drains—Advantages and Disadvantages
- Trench—liquids flow relatively short distances, sloping fairly simple, but can weaken floor structure
- Central draw point(s)—compromises floor structure less than trench, but sloping can be complicated
- Sump to sewer or waste tank—necessary for involved waste systems, but messy when pumps fail

QUALITY ASSURANCE/CONTROL
Levels of Inquiry and Intervention

20

Let's back up a bit. Quality Assurance or Quality Control, whatever you want to call it—QA or QC—is a system of analyzing or appraising your beer in order to determine its suitability for market. It isn't exactly like the frog you need to kill in order to understand its inner workings, but analysis in itself won't get the job done properly to begin with. It won't bring the frog—or your beer—back to life. I remember many years ago visiting a medium-sized regional brewery that sent beer pretty far afield in draft and bottles, and being proudly shown a tunnel pasteurizer and blinded and partitioned sensory analysis area. The trouble was, stable as it may have been going out the door, much of the beer in the market was infected—the IPA tasted more like hefeweizen. The problem was upstream in the realm of brewing process and sanitation. This could have had something to do with the policy of cleaning only with hot, and hard water, but I digress. Downstream of the actual brewing, the analytical tools and training were insufficient to recognize problems evident to consumers—consumers who were now being offered more choices all the time, and were quickly learning the difference between them. For this and other reasons, this brewery is no longer in business.

One of the first aims of the commercial brewer, or even the devoted homebrewer, is consistency. To be able to duplicate results is essential to the satisfaction of customer expectation and the establishment and maintenance of brand and reputation. Like a lot of good ideas it sounds obvious, but accurate record keeping is one of the most important aspects of this. A good brew sheet, with spaces to note and annotate everything—not just recipes with amounts, temperatures and changes throughout brewing and fermentation, but everything else that happens too—is perhaps the brewer's most valuable tool. Brewers' logs speak across the ages, sometimes in archaic expression and without analytical measures we are accustomed to today, but it's possible to look at a document hundreds of years old and brew a pretty good approximation of beers that were knocking them out in the time of Dickens, or Luther.

The codification of SOPs, or Standard Operating Procedures, is instrumental to the consistent application of accrued records. For unless you plan to do all the brewing, cellaring and packaging every day, yourself, forever, it will be necessary to ensure that things are done a certain way by getting it all on paper. There are limits, of course; not every idiosyncrasy of procedure needs to make it into such a document. Some people are left-handed, for example. But ensuring that all procedural boxes are checked along the lifeline of a batch of beer goes a long way toward ensuring it's pretty darned close to the previous batch.

I'm not going to take you through every step of cleaning and sanitation. I'm presuming that either you know the basics now, or will learn them from someone who has established SOPs for such things, even if it's your chemical salesperson. I do feel it necessary to point out that these phases of process are the surest to succeed or fail, depending. A lot of this is left to conscience—you know, for example, that black mold growing in the corners of your cellar isn't a good thing, and that dropping a gasket on the floor means going to get a clean one. You know that being thorough and consistent is important. You also probably know that you can drive yourself crazy wondering, doubting and suspecting where cleanliness is concerned. Like so much else it's a matter of balance and the deals you make with yourself.

Within You and Without You— Tools of Analysis

Like other more physical tools, those of analysis are fundamentally an extension of our capabilities as human beings. As a hammer focuses the force brought to bear on whatever it's striking, so a microscope or hemocytometer, even a thermometer, more precisely quantifies our physical capacity to observe or measure. And on from there. Instrumentation always has the potential of becoming an addiction, but it does, in its way, open the doors of perception where understanding the makeup and processes of beer are concerned. Probably most to the point, it standardizes the parameters of well- (and poorly-) made beer, providing a scalable, black and white, universal reference.

That said, the senses are probably the most useful and best-honed tools any brewer has. People have made beer for centuries, after all—some of it presumably delicious—armed only with the empirical knowledge of their experience and what they had picked up from others. We remain a largely self-taught movement. We may in many cases be better educated and better equipped than those from brewing's agrarian age, but we rely primarily on the same front line of perception: our noses and our taste buds. As apprentice home and professional brewers we smell and taste constantly, eager to pick up change and divine a finished product, making choices along the way informed by what we

think we're perceiving. As we gain experience and attempt more ambitious projects, we do the same. The closest assessment of quality and preference comes from tasting our beer and our brewing water daily, smelling hops and yeast ready for pitching, and sampling our brewing malt.

Naturally we choose to check things as we go, with such things in our earliest and least secure phases as iodine to check starch conversion and pH strips to make sure that yes, it's gradually dropping. Thermometers and hydrometers, too, are of course basic equipment in validating the correctness of our processes. Later, as curiosity (and perhaps risk) grows, we move a bit into microscopy. A close look at a simple hemocytometer (a gridded glass slide on which individual yeast cells can be discerned and counted) gives us an idea of pitching rates. Dye-staining cells allows us to check viability and instances of mutation and infection. By building such evaluation into standard procedures we build a greater body of knowledge, also empirical but more objective than that of our forebears' swiping the head off a ferment or deciding when the surface of heated water becomes glassy.

Basic lab tests also offer a window into what has already happened. While in a pub setting, such analysis may often be academic, as the beer in question may already be on line, the tank half empty. But it still informs future procedure, such as whether to repitch a particular yeast or not. Hsu's Lactobacillus-Pediococcus (HLP) medium is easily mixed and easily inoculated, and within a few days can show the presence of two of the most common and compromising wort-spoiling bacteria. Other simple tests are readily available from brewing supply houses such as Brewcraft and GW Kent, or from yeast labs such as Wyeast, White Labs and Lallemand. Their staffs are also a wealth of suggestion and guidance when it comes to picking the testing media and equipment appropriate to specific inquiry. These companies may also offer services for wort, beer and yeast analysis, potentially ratcheting up the level of detail available, for a price; things like yeast viability, analysis of morphology, attenuation, alcohol content, IBUs, calories and other categories can be helpful in evaluating process. Other analytical companies exist as well. As an augmentation to basic understanding and experience, it's sometimes worthwhile along the way to pay the money and be certain of the result. Sometimes a larger or more established brewery in your area can be tapped, discreetly and deferentially, for help with such analysis. Some of them make it a part of their business.

If your brewery is sending packaged beer into markets even a state away, or perhaps if you choose to devote the wherewithal to maintaining consistency closer to home, even within your own four walls, you will probably want to invest in some kind of tester for levels of CO_2. While somewhat expensive when new—over a thousand dollars, but they are occasionally available used—the basic Zahm-Nagel tester is the most common such device, and will help in determining volumes of CO_2 appropriate to the beers you make and sell. It isn't completely foolproof, and can be somewhat tedious to operate, but it's an important step toward eliminating the curse of many brewpubs: flat beer. More sophisticated and expensive CO_2 meters are available for faster and more frequent readings, if that becomes necessary, as is equipment for measuring dissolved oxygen. A properly outfitted lab will always seem to need one more thing to offer a more comprehensive picture: a gas chromatographer, for example ($\$\$$), or even an Anton-Paar Multiparameter Measuring device ($\$\$\$$), which spits out information so amazing, it will suddenly seem you could never have done without it. As a startup, however, you're probably a little way off from that.

A Little Knowledge…

Many empirically accomplished brewers get into the business so fast, and find themselves occupied so completely at the outset, that perhaps paradoxically, they don't get training first. I used to say in fact, only dissembling a little, that I would have had to quit my job in order to be trained how to do it. Folksy wisdom notwithstanding, it's a good idea to pick it up where you can, whether it's part of your startup process or whether you go to night school, so to speak. Seminars and courses exist in all shapes, sizes, lengths of time and levels of technicality, covering all or specific aspects of making beer and bringing it to market. Often shorter

ones are offered before, after or within festivals and conferences such as the Great American Beer Festival (GABF), the Craft Brewers Conference (CBC), and the meetings of the Master Brewers Association of the Americas (MBAA) or the American Society of Brewing Chemists (ASBC). Membership and participation in all of these goings-on cannot but help to fill in some of the gaps in knowledge and experience that nearly all of us have.

Making sure of the knowledge, training and its application by your various staffs is also vitally important in making sure not only that your beer is being properly made but cared for and presented in its best light and context. You can either undertake this yourself, perhaps holding regular meetings and talks to explain brewing process and the specificity of new releases, or you can hire out for it. On the brewing side this can involve courses at, for instance, the Siebel Institute in Chicago. Where front of house and wider-world sales is concerned, a relatively recent development is the Cicerone program, which involves instruction, testing and certification on a few levels, from basic stylistic awareness and appropriate presentation to unstinting, hawk-eyed competence on par with the master sommelier.

But back to those gaps in our knowledge. Instrumentation, reading, even procedural instruction can help to trace the outlines and even 2-D makeup of a theoretically successful beer. It takes the guidance of sensibility to inform a fuller recognition both of rightness and wrongness where flavor and flaw are concerned. And there are gaps in sensibility as well, based on experience, sentiment, personal preference and innate gift. For instance not all people, brewers and otherwise, equally recognize and object to the rich and buttery presence of diacetyl in finished beer. I myself have come to recognize a certain weakness where highly elevated levels of corny and sulfurous DMS (dimethyl sulfide) come into play. These deficiencies too can be recognized and schooled either by flesh-and-blood instruction or through the use of the sensory kits available through such outfits as Flavoractiv. These constitute a sort of sensory encyclopedia, with vials that contain specific flavor and aroma components potentially occurring in beer.

In the past such kits have been expensive, inspiring cooperative purchase via brewers' guilds and other groups, but as with so many other aspects of our trade, more economical versions have lately been tailored to fit our often more modest needs.

Go or No-go—The Collective Emperor's Thumb

To bring staff education a step further, you may eventually consider establishing sensory panels to adhere to a consistent brewery stewardship, even zeitgeist, where the parameters of brands, and groups of brands, are concerned. In such settings individual panel members are isolated and given samples of batches of beer under final review prior to release into the market. Based on the opportunity to detect and describe discerned flavors and aromas and the answers to specific questions, they determine whether the batch in question is true to style and appropriate for commercial release. None goes into this stage of evaluation totally blind; presumably and preferably, instruction has come first, relying on discussion, evaluation and consensus to establish the standards of individual brands and overall house flavor.

One interesting aspect of this kind of evaluation is that the panelists need not be experts, or even brewers. Discerning palates often also sit behind desks and drive forklifts. Not only does such diversity where the skills and backgrounds of potential sensory panelists give a more confident and comprehensive look at the beers in question, it provides an opportunity for company-wide esprit de corps. There are courses and sources of information as well for the establishment of such groups and procedures. There are people walking around our various gatherings willing to share their rudiments. If nothing else, simply getting your staff to recognize the elements of the beers they serve is a step in the right direction to ensuring product consistency and deliciousness.

Chapter Highlights

Inexpensive Tools for Maintaining Quality and Consistency

- A good and complete brewsheet
- Well-defined SOPs (Standard Operating Procedures)
- Even a simple program of sensory analysis
- HLP medium and plastic test tubes

More Expensive Tools That Come in Handy

- A hemocytometer and a microscope to read it
- A CO_2 tester such as a Zahm-Nagel

Even More Expensive Tools Pretty Much Essential in a Packaging Brewery

- A better and more easily and quickly readable CO_2 meter
- A DO (Dissolved Oxygen) meter

SECURING RAW MATERIALS
Who Are You Calling a Pawn?

21

Looking through the brewing logs of past centuries, there's a striking lack of specificity where raw materials are concerned. So many loads of malt, so many pounds of hops, without designation as to type or variety. Of course back then, malting was undertaken by breweries themselves; the malt you used was your malt, and not the malt of a half-dozen other nearby brewers and maltsters. Some of it might be roasted, but it was still the same beginning product: malt. Hops were, well, just hops. If there was any designation it was geographical: Hallertau or East Kent, perhaps, but most often a recipe didn't even go that far. You used what was available locally, perhaps on your own farms.

Even by the time of our new Eden, the legalization and spread of homebrewing, and the craft brewing movement which followed, things were not a lot more sophisticated. Choices were few where malt was concerned. There was two-row, which you used for ales, and there was six-row, which was what the big brewers brewed with, and which was cheaper but harder to use. Since the UK had begun their homebrewing movement before ours, there was some English malt available. There were also a handful of international hop varieties: a couple of English, a few German and Czech, plus two or three domestic types from Washington and Oregon. Yeast was also very limited: brewer's yeast for the choosy, and a lot of stories about people

paring slices from a bakery-sized brick of Fleishmann's. Even professional brewers mainly used dried yeast. It was an innocent time, but it got to be kind of boring. And it didn't last.

Before long, hop and malt merchants noticed craft brewers, and they started to come calling. They talked up an expanded selection of imported malts, and spoke of fledgling specialty production schemes in their big domestic malt houses. New hop varieties came along too—more from other countries, like Slovenia and Australia, and some others from here, too; variations, essentially, on what had been available before, but which allowed us to display a more sophisticated awareness. Everything was cheap, too. Boy, was it cheap. And availability almost wasn't an issue. You made a phone call, you got your hops and your malt, and you paid a little money.

This is a modern narrative, so the snake that inevitably appeared in the garden wasn't all bad. He brought choice, variety, and lots of ways for us all to be enormously creative. But there were suddenly an awful lot of us, running to and fro en masse, and we did to stability what shifting of weights and tipping of balances always do. Supplies which before had seemed unlimited ran short here and there; the innocence of spontaneity became a riskier proposition. Oddly, prices remained low for a time, likely held down by dictatorial big brewers. Our ranks continued to grow, and we encouraged brokers and farmers to provide us with fascinating new products so we could emulate the success of other respected brewers and strike out on our own.

The hop crisis of 2007-8 (and less famously, the accompanying malt crisis) was the result of several factors. Farmers found that their dependence on a certain way of doing things could no longer last. The low hop prices dictated by the big brewers made other crops more attractive, and acreage was decreased, favoring the more efficient cultivation of high-alpha hops. The more esoteric aroma hops beloved by small brewers (who, after all, only commanded a small part of the market, yet a disproportionately large percentage of aroma varieties) came to be luxury items, requiring commitment and risk, scarily vulnerable to the roving eye of fashion. Crop failures in other parts of the world created a huge and specific demand for hops from the Yakima Valley. The brewers running to and fro now came from all over the globe, the largest of them continuing to consolidate and foster more efficient operations, resulting in another alteration of pattern and demand. Prices soared. Then there were fires, and a suddenly sagging economy. The sequence and severity of misfortune came to be almost biblical in scope and correspondence; the term "perfect storm" became vastly over-used. And always, there were more of us.

A Difficult Pump to Prime—Establishing and Maintaining Relationships

New brewers arriving on the scene today face immediate challenges where the procurement of raw materials is concerned. As with many new businesses, payment must be made in advance, at first. But with so many new and gradually seasoning customers crying out their specific wants like so many stock traders, it can be difficult to get a word in edgewise. It's not as simple as making a phone call, especially where hops are concerned. Bagged malt can generally be had for the ordering, but in times of scarcity and crisis existing customers are helped first and the newcomer goes wanting. It will likely take unforeseen creativity to come up with recipes based in market reality, at least at first. Once you've placed a few orders and

paid a few bills, your voice will begin to be heard, but perhaps not until the next harvest year approaches. At which point you might consider contracting for your hops.

Committing to the usage of (and payment for) very specific quantities of anything might require the small brewer to relinquish any notions of an unfettered self-image. But with all the regulations, compliances and impositions of taxes to which you are already forced to submit, you might as well admit it: you're fettered anyway, so what's one more agreement? Having established a baseline of consumption by however long you've been doing business, it's a simple exercise of arithmetic and extrapolation to figure out how much of particular hop varieties you're likely to use in the coming harvest year. Combine that with the certainty that a handful (and perhaps more) of the most sought-after varieties will at various times along the year's timeline cease to be available on the un-contracted, or "spot" market, and you've got ample reason to do the math and put your name on the dotted line.

Another common libertarian reason for not wanting to contract for hops is the volatility of the spot market. For if you've contracted for Hop X at ten dollars a pound and its value sinks to four or five as the season wears on, you've paid five or six dollars too much. Theoretically. Never mind that a spate of new brewers hell-bent on producing a line of single-hop-X beers might drive that price up instead of down, or exhaust supplies altogether. Lately, the big brewers have also taken interest in some of the varieties we have always considered our own. In truth there's a lot you can't know as you enter into an agreement. What you can know is what you'll be paying almost no matter what, and that you'll get a chipper affirmative when you call to place your order rather than a door in the face. Besides, do you want to spend your time making and selling beer or uneasily monitoring markets?

Contracts are a way of communicating between brewers and farmers, providing mutual assurance of price and availability and establishing a history of supply and demand that can serve to plot a more secure future. Anyone who weathered the crisis of 2007-8 will see the benefit of this, and if they've been paying attention since then, they're also aware of some of the ups and downs that have ensued. Let's also consider the plight of the farmer. Hops are only one of the things we worry about, and sure, we don't want to go broke following a capricious market, but growing hops is the exclusive livelihood of many in the Yakima and Willamette valleys and elsewhere. They deserve assurances of solvency, or at least profitability for the commitments they've made to put certain things in the ground. When at all possible, the big brewers kept prices low for themselves, and while this isn't entirely satisfactory, it did impose a kind of stability. But those guys are busy now trying to post short-term profits in order to show that they know what they're doing, and they've withdrawn a great deal of monitoring and maintenance muscle. It now falls far more to us, collectively, to step up to the table. It may turn out that we pay a bit more in the long run for hops guaranteed by contract; or it may not. But even making use of such a contract provides us a more grown-up role in the planning process. No more of that dashing past the table and snatching whatever variety is tastiest or closest to hand.

Nor do you need to contract for all of your hops. Not all varieties typically run short. In addition, if you feel you know what you're doing (and that's the kind of thing you're into, you riverboat gambler you), you can contract for a percentage and take your chances with the rest. You may not have been reading the Brewers Association Forum during the crisis when startups (and even some more seasoned) were writing in begging for hops, any variety, pellet or whole, from the unused stock of their brethren, but it gave one pause to see such desperation.

The aftermath of the shortages and price hikes of a few years ago have brought about greater communications between brewers and farmers not only through contracting but through simpler conversation and contact. I know I've had more direct visits from farmers in the past couple of years than I'm used to; many of them now seem willing to negotiate directly. Most often, however, they're offering un-contracted surpluses. It's still the brokers who typically offer contracts, and it's the brokers who have worked the hardest to try to win back trust. For desperation brought

out a darker side of their end of the business. There were variously leveled charges of opportunism and arbitrariness, fear-mongering and other manipulation. New structures have arisen—and particularly where the smallest brewers are concerned—circumventing longer-term uncertainty and its accompanying bad behavior. Contracting a few years out may make you nervous, but just as you can take your chances with market fluctuations in the term of a single season, it's not a bad strategy to tie down diminishing percentages of anticipated usage in the approaching couple of years, then revisit and evaluate when the time comes to make further moves, if necessary.

The Wind that Shakes the Barley— Malt Contracting

Malt is a bit of a different story where contracting is concerned. If your operation is small enough to deal exclusively with base malt in bags, you may not need to read any further, as to date, contracts are not generally offered for bagged malt (there are, however, exceptions, and times are changing). In this case you'll pay the current market price as you go, and as availabilities hold. But if you plan to receive bulk malt in a silo, you're suddenly part of a huge community of farmers, maltsters, brewers and politicians engaged in a balance of fortunes and continents. It's funny to think that something as distant-sounding as the Canada Wheat Board (should it still exist by the time you read this) would have a bearing on your life as a brewer; but as a governing body which determines the currents of grain-related commerce and cultivation, in that vast supplier to the North, it just plain does. More humbly, so does the weather. Simply put, it is largely factors beyond your control that determine what you pay for malt year after year. Still, a contract is once more a worthy instrument to assure yourself of a consistent price and ongoing availability according to projections put together between you and your maltster.

If you've been paying attention, you'll notice a difference right there. The sale of hops is typically arranged through third party brokers who in simpler times might have been farmers themselves, representatives of a true cooperative, but who today are essentially independent entities. Malt is tendered by those who process it; not farmers either, strictly speaking, but proprietors of massive facilities in the Northwest and Midwest who procure, monitor, malt and blend grain shipped from massive fields across the continent. Malt prices between farmers and maltsters are hotly negotiated year after year, and are subject to the price fluctuations of other, potentially competing crops like wheat, soybeans and corn, which could just as easily be put in the ground instead of barley. With such uncertainty, contracts for malt are typically not offered for multiple years; in fact, until factors such as weather and expected yield are at least partially known, malt contracts in general are not undertaken until farther into the growing season than you'd see for other things, like hops. The size of the areas covered and the scale of the risks involved just make the machinations of malt move a little more slowly.

Once more it's a baseline of usage established by having been in business awhile that is the most useful determinant of your contracted amount of malt. If you're just getting started you'll probably be content to just pay as you go, absorbing or benefitting from the variance in price as the year wears on. Similarly Catch-22-ish to the establishment of a relationship with a hop broker, being taken on as a new and unproven customer can be a challenge in an increasingly tight and populated market. There's something to be said, along these lines, for having been in the swim for a number of years working for others, but if you're a new face you'll find that knowing a bit about how things work will help at least get discussion started.

The Gift that Keeps on Giving—Yeast Procurement and Management

Perhaps more than any other of the basic materials of brewing, yeast presents countless choices for the formulation both of individual beers and the groups of them that constitute a product line, and there are relatively few issues with availability. The main reason for all of this is that, quite simply, yeast is magic. It literally dropped from the sky in all brewing regions of the earth, was harnessed under varying circumstances and with widely differing results, and now exists in so many different forms and combinations (and from so many sources) that barring some sort of science fiction-type cataclysm there will never be shortages. In addition, with its tendency both to adapt and mutate, it could almost be said that each individual yeast morphology exists uniquely in every brewery that uses it. And that, my friends, is a lot of permutations.

If yeast is information, comprising yeses and nos of flavor, aroma and behavior in apparently endless combination, then like anything posted on the Internet, it wants to be free. Thanks to a sort of informal and universal expatriation by brewing yeast collectors, varieties once used to make specifically recognized beers and beer styles have spread to general availability. This transport can occur through legitimate channels of commerce, as in the case of the dried Whitbread yeast that went from a relatively early homebrewing choice to the dominant yeast of 1980s California brewpubs. But it can just as readily arrive in a plastic vial in some nameless beer enthusiast's luggage, collected with or without permission (and perhaps risk) from some venerated, likely European source. Used, isolated and stored, these yeasts have become part of the lexicon familiar to anyone who knows and can generally procure them. And as we see with hops, more yeast strains are becoming available every day. The sales circulars of every prominent yeast lab boast of new varieties, winkingly described in terms specific enough to be at least fairly closely geographically recognized, but vague enough to avoid litigation. Rumor and conversation take care of the rest as far as probable identification is concerned.

Unlike raw materials produced by the earth, yeast is husbanded and maintained in the laboratory or the brewery, where no less natural processes bring about its reproduction apart from the vagaries of politics, weather and other material happenstance. The mercantile sensibilities of the world's earliest brewers might be offended at the idea of paying money (or skins, or beer) for something that exists naturally and for free, but we are a fussier and more taxonomic lot, brand-dependent on consistency. We don't mind paying for something we can watch take its first stumbling steps and then get into full stride, producing for us something we have envisioned just so, especially as the cost can be amortized by multiple use.

A number of commercial yeast labs exist, each providing an array of yeasts lager, ale and otherwise bacteriological to any brewer knowing enough to place an order. Yeast can be obtained in liquid form, either in a quantity sufficient for full batch-sized pitching or, less expensively, grown in one or a succession of worts to the eventual same cell concentration. It can also be procured dried, a form which despite its sometimes-disparaging identification with simpler times, can be a perfectly creditable option, with many of the same style varieties. Maintaining yeast cultures in your own lab represents greater initial cost but likely long-term savings. This way yeast becomes truly yours, under your control, to be summoned by your manipulation to do the work you need it to do.

The Leaner Beast—Considering the Options

The mention of lab equipment brings up the subject of the balances and choices to be considered when putting together systems. As a beginning commercial brewer you may or may not have the training or inclination to undertake growing yeast up from single cells, or including a yeast propagator in your initial equipment. Malt handling and the design of brewhouses can be simplified as well, leaving out certain items to bring startup cost down, perhaps to be introduced later. Pre-ground malt is available, for example, thereby reducing or eliminating the need for a grain mill; similarly there are those who have elected to purchase malt extract for use in their commercial kettles, cutting a mash/lauter tun as well out of the configuration. In both cases, relying on the processes and decisions of a supplier of a pre-processed product makes things easier, but removes many of the choices in crafting your own brews. At this point, it's impossible not to mention the Granite City chain of brewpubs, all of which lack both of these items in their individual restaurants; they are supplied by conventionally produced wort from a single production center, which is then trucked to each of a few dozen locations. This isn't a startup model, to be sure, but an illustration of a way to generate trimmer brewing operations in restaurant spaces.

The hop crisis of 2007-8 brought about a lot of soul-searching, reflection and reevaluation of process and conception. Many brewers altered recipes both simply to lessen usage and to make use of varieties that were available once other stores were exhausted. General recipe focus for new beers also tilted a bit in favor of less strong and less hoppy session beers. But lupulin, if not a physical addiction like heroin, might be compared more directly to oil: it's a lifestyle choice, and a hard one to give up. Breweries widely discussed and no doubt here and there implemented the idea of retaining the ability to use whole hops rather than pellets. There are many farms and other sources for whole hops, but relatively few pelletizing plants (most of which are in the hands of brokers); to be able to brew with whole hops opens source potential substantially and reduces dependence on the most crowded part of the market. What this means in brewhouse design is mainly to lessen reliance on the pump-enabled transfer and whirlpooling of hopped wort. The ability to use a strainer of some type in removing the post-boil wort from the kettle would also aid in making whole hops at least a possibility. Hop extracts are also an option for reducing kettle material while maintaining desired levels of hop character. Take a look at the brewhouse design section of this book for further thoughts on these possibilities.

These days, thankfully, we have many options in the selection and availability of brewing's raw materials. Our movement's pioneers had to literally beg for suppliers to hook them up; then, once given the nod, they had to somehow deal with receiving the goods in improvised ways. Ken Grossman of Sierra Nevada tells a story of pulling his truck in under a malt hopper, receiving a brimming bed full of malt, and driving back to his brewery with his front tires only intermittently in contact with the road. What's more challenging these days is spotting trends far enough ahead to keep the supplies you need flowing in and beer flowing out. In contrast with the country's—indeed the world's—largest brewers, there aren't just a few of us making all the decisions. In some ways we think with a collective hive consciousness, but insist on our individuality. It may be easier said than done, but we need to keep options open without finding ourselves holding the bag. And like so much of what we do, the ways to balance all this are as numerous as we are.

Chapter Highlight

One Piece of Advice:

- If at all possible, contract for your malt and hops.

SECTION VI

BREWING

CRAFTING YOUR PORTFOLIO
Revolt into Style

22

When I was having my earliest fantasies about someday having my own brewery, I wanted things to be simple. I would make two beers, an ale and a lager, and they would be strong and full of character. Inspired by a passage in *The Long Ships*, Frans G. Bengtsson's great Viking saga, in which the best and strongest ale is saved as a reward for the hardest work—portages—I would call them Portage Ale and Portage Lager. Yeah.

Times were simpler then. The whole idea of "microbrewing" was so recent, relatively speaking, that style was not yet a matter of general awareness. It was not odd for an emergent packaging brewery to come out with only one beer, perhaps only called "ale" or "lager" beyond the brewery's name. Pubs typically served only a few styles, often mainly differentiated by color; a common triad, whatever the beers were actually named, consisted of a pale, an amber and something dark. So my schematic was spare, but not at all unprecedented.

Soon, however, we all became educated. Books like Michael Jackson's *World Guide to Beer* and then the Brewers Publications Classic Beer Style Series, taught brewers and other interested readers about specific style traditions and subcategories. Pale ale, for example, was not just the lightest-looking beer on offer in the store or at the taps, but a style with many different variations. Pilsner and porter too had different interpretations based on history

and geography. At the same time, the Beer Judge Certification Program (BJCP) and the Association of Brewers (AOB)—through its management of the Great American Beer Festival (GABF)—codified style for purposes of competition. Accurate emulation came to be a way for brewers to show their grasp and mastery, and gauging their efforts a way of evaluating and ranking their success.

Then things got more complicated. New ingredients (for Americans) such as wheat and rye forced the consideration of new styles and interpretations. Styles practically extinct in their countries of origin were exhumed by craft brewers, spurring a spate of "new" styles; these reinterpretations may not have been recognized as authentic by beer history buffs, but still served to shed light on worldwide beer heritage and culture as they took on new life of their own. Extra-strength versions of regular styles such as Double (or Imperial) India Pale Ale brought about further branching. And of course there were new stylistic inventions which defied classification.

All of this testifies to a dizzying expansion in the awareness of styles, and with it an increasing demand by both brewers and consumers for an array of products far beyond the tight little nexus of the movement's dawn. However brilliantly conceived, executed and appreciated Portage Ale (or Lager) may have been in the late 1980s, it would probably not be enough with the passage of time.

Look at the largest, most established and successful craft breweries and you'll usually identify them with a single product that made them so. Sierra Nevada Pale Ale, Brooklyn Lager, Widmer Hefeweizen, New Belgium's Fat Tire, Samuel Adams Boston Lager; these are the beers that caught people's attention, that became the pillars on which the craft brewing movement was built. But though they remain mainstays, they are no longer alone in the portfolios of these pioneering breweries. Any successful business, after all, needs to flex with the times.

So as a prospective professional brewer, you are entering the market and the community at a time of particular historical significance. Whether you choose to fit in with or rebel against whatever else is out there, you will need to consider how you place yourself and your products. A handful of undistinguished beers amateurishly marketed these days cannot rely on novelty for attention as it might have twenty-five years ago; today it would show a lack of inspiration. With over 2,000 US breweries currently open, and no doubt at least a few—quite likely a few dozen—in your prospective market, you'll need to distinguish yourself. This doesn't mean that each beer you produce needs to be something never before seen or attempted. It does, for starters, mean that each of them needs to be a top-quality example of whatever styles you've chosen to emulate or create. With the maturing of the craft brewing movement has come customer discernment. We aren't the only ones who know what we're doing anymore. They know what we're doing, too.

Brick, Sticks or Hay—
Building Your House Brands

There are several considerations when putting together your portfolio, whether it consists of a few core brands to be released in bottles or draft, or the first of dozens your brewpub will produce as it endures. The first, lest our analysis seem too grown up, is what you yourself want to do. Yes, beyond being smart about how it's all going to fit into a wider world, you are the heart of your own brand; if you aren't passionate and enthusiastic about what you plan to bring into the market, why are you bothering? And I'm going to leave that part to you. If as a homebrewer you've developed a line

of compelling and flavorful beers with nettles as a core ingredient and you believe that based on your research and gut feeling they're going to soar in the market, I'm happy to get out of your way. Ditto if what you want to make is a pilsner that Emperor Franz-Josef himself would look forward to at the end of the day. There's no harm in a little ego when determining what you make.

Specialty beers often require specialty equipment. Or put another way, the equipment you choose to install (or happen to have on hand) will in large part determine the type and number of beers you're able to produce. Lagers and other more deliberate styles take more time (as you no doubt know), requiring the extended occupation of their designated tank space. In addition, they are best crafted with brewhouses specifically designed to produce wort for lager fermentation and conditioning. This isn't a bad thing; it simply is. You'll just need to remember the restrictions your plan and vision have placed on your equipment when configuring it. Nettle beer probably turns around pretty quickly (I'm assuming it's an ale), but that Franz-Josef Pilsner is going to displace a batch or two of ale from the rotation each time you brew it.

An analysis of your likely clientele is also in order when choosing the beers you brew. Is your pub in a university area? What kind of students will you be serving? Hopefully graduate students and upperclassmen, if you intend to stay in business. You'll also probably see some international students. What styles of beers will they respond to? Ales similar to the ones they recall from back home? Or can you get them to branch out, to try new things of your design? Or is your place in a shopping area, either a mall or a cluster of businesses? Who shops there, in what kind of stores, and how long do they typically stay? What other types of neighborhoods nearby will you draw from as people come into your zone to do their other business? You get the idea.

Geography, though not as restrictive as it once was, can also be a determiner of style, if only to prefigure your most popular beers. Craft-brewed lagers are more popular in the mid-Atlantic Coast—Pennsylvania, Maryland, New York—and on into the Midwest, than in many other parts of the country. Wheat beers are also big in the Midwest, especially as you move farther west. Bell's Oberon, from Kalamazoo and Comstock, Michigan; Goose Island's 312 in Chicago; and Boulevard's Unfiltered Wheat Beer in Kansas City are all flagship wheats for these quickly growing Midwestern regional breweries. Some loyalty to style can be attributed to the immigration patterns of long ago, which in turn determined the location and spheres of influence of our largest breweries. Such legacies affect us, too.

And then there's the West Coast, where the earliest craft brewers were founded and where, as it happens, nearly all of the nation's hops are grown. Beers in these areas tend to be bold and bitter, from Washington and Oregon down to northern California and on to San Diego. In Portland or Seattle, for example, it's not unusual to find multiple IPAs pouring at all but the corporate pubs, and often as many as three or four (one of my breweries recently poured nine). Oddly enough, parenthetically, a quick trip across the northern border into British Columbia presents a decidedly maltier array of beers, despite being, like much of Washington, within sniffing distance of the hop fields of the Yakima and Okanogan valleys. But that too is changing as brewers there keep an eye on their brethren in other regions. An increasingly style-savvy public ultimately dictates everyone's best efforts.

Your fledgling packaging brewery will probably start with a small cluster of brands: your flagship; one or two others that sell substantially less, but strongly; and a seasonal offering. Seasonals are not only engaging and gratifying to produce—you've got to have some fun interpreting your addition to the fall, or summer, or holiday pack—but they are very often your most popular style according to analyses undertaken by the Brewers Association and other evaluating entities such as IRI and Nielsen. IPAs have come on strongly over the past several years, as fiercely hoppy northwest and southern Californian interpretations of the nearly extinct English style have reached and influenced other regions. Belgian styles, once the nearly exclusive province of the courageous few, have also proven irresistible to brewers looking for a challenge, wherever they happen to live; witbier in particular (and partly because of the shrewdly-managed strength of such

big brewer brands as Hoegaarden, Shocktop and Blue Moon) has proven to be a style with legs, appealing to a broad group of drinkers. In any case, differentiation is the key: not to put out three beers that differ in color but little else, but to present potential customers an interesting choice that will show them not just good beers but a strong brand. Quality in any individual beer is essential; consistently maintaining that quality inspires trust.

Altering your lineup in a pub setting is easy. If you've already designed and ordered packaging for that lineup, and invested marketing time and money in it, changing things up is a bit more complicated. Just the same, you'll need to pay close attention to the performance of individual brands, and be prepared to roll with the results of your analyses. Maintaining and re-thinking your portfolio in the course of years may not be too much of a concern during preparation and actual startup, but it's important not to get too comfortable sticking with the same thing. There are notable examples of breweries so committed to brands and strategies in particular that their relevance and vibrancy has faded. The most successful brands have weathered—indeed, flourished—in a climate perpetually in search of change.

Chapter Highlights

- In order for a brand to survive, the beer must be of top quality.
- Whether conforming or innovating, your portfolio has a place in the brand spectrum.
- A portfolio must be flexible enough to change with the times, and with inclination.
- Your equipment can dictate the types of beer you are able to make, and vice versa.
- The types of beer you choose to make are determinants of production volume.

WASTEWATER ISSUES
Down the Drain

23

Many brewery projects, both startup and expansion, have been stalled or derailed by inattention to wastewater issues. As with other aspects of making and selling beer, it is essential to know going in what restrictions and requirements are in place before putting any wastes down the drain. For there will be waste: water; spent grain and yeast; trub (coagulated protein from the boiling of wort); hop material; cleaning chemicals both basic and acidic; diatomaceous earth and other filtration materials; as well as the inevitable debris of packaging. It should be obvious to check with local authorities on the degree to which your prospective brewery is beholden to wastewater strictures. Doing so may bring challenging news, but forgetting could prove fatal to the continuance of your project. Having things reasonably under control will also save you a great deal of money.

While every municipality will no doubt prove different in the specific requirements for the treating and monitoring of its wastewater, size is an operative factor where such issues are concerned, both of the brewery and the civic entity involved. It may seem paradoxical, but large cities are the places most tolerant and accepting of brewery wastes. A greater diversity in city populations above street level makes for a more complex and tolerant mix in their sewers. This doesn't mean that anything goes. It does mean that it takes more to meaningfully

tip the balance. Small towns and rural districts are going to be more noticeably affected by the disposal of specific waste, and because of their size and custom, less able to deal with the potential extremes coming from a brewery. They are therefore more likely than larger cities to simply say no rather than to impose a doable but perhaps expensive solution to brewery effluent challenges.

There is certainly a size balance—a small brewery in a big city, say—where requirements will be minimal. There is also a time factor, meaning mainly that what is not required today may well be tomorrow. Inspectors won't be nosing around every week; it may take them years to get back to check on things. When they do, however, you will probably have grown and regulations will likely have become stricter. We will therefore proceed on the assumption that good faith measures should be implemented for both reducing the cost of waste, and its responsible treatment. If such restrictions do not apply in your area, so be it, but environmental regulations can change quickly and drastically.

For it remains a simple fact that even if allowed, the dumping of wastes can be an expensive proposition. Vigilant sewer authorities charge not only for the volumes of water entering their systems, but for the types and amounts of solid and chemical waste. It is therefore recommended that you separate and neutralize as much of your waste material as possible, especially in a setting where not to do so will be both expensive and taxing.

Job One—Reducing Water Usage

When the Magic Hat Brewery in Burlington, Vermont moved down the road to a larger facility in South Burlington, it was assumed that sewage requirements and rates would be more or less the same. What they discovered, however, very nearly put them out of business. South Burlington, it turned out, was neither as tolerant of waste nor as able to deal with its volume as had been the city of Burlington proper. It took time and a great deal of money, as well as the implementation of systems in several stages, but Magic Hat survived to tell the tale. Many of the steps they took along the way, such as trucking wastewater to municipalities that did allow dumping it (for a price), may be beyond the scope of this chapter. But one is certainly relevant: perhaps the most important program they instituted in their new brewery was one of simply reducing water usage.

Water in many parts of the United States has traditionally been an inexpensive resource, a fact that's served to discourage its conservation. With population increases and a generally rising rate of demand, three times as much water was used in the US in the year 2000 than in 1950. It is widely predicted that within the next couple of years up to 70% of the United States will experience some water shortage, and that by 2025 roughly half the world's population will live in conditions of severe water distress. Twenty percent of all energy expended in the state of California goes to moving, usage and treatment of water. Municipalities typically charge a percentage for wastewater pegged to incoming usage; therefore, the best way to save water and the money it costs is to minimize the amount you use.

The proportional amount of water used to make beer, which includes not just beer's liquid component but its use for brewing, rinsing, cooling, cleaning, packaging and whatever else, can vary from an abstemious three-to-one ratio, to six- or seven-to-one and more. This difference, needless to say, can be substantial in terms of cost and efficiency, especially in places where water comes at a premium. Just as obvious can be some of the ways to save in water usage, once sensibilities are attuned to such a mission. All you have to do for starters is watch someone play a hose back and forth across a brewery floor seeking to push an inconsequential bit of debris or residue in the direction of a drain. My friend John Mallett of Bell's Beer refers to this use of a hose as "the brewer's broom," the hypnotic result of which is not only inefficient but expensive. Efficient use of water in the brewhouse can reduce not just liquid volumes sent to the drain but solids as well, as spent grains are over-sparged and excess sugars and other materials are washed away rather than composted or fed to cattle. The capture of certain rinse, or "grey" waters for eventual reuse in CIP (clean in place) systems is another way to reduce overall usage, and once used for cleaning, the titration and pH adjustment of chemical solutions for continued use is another. Using water three and four times in the course of your operation can potentially reduce its cost by a similar factor.

Even a simple CIP system consisting of vessels large enough to recapture used chemical solutions for continued use is helpful to the cause. Serial use of chemicals pumped tank to tank is fine, but necessarily results in fewer uses. Correspondent to the size of your operation, nearly anything will serve: cut-open kegs, stainless steel drums, plastic rainwater or caustic barrels, an old decommissioned brewing vessel or something manufactured for the purpose. Having a place to park your cleaning solutions will save both on water usage and chemicals. Remember that water's very physicality makes it a mechanical cleaning medium as well as whatever chemical effect has enhanced it. Nor should elbow grease be discounted as a contributor to cleaning regimens and reductions of water usage.

Precipitation—Letting Time and Gravity Work for You

The most commonly watched factors in wastewater are pH and the biological oxygen demand (BOD) and chemical oxygen demand (COD) exerted by suspended solids. All are things that affect the balance of sewer systems in their march toward a tolerably neutral range, and which place demands on the natural processes of decomposition. Avoiding undue influence on all these processes can be fairly simple, beginning with as much dry removal of materials as possible and the straining of liquids on their way to holding tanks and drains.

A cone-bottomed plastic tank configured with a drawoff point sufficiently above the bottom to allow the sedimentation of solids is perhaps the most important piece of water treatment equipment. With time and perhaps minimal and periodic adjustment, many brewery wastes will combine and neutralize themselves. Agitation hastens these processes, such as by employing used caustic in fermentation blowoff buckets. The bubbling of fermentation CO_2 through the highly alkaline liquid will mitigate its strength by both agitation and chemical contact. In any case the combination of wastes in a settling tank will allow grain and other incidental solids to either fall to the bottom or rise to the surface and bring acidic beer and sanitizing solutions in contact with alkaline caustic. This process takes passive steps toward achieving an allowed pH range, minimizing the need for further adjustments. Larger systems will be required to have logbook or electronic monitoring before dumping; smaller ones often simply to have systems in place. Once drained of liquid, solids can be discarded along with other materials such as spent grains or hauled away separately. Especially with regard to small systems, sieves and strainers employed on the way either to drains or settling vessels can also greatly lessen later removal and neutralization efforts.

Treatment 2.0—More Involved Systems

Size once again comes into play when employing systems beyond the basic settling and neutralization programs ordinarily sufficient for the treatment of liquid brewery waste. Even a rapidly growing brewery will find itself generating more waste than simple systems can accommodate, and a brewery of any size in a rural or small town setting may be called upon to take commensurate action. Employing low-tech, less efficient methods for waste treatment can nonetheless prove effective in satisfying local authorities.

A now-defunct rural brewery of my general region used not to be able to put its chemical waste down the drain at all. Instead, they employed a leach field, simply dumping used caustic onto a patch of ground adjacent to the brewery for eventual denaturing. This offends sensibility—you wouldn't want to grow lettuce there—but it isn't so different from a series of outdoor effluent ponds. These sequentially reduce contaminants to the point at which plants and fish can serve as the final purification before the liquid, which entered the system as rinse water or spent cleaning solutions, can perhaps be used to irrigate the brewery farm or hop yard. Once more, agitation and/or oxygenation can serve to hasten the process, and may help to guard against general septic funk. It should also be mentioned that prolonged surface introduction of chemical wastes can result in salt and other possibly harmful accumulations. Also note that implementing such a system would still require the approval of local authority.

Self-contained systems bringing together the technologies of the stone and space ages can involve biofilm-coated stones, wooden slats or finned plastic balls. These assist in neutralizing wastewater requiring microbiological interaction before it is released to the wider world. It all reminds me of the hobby I forsook when I started brewing: salt water aquariums, in which microbiologically-charged filter beds and a balance between impurity and regeneration keep the whole system in function. This introduces the notion of anaerobic processes for balance and purification—all the others we've looked at above have relied on the presence of air to aid in neutralization and degradation. While the notion of a big and self-sustaining aquarium-type system for processing brewery wastes may be conceptually appealing, the sheer size of such a thing would be prohibitive for most. More commonly employed are activated sludges and filtration media. Some larger craft breweries such as New Belgium, Sierra Nevada and Magic Hat have anaerobic digesters in place, capable not only of processing waste but of generating usable methane, along with other byproducts. Systems for aerobic or anaerobic treatment of as little as a thousand gallons a day are commercially available, but the costs associated with setting them up is likely beyond the reach or need of the average startup. By the time your brewery is considering such a system, you likely won't be consulting this book.

Chapter Highlights

Basic Wastewater Wisdom

- A brewery's wastewater impact is greater the smaller the municipality.
- Reducing water usage is the most important step in minimizing impact.
- Reusing water is reducing usage.
- Settling and removing solids will reduce BOD.
- Time is a neutralizer, but also a luxury.
- Introduction of chemicals for pH balancing is often necessary.

SUSTAINABILITY
Sustainability as Sensibility

24

Like synergy and organic, the term sustainability can be turned to such a variety of purpose, it can at times seem nearly meaningless. People use it generally to refer to and perhaps justify their environmental responsibility. But like these other buffeted and overused words, that isn't sustainability's fault. It just happens to be in the right place at the right time, again and again, as people strive to do the right thing.

While it may literally have to do with maintaining or holding things up, sustainability most often carries a connotation of conservation and general environmental rightness. It can pertain to efficiencies in the production of beer, such as limiting water use or using energy sensibly; it can apply to methods of cultivation and further processing of malt and hops; or it may describe fuel consumption demands and refrigeration associated with transport and storage. Sometimes it's just about garbage or what goes down the drain. It may, in these polarized times, have taken on a political sense, but let's go back to its actual meaning, of bearing and maintaining systems frugal and responsible, things that any business should strive to build into its ongoing operations.

States of Matter and Energy

It's easy to get a little discouraged when contemplating the exemplary efforts by some of our largest and most conscientious colleagues in craft brewing. But no system is too small for any sustainability effort to bear fruit. Such things as cutting water and energy usage—turning off the lights, for Pete's sake, or fixing a leaky faucet—can be implemented simply and effectively just by making people aware. Sustainability is in fact a sensibility. It includes solar arrays and anaerobic digesters, but it also involves sorting trash and being aware of where things go when they leave your sight. Its main efforts involve energy conservation and the treatment and consideration of solid and liquid wastes, but its sensibilities can also spill into areas one might consider more directly related to human resources, such as the treatment and encouragement of people.

Water treatment on its way to the drain is elsewhere discussed and conservation of course mentioned, but the best way to deal with waste is to minimize its creation in the first place. Profligate water use even in places where it is plentiful is not only expensive but unconscionable as well; there are always ways to cut down. Even slow leaks in pipes, faucets and along hose runs waste an amazing amount of water. Overzealous rinsing of tanks, kegs and of bottles on their way to being filled or afterward can be corrected by a little analysis and awareness. Just how effective is a rinse conducted in half the time, with half as much water? Could the nozzle size on a bottling line be reduced or a timer installed to keep it from running continuously, or the water reclaimed for other use farther along in the process? Naturally, you still need to get the job done properly, but it's worth experimenting and testing to see if the same task could be accomplished with less water. Breweries larger and more involved than the typical startup may have automated systems built in to monitor and temper amounts of water being used for any number of processes, from mashing in and sparging to cleaning and rinsing. In a case like yours, however, the same creativity and ingenuity that gets you up and running can serve to improve systems along the way.

Reclamation of CO_2 is something that often comes up in discussion, but is nearly as often tabled, owing to the fact that, like water in most parts of this country, it is so inexpensive to buy. For even a large-ish craft brewery, the return on investment pencils out to several decades at least. Should carbon and energy taxation be reformed, however, and charges for inordinate use be put into place, such programs may suddenly make a lot more financial sense.

It may be obvious to say so, but a monthly look at your utility bills will first of all establish a baseline from which to improve and mark the progress of any programs or repairs you undertake to save both water and energy. Another useful conceptual tool is tying water and energy usage to production. If as you grow you can use a lesser proportion of either or both, you're winning. Costs per barrel go down and you make more money. The average production brewery uses as much as seven times the amount of water as it produces in finished beer. With the gold standard of such usage more like 3.5 to 1, you've probably got your work cut out for you.

Equipment repair keeps things in good running order, of course, which includes more efficient function and lower energy use. Compressed air systems are almost invariably riddled with leaks, which not only hamper their function but turn a resource often viewed as free into a substantial waste of energy. Ours is an industry segment built on the leavings of others, and we often start out with equipment older and less efficient than we might have with a bigger budget. Greater energy efficiency tends to pay for itself over time. If it helps your conceptual grasp and cures you of misplaced frugality, do a little back-of-the-envelope examination of the return on investment next time you're thinking of replacing something, and in many cases you'll be surprised at the rapidity of recoup.

Traditional breweries employ such truly free forces as gravity and natural light as much as possible, minimizing the need for electric power to run pumps and illuminate interior space. Programs to recognize differences of demand based on time of day and day of the week can suggest remedies such as timers to avoid lighting unoccupied rooms or to take advantage of greater levels of natural light. Light wells or tubes can provide the clerestory effect of an earlier age of industry. Many of these things are merely steps in awareness, and not necessarily expensive programs. Bringing your staff in on the fun is an important part of the whole game. Everyone wants to increase efficiencies and save money for more vital and exciting plans of improvement. A team of in-house "efficiency experts" will find more ways to conserve and improve systems than a single person walking around with a clipboard. But even the clipboard is a start.

Restaurant operations can be enormously demanding on waste and energy systems, from the inevitable waste of food both prepared and cleared from tables, to the need to be ready to serve at all times. Dishwashing and icemaking are two areas almost always in need of improvement, as is the thawing of food by waterflow. Solid waste sorting and garbage and recycling collection are essential to ongoing operation, as is the removal of spent grains from brewing. These days, used cooking oils can usually be taken away by arrangement for conversion to biodiesel. Hopworks Urban Brewery in Portland, Oregon fires its kettle with it. Once again, the early lives of pub businesses are undertaken with a lot of used equipment: refrigerators and freezers that cost less up front than they do to run for even part of a year, inefficient and ill-calibrated ovens and stoves, stuff that in many cases should have been left on the auction house floor. If you can afford them at the outset or down the road, Energy Star certified appliances put you ahead of the game. On-demand water heaters and boosters can cut back ongoing energy costs substantially. The National

Restaurant Association can provide help in increasing efficiencies through its Conserve Sustainability Education Program.

And speaking of helpful organizations, our own Brewers Association is on the verge of providing members with extensive manuals on sustainability and the implementation of its systems. Available online to members, these documents will cover everything from snapping off the lights to examining the feasibility of renewable energy systems. In addition, cases studies and examples of breweries large and small—some probably hardly bigger than your own—and the considerations and programs they've undertaken toward achieving greater sustainability are inspirationally larded throughout.

Spent Grains—Its Own Beast

Whether your brewery generates them by the bucket or by the silo, the disposal of spent grains from the brewing process is a subject that can't be ignored for a moment. Right up there with floors and drains, it's a subject of endless chatter and entreaty on the BA Brewers Forum as newcomers to the arena of craft ask advice on what in the world to do with all that material.

The good news is that there's a great deal one can do with spent grains, whether some is retained for pizza crust or growing mushrooms, or it's all hauled away for compost, livestock feed or even ethanol production. Establishing a solid relationship with someone who can regularly take it away is as important as any other agreement you might forge with vendors or tradespeople. Storage can be an issue, of course, particularly during warm weather and in the city.

It's a bit odd, but spent grain removal can be a revenue stream, a cash-neutral proposition or a drain on finances. Larger producers are often able to sell their spent grain; and smaller ones can usually donate it to community gardens or supply some of the feed needs, gratis, of dairy or pig farmers. It's in the middle that things can get more challenging. Even a busy pub can generate a few dozen 55-gallon drums of spent grain each week, some of which invariably seal improperly or get so banged around that they leak and are difficult even to move. Skip a single pickup and you can have sixty or seventy smelly barrels taking up

valuable alley or parking lot space. My company went from having grains hauled away for free to having to pay up to five dollars a barrel to have them removed. It's a good thing that in those days we didn't have residential neighbors—we do now. A few expensive iterations of bin and dumpster later, a fair amount of complaint, and we've finally developed a stable and sustainable system for each of our locations. Our pubs' systems involve bins of varying size picked up whenever necessary; our production plant has a trailer conveniently isolated by some railroad tracks. The small ones we pay for, the trailer we don't.

Talk occasionally arises identifying processed spent grains as the answer to every food, feed, fuel and sustainability issue out there. I've heard presentations by outfits assuring me that within several months the means of drying and compacting our grains for fuel use will be ready to roll, and I've read credible reports of small-scale systems for growing mushrooms on spent grains for use in brewery-allied restaurants. Alaskan Brewing in Juneau dries their spent grains of necessity, given Juneau's relative lack of accessibility, using them as fuel in a specially designed furnace which powers the majority of the brewery's operations. I have no doubt that future creative solutions to this ongoing issue will one day benefit all of us.

Tickling the Warp Core—Using and Generating Energy

Carbon footprint is another of those terms whipped into endless service, but as a concept it is simple enough to quantify energy expended by chains of process. New Belgium Brewing, one of our industry's pioneers where sustainability is concerned, conducted a study a few years back stacking up all the energy used to produce and market a six-pack of their flagship brand, Fat Tire. Beyond simply taking a look at the various usages within their very efficient brewery as the beer was brewed, fermented and packaged, they included the processes on both the front and back ends of direct involvement: things like tillage and pesticide use in fields of barley and hops as well as the fuel used in trucks and railcars bringing finished beer to distributors' warehouses and eventually onto the shelves of stores. Somewhat surprisingly, among the highest-level burners of energy in the whole chain was open-front refrigeration in stores and the fuel burned by individual consumers on their ways to and from picking up that six-pack. So much of sustainability, after all, is about awareness, and what can be done about it.

While examinations like the above are valuable in big-picture conceptualizations of what we all do, it is up to each of us to close as many loops as possible where energy use is concerned. Boiler efficiency is an area of great potential waste, and properly tended to, savings. Greases and oils can be sold or donated to biodiesel concerns, or perhaps used (to great public relations effect) in brewery delivery vehicles. Pallets, plastics, aluminum, cardboard and glass can all be turned to second use and beyond, mitigating energies of removal and processing.

Some businesses elect to further balance energy use by purchasing renewable energy credits from utility companies. Others generate or subsidize the production of a portion of their own electricity with solar arrays, wind turbines, anaerobic digestion and other laudably sustainable systems. You might think a certain size of operation necessary for the costs of any such systems being, well, sustainable, but companies as small as the 10-barrel Standing Stone Brewery in Ashland, Oregon take a hand in generating some of their own power.

Sustainability as a State of Mind

It may seem a trifle touchy-feely to think of styles of operation and management as variously sustainable, but consider the benefits of staff longevity and loyalty and, conversely, the difficulties that can arise when such things are given short shrift. There are those, in fact, who hardheartedly believe that staff attrition and even discontent are things to be shrewdly maintained in order to avoid jadedness and institutionalized resistance to change, but I'd like to believe that they mostly don't work in our industry. For human energy is a resource as well, not simply in quantifiable ergs and joules of physical effort, but in less tangible areas such as spirit and satisfaction. These things are an end in themselves, of course, and while perhaps not directly reflected in the bottom line, they bring both

real and perceived value to companies that care. Very often it's institutions that foster conservation and the generally considered use of energies and raw materials that have an eye out for the well-being and contentment of co-workers. To involve co-workers in the formulation of plans and policies empowers them and closes yet another loop of energy and sustainability.

It's all very well to talk of essential programs for sustainability when the struggles of a young business invariably aim at simply keeping the doors open. Perhaps in your particular situation, sustainable change isn't affordable—yet. But keep things in mind, maintain a conscience not just of sensibility but eventual return on investment in things tangible and otherwise, and pieces that bring both efficiency and the rightness of human and earthly stewardship are far more likely to eventually fall into place.

Chapter Highlights

- Implement plans of awareness where the use of water and energy is concerned.
- Whenever possible, make use of free and natural forces such as light and gravity.
- Reuse or recycle everything possible.
- Maintain equipment, and keep an eye to replacing inefficient equipment and appliances.
- Be conscious of energies expended before and after your own processes.
- Even a small amount of energy generation is a step in the right direction.
- Remember that human spirit and energy are resources to be maintained and cherished.
- Keep the doors open first, but improve systems as you can.

PACKAGING AND PRESENTATION
The Tao of Your Beer

25

If there is a best way to sell beer, it's almost certainly at odds with the best way to care for it. Bringing your lovingly-crafted product to your customer involves compromise: whether you put it into bottles, kegs and cans of particular type and size, shipping it far from home in containers shuttled here, there and all over the place; allow it to come to rest in distributors' warehouses and retailers' coolers and ambient aisles; or even pour it at your own bar into a glass you've chosen yourself. You can't just leave it in the tank, however, to gradually retire untasted, unappreciated and unpurchased by those who would keep you in business. It has to get into people's hands somehow, and in the best condition you can manage. It is possible to keep a crown on all that chaos, to make choices that can at least head off difficulty, disaster and above all deterioration—we'll now look at how to present and sell your beer in its best possible earthly light.

One of the first questions you'll be asking yourself, even as you craft your business plan and develop your concepts and ideas, is whether to package your beer at all. And I'm not talking about the difference between a pub and a production brewery. Many pubs package, and some production breweries devote their attentions entirely to draft. Two of the biggest breweries in my area, for example, Georgetown Brewing and Mac and Jack's, each produce in excess of 30,000 barrels annually, all draft. Perhaps Seattle is just curmudgeonly when it comes to the package. Mike Hale, another local pioneer, and I were both quoted in the same New York Times article once, declaring that our breweries would never bottle. We've both since recanted, however, in both 12s and 22s.

Draft 101

Why draft over packaged? Because it's easier to control draft beer, especially if it's coming through your own taps. In a pub setting, you're continually aware of clarity, freshness, levels of carbonation, even the reception your beer gets from the customer as it's served and consumed. Anything that goes out the door disappears, in a way; all too often the only time you hear mention of it again, it's because of a problem. Which may not even be your fault. Beer that's stored warm won't thrive away from home, and if the beer lines in someone else's tavern aren't kept clean, savvy customers can form opinions about your quality control that have little to do with your efforts and mastery.

Line cleaning is a subject unto itself, and represents one of the softest underbellies of presentation where your beer is concerned. There are states, such as Oregon, where regular line cleaning is the law. You can imagine, however, how stringent enforcement must be. Some states allow breweries and distributors to provide retailers with line-cleaning service. Others, like mine, forbid it, on grounds that it could potentially be used to secure custom, or even sabotage rival presentation. You can also imagine, in both cases, muddiness of interpretation. Some might ask, why lock one's self into providing a service to an account which really should be taking care of things itself? Conversely, it's heartbreaking to go into a place and taste your beer in lamentable condition because of a funky beer line, or worse, a system that pushes its beer by means of an air compressor rather than neutral and life-preserving CO_2—and this in the 21st century.

The *Brewers Association Draft Quality Manual* is an invaluable resource not just for gathering information on cleaning lines, but in connection with all aspects of presenting draft beer. It was compiled over a long time and with a great deal of care as a service to BA members and brewers of all sizes; it was also shared with retailers, offering the information it contains as a procedural olive branch, showing them the way without calling them out. In your own place, it can serve as a manual for setting up and maintaining your draft system, from size and equipment choices to ready information on such things as CO_2 absorption and hydrostatic pressures.

Lines should be cleaned no less frequently than every other week. It can take the better part of a morning for a single person to attack a reasonably extensive lineup of taps and lines, so allocate the necessary man-hours for it. No wonder many bars drag their feet. Typically, caustic chemicals are circulated either by means of a pump or a pressurized keg, and then lines are rinsed clean. An acid cycle can also be introduced to vary pH and help remove deposits like beer stone. Trade shows sometimes display systems which send a tiny cleaning sponge ball racing through the full line interior; but so far, impediments like hardware uniformity and faucet restriction have kept them from coming into general use. A comprehensive cleaning of lines should also include disassembly and brushing of all taps.

Where beer lines themselves are concerned there are a number of options. One bar I know keeps things simple for their several dozen: each keg is arrayed in the cold box no more than a few feet behind the appropriate tap; when it's empty they remove and discard the line, starting fresh with the next one, whatever the beer. They aren't a brewery, but as some pubs keg all their beer, it's a noteworthy, albeit wasteful model. Fairly common is the scenario involving a mix of kegs and serving tanks all feeding into a bundle of lines accompanied by send-and-return lines for glycol or other coolant. These bundles can be purchased pre-made from companies specializing in draft systems, and they come in color-coded groups of four, six, twelve or however many. Once you start researching all the questions you'll have about line gauge, length and configuration, some of your craziest notions will be dispelled and you'll see the wisdom of a simple run. Once again, the BA *Draft Quality Manual* is a good place to start.

I've long maintained that the fewer times beer is touched between production and serving, the better. Endlessly broken down into a mix of bottles and kegs, with perhaps the remaining amount to be served from a tank, not only is the potential for waste greater, it's easier to lose track of where all your beer went. Just the same, that's the reality in many settings, for the purpose of selling more beer more quickly, while ensuring both freshness and the practices of good business.

Whether they have serving tanks or not, many pubs keg their beer; production breweries certainly do. Where kegs are concerned there are far fewer choices than there used to be. This is a good thing. The primitive Golden Gate keg, with its simple, yet temperamental twist-operated openings at the top and bottom, and the lamentable Hoff-Stevens configuration—really an R & D step along the way to the development of the these-days dominant American Type-D Sankey—are devices best consigned to head-shaking historical awareness. He who does not know the history of draft systems, after all, may be doomed to repeat it if a cheap lot comes up for sale. Golden Gates have enjoyed a second life, since they are adaptable enough to use for cask-conditioned beers, but tapping hardware is more difficult to get with each passing year. Occasional lots of used Hoff-Stevens kegs even today occasionally come on the market, but as tempting as the price may be, try to resist, both from the standpoint of reduced function and the increased unlikelihood of taverns even owning the associated hardware. Let me quickly relate an experience I had when we were contemplating the appropriate route to take, and which decisively resulted in the bullet-biting purchase of Sankey kegs. A keg at a party I attended failed in all three ways a Hoff-Stevens can: the disappearance of the 8-shaped tapping gasket, the absence of set screws on the collar which keep the whole structure sound, and a puncture in the interior plastic draw tube. We ended up pulling the bung and serving the beer in a bowl. Type D Sankey kegs are far more practical, cleanable, available and sound, fitted with reasonably reliable click-down tapping, an unambiguous in-and-out configuration where the flow of beer and gas are concerned, and a sturdy stainless steel tube of sufficient diameter to draw beer from the bottom of the keg.

Other European keg and coupler types exist, but are not considered an option for domestic use. If yours is a pub pouring guest beers, my guess is you will eventually come in contact with them. Anchor Brewing uses a "Type G" variety fairly common in England, but their decision to do so had mainly to do with keeping their hardware more identifiable in the marketplace in order to make recovery easier. The European-type Sankey looks just like the American "Type D," until you engage the mechanism and expose a longer draw shaft (which then refuses to couple with the American Sankey).

In addition to types of kegs, there are a few standard sizes available and in use in breweries and bars throughout the land. Gone are the days, thank God, when there were one-barrel, 31-gallon kegs to ruin the backs of delivery personnel and break through walls. You may occasionally see one in a western scrap yard—a rare view of the Age of Giants, like catching a glimpse of Thor's boots. 15.5-gallon half-barrels are most common, with probably the five-gallon "sixth-barrel" (or "sixtel" or "log") the next in ordinary use. As tall as a half-barrel but with a smaller footprint, they have been in use since the mid-nineties and are popular in bars with small refrigerators that still want to offer a reasonable array of beers. We did it to ourselves, I suppose, always willing to find new ways to sell beer. The sixth barrel is tailor-made, however, for

specialty beers and available only in limited quantities which can also be priced accordingly. And speaking of pricing, because they have the same hardware and require equivalent amounts of labor and manufacturing time (if not material), sixth barrel kegs don't cost that much less than half-barrels. On the way out is the 7.5-gallon quarter-barrel, and especially the squat configuration, which takes up as much space in a refrigerator or walk-in as a half-barrel and holds half the beer. Another less commonly taken option is the 50-liter/13.2-gallon keg, sometimes available in large lots from liquidations or hardware conversions by European breweries. I'm not judging, but it's not at all unheard of for breweries to occasionally switch their whole stock from half-barrels to 50-liters and not change the price, thereby (obviously, duh) effectively raising it by nearly fifteen per cent.

Aside from the type and size of keg to be used, there are also keg ownership options. At a cost approaching two hundred dollars per newly manufactured keg, this can be an issue worth kicking around. One hears of keg cooperatives, in which a pool of kegs is owned by a group of breweries and filled and distributed according to both happenstance and predetermined pattern. Additionally, companies like Microstar provide a rental service based on distances and turns of use. Subscription to such a service—which at times is withheld from new customers, or even restricted for existing customers based on hardware infrastructure—involves the contractual codification of prediction, projection and anticipated luck, and can be a thorny thing to manage. It's also a service that doesn't come cheap. But kegs tend to disappear over time no matter who owns them, unfortunately; as much as 10% per year, according to study by bigger brewers. (All those homebrew kettles and lake cottage buoys come from somewhere, after all.) Managing such shrinkage by spreading out the risk may turn out to be an advantageous choice. It should be noted that it is simply unethical to appropriate the cooperage property of another brewery, whether as private citizen, homebrewer or fledgling brewery owner. Whether they are taken from the alley behind a tavern or deemed personal property on the grounds of having paid a deposit, such acquisition is stealing.

Kegs do not belong to you unless you have actually bought them from a manufacturer or another brewer.

Confining the Genie—Bottles and Cans

Bottling beer can be intimidating. It's something grown-ups do. For the start-up professional brewer of limited means, its hardware is all but out of reach, costing, according to the whispered reports from those within the industry, hundreds of thousands of dollars just to ante up. At this stage of the game, the memory is generally still fresh of the day in one's homebrewing history when the siphon hose and racking tube were discarded in favor of the liberating soda keg: one vessel to fill instead of fifty. To be sure, the blinders of draft-only can be insistently worn into grizzled professional maturity, but most breweries do eventually work around to some kind of packaging.

There are a few compelling reasons for this, having generally to do with there being a big wide world out there full of potentially profitable retail opportunities untouched by the tavern trade. There's also something just plain compelling from both an individual and a marketing point of view of a discrete, branded serving of beer you can hold in your hand. Regrettably, the warmth and general rightness of this feeling makes no headway against the challenges of affording it all.

Though I may not have been as polite as I could have the first time our local itinerant bottler approached me with the prospect of bringing his equipment in to answer our putative bottling needs, such an arrangement has made it possible, in our area at least, for breweries of nearly any stripe to get a toe into packaging without committing to the acquisition and maintenance of equipment. But that was back when I would never dance. The reversal of my earlier decision came initially not because I was so enchanted by the siren call of the grocery case, but simply because—another harbinger of maturity here—our distributor needed sample bottles for its sales team. Fast forward to a few GABF medals won with bottles properly filled (not by hunching over our little lame counter-pressure piece of dreck) and I was sold.

I don't know why there aren't a hundred of these itinerant bottling guys. Our packaging savior now services dozens of Washington, Oregon, and now Bay Area breweries, and there's no reason many other areas couldn't be similarly catered to. All that's required in terms of potential market is a geographical concentration of breweries—any places you can think of where that's happening?

As a concept such an arrangement is certainly sound. Anyone who weighs the custom bottling option responsibly, however, needs to be aware of a few things. Realistically speaking, no mobile bottler is wheeling in 72-head fillers of sterling Teutonic make. Nor, to be fair, do they suggest the work be done by the one- or two-head manual hand fillers often used by startup brewers. The reality is in between, with (most likely) a four- or six-head filler almost certainly produced by Meheen Manufacturing. The output per minute can't touch the average of a big-boy bottling line, but these machines make it possible for many breweries to get into bottling at all. Like any bottling line, they require a great deal of ongoing maintenance, which is another reason to consider securing the services of someone else's—providing, that is, they properly care for it. This might make some brewers nervous, as might the trust needing to be placed in the sanitation techniques of the machine's owner/proprietor. As with so many things, you just need to get to know the options, as well as the people involved. And when it's not on the job, this traveling machinery doesn't take up any of your precious production space—it simply wheels out the door. For the right set of demands and limitations, this can be an excellent solution, offering the opportunity to get into the packaged market without giving your company or floor plan a total re-think.

Linear machines such as the Meheen line fill and crown four or six bottles at a time and can put out about fifty 22-ounce cases an hour. Properly maintained, they do a creditable job of putting beer in bottles without overly distressing it by oxygen introduction. They are a relatively affordable alternative to machines that can fill several hundreds of bottles per minute. They are also relatively compact. They make sense for a 5,000-barrel-a-year brewery evenly split between package and draft. Much larger, and their use and maintenance will likely become a bottleneck (so to speak). It is at this point that figuring out a way to afford something faster becomes a priority, and as

Craft matures as an industry segment, in-between rotary machines have become available only in the last decade that fill a niche demand. These can generally be switched over to fill bottles of varying size.

While there are different shapes and styles of each to consider, the most common sizes for bottles available to American craft brewers are 12 and 22 ounces. In a way the differences between them tell a simplified story of the craft brewing movement itself. Forced in its earliest days to occupy the tall grass at the edge of the commercial veldt, craft in many cases opted for the package that didn't seek to vaunt the shelf space well-protected by the big brewers and could get along tolerably well up at the top there, next to the milk. Soon it became a mark of outsider status to crack the rank of craft brands so displayed; many sympathetic consumers went first to peruse the lineup of the new and interesting. Before long, however, craft brewers assumed both the desire and the effrontery to put themselves alongside the 12-ounce offerings of their industrial compatriots. This resulted in the slight relegation of brewers still in the 22-ounce game to a kind of top-shelf ghetto; if you were a brand with a bullet, you were in six-packs. But after a certain thinning, 22s roared back as a new retro package. Tune in next week for the latest in this gripping story.

Simply put, the attraction of the 22-ounce package is its profit margin. The larger bottle seems able to command a somewhat disproportionate per-ounce price when compared to smaller bottles, both because consumers of craft early on got used to the idea that it cost a bit more than so-called macro, but also because a bottle that looks a lot larger should logically be more expensive. Some in our industry have tried to steer public perception away from what the "bomber" name suggests: ruffians downing its whole contents in one go, rudely wiping their mouths and homicidally brandishing the shattered end. But until something other than "dinner bottle" manages to take hold, "bomber" or "deucer" it shall likely be.

The 22-ounce bottle just is. It stands alone as its own display material where the 12-ounce bottle requires five others to go with it, snugged into a six-pack carrier inevitably expensive to design, produce and stuff. There's no doubt that given sufficient wherewithal the six-pack market is worth pursuing, but for getting into packaging from a startup point of view, there's a lot to be said for the big bottle.

Increasing numbers of brewers are these days entering an elite stratum of market, putting super-premium beer in super-premium packaging more closely associated with wine. 25.4-ounce cork-finished bottles of something special from brewers of high-tone reputation are here and there commanding ridiculous resale prices, but inevitably to the consternation of the brewers themselves, completely leaving them aside where resultant profit might be concerned. Van Gogh sold no paintings during his lifetime, after all; the hundreds of millions they've commanded since his death have gone only into the pockets of dealers and collectors. Swing-top Magnums, Jereboams and Methuselahs of special beers would seem to be more collectible than lip-smacking, but they can provide an occasion of ritual largesse in the right setting. One caution I'd offer to any of these possibilities is that if something is heralded with a clarion call of drop-dead desirable packaging and rarity, the contents had better truly be something notable. One shake of the lamb's coda where package size is concerned is the six-ounce "nip" for beers of strength and seasonal rarity, such as barley wines or Imperial stouts released in winter. However, such oddities—as those above—generally require hand bottling. All caution voiced, these off-beat sizes can prove a pretty good profit center.

Cans as well have traced an arc of attitude in the craft brewing movement. In our earliest embryonic days, every single one of us might have been quoted in the New York Times saying that we would never can. Why would we? Cans are what unremarkable beer came in, right? But as we grow up, we want the appurtenances of maturity, and mercantile wisdom. Besides, as it will, technology has marched right along, answering one-time charges of tinny flavor and environmental heedlessness to provide a product as tasty as that poured from a bottle and arguably as sustainable. Sixteen-ounce cans of craft have become popular of late, and the numbers of breweries getting into cans has ballooned beyond the point of novelty. Proper canning hardware is extremely expensive, to be sure, but low-flying alternatives are available, making entry into such a niche at least a priority consideration. I've even heard of mobile canning outfits answering the demand for what might once have been considered a perversity célèbre. Craft isn't just our beer anymore, it's true. It's where we want to go and how we choose to present it.

Chapter Highlights

- The fewer times beer is moved in any state, the better.
- Beer line cleaning is a vital but difficult beast to tame.
- Stainless steel Sankey kegs are the only viable draft option.
- Despite some limitations, itinerant bottling outfits are a boon to the industry.
- More packaging options exist all the time, in different price ranges.
- Aside from in-house draft, the 22-ounce bottle can be the most profitable way to sell beer.
- Cans are no longer anathema, nor are they a novelty.

SAFETY
Accidents Waiting to Happen

26

Accidents of all kinds are surprising by their very nature. Sometimes they would seem to be unavoidable, the result of confluent happenstance. Not everything, after all, happens according to plan. But avoidance plans can be made, too, to minimize the possibility of accidents and prescribe behaviors that protect by avoiding risk. Because what's often most surprising is how such a thing, whatever it is, could have been allowed to happen in the first place.

In general, startup breweries and other cottage industries are like hermit crabs, moving into previously occupied spaces, and with a little wriggling and adaptation, making them serve. Vision, creativity and the ability to improvise can turn former industrial, retail and restaurant spaces into breweries. Sometimes the fit isn't perfect: inadequate wiring or plumbing, support structures insufficiently burly to support weights of storage and production, spaces not quite large enough to allow free movement and unencumbered use; these may all necessitate decisions that will bring a space and its various functions into line. We've all seen the result of taking too many shortcuts, either motivated by tightness of funds, or sometimes by mere laziness. Such decisions assume risk; to products, structures and systems, and to the people working under such conditions.

Of course there are codes to enforce standards of function and safety, during construction and on into day-to-day operation. Agencies such as the Occupational Safety and Health Administration (OSHA) oversee workplace systems and conditions of safety. States also maintain such oversight. These are the groups to whom you'll be accountable when establishing and maintaining safety protocols in your brewery.

Breweries, we all know, are potentially very dangerous places. Large volumes of boiling liquid and steam create scalding hazards; cleaning chemicals pose dangers of burns; CO_2 from fermentation, carbonation and draft service can accumulate and potentially asphyxiate the unwary. Add in wet and slippery floors, the basic hazards of electricity, hot water, gravity, glass and physical strain, and one begins to see the scope of the risks involved. This is why insurance for breweries, both private and publicly mandated, is expensive. We may at times feel essentially connected to the hobbyist's passion and the freedoms of creative expression, but we need to remember that the expansion of a concept creates its own challenges and responsibilities.

Larger brewing facilities will often automatically trigger inspections and walk-throughs by OSHA by their permit processes. While this may cause concern, it also provides guidance as to what is needed to provide a safe workplace. It's the smaller ones, the vest pocket pubs and garage operations, that are often overlooked, allowed essentially to operate without oversight or enforced conscience. Unsecured gas bottles, chemical containers sitting directly on the floor and perhaps used without eye and hand protection, unventilated cellars and fermentation areas; these are the things that can easily be overlooked or considered unimportant by brewers and brewery owners. And while mainly we seem to be a lucky bunch, many of us nonetheless have scars to prove our passion and the risks we have unthinkingly undertaken. Nearly everyone I know has been burned at some point, whether by protein lobbed out of a heaving kettle, uninsulated steam pipes, or hot water. Nor are we strangers to chemical burns; usually it's just a spot here and there, but occasionally much worse. It's something we generally shrug off as part of the job. But we owe it to ourselves and our co-workers to implement plans and programs to avert such occurrence.

Safety Officer may sound like a do-nothing title, sort of like the secretary-treasurer in a kids' club without dues who doesn't take minutes. But even if it's just a person who takes a safety-minded walk through production areas and lists things to be improved, appointing such a person provides a valuable safeguard against sloppy accident avoidance policy. Bigger plants have people whose full-time jobs are implementing safety procedures and protocols, establishing barriers, enforcing the wearing of protective gear and clothing—they're there to think of everything. In your brewery it might just be you and a clipboard. It's surprising how easy it is to find things needing improvement once one bothers to take a good look. It's easy, in fact, to get a little obsessive about it. The bottom line, however, is that workers, customers and other visitors must be protected from injury no matter how small an operation you're running. You wanted to run a brewery, right? This is merely one of the things that goes along with it.

It's tempting to list some of the terrible things I've seen over the years, to recount some of the horror stories. Hazardous situations often go unchecked, and people are hurt and occasionally even killed working in breweries. It's something we should all consider and fear. Not having a systematic way of improving workplace safety means you're just waiting for something unfortunate to happen.

It makes sense from an obvious, practical point of view, but a program of regular equipment inspection and maintenance is an important part of adhering to safety standards. Especially in a DIY kind of setting (as with most small breweries), it's vital to continually check things like hose clamps and other fittings before proceeding with, well, anything at all. It's valuable as well to conceptualize what it is you're about to do in order to feel absolutely sure when you flip a switch or turn a valve: Is the tank properly vented? Could caustic somehow find its way into the beer? Don't bother feeling silly about talking to yourself. Call it a loveable quirk in your campaign to keep us all alive and enjoying beer. If a disaster fantasy helps in your adherence to protocol, by all means indulge it.

The immediate consequences of accident are obvious. Perhaps not so concretely visualized are the things which can follow, such as investigation and, in some cases, prosecution. Repeated mishap cannot but attract attention, especially as workplace-related accidents are generally required to be reported, such as during visits to the emergency room. Labor and Industries and Workers' Compensation insurance is a godsend in providing coverage for injured workers, but draw on it more than a couple of times and you'll discover how it's financed. It can take years, in fact, to recover from the rate hikes imposed by immoderate occurrence of accident. As with so many things, once you are on the radar you can expect regular visits and reviews by any agency you may have rubbed up against in the course of dealing with unfortunate, perhaps avoidable, happenstance. Owners of businesses, by the way, are not covered by Workers' Compensation—yet another reason to stay safe.

It's a bit of an odd subject, but being accident-prone is also something to protect yourself, your co-workers, your equipment, and your products against. This condition, most common in young and heedless males, involves a certain self-abusive bravado that would seem to center a cosmic attention and exercise of mischance on the innocent execution of routine. In short, some guys are amused, even proud of having passed through repeated accident, to the extent that it seems like they practically invite it. There are one or two of these targets in every crowd, and not only in the workplace. Bike, skateboard and motorcycle mishaps also seem to attend the chronically scalded and sprained. To some extent these are our boys, snips and snails and all that; but we also have a responsibility, as far as we can execute it, to save them from themselves. Lectures about general behavior can be awkward, especially regarding things that happen off the job—it really isn't any of your business. But you need your co-workers healthy and on the job, too. I've seen people shape up and take better care of themselves; I've also fired a few who seem incapable of avoiding injury to themselves and the equipment they work with.

Aside from general vigilance and the institution of standard operating procedures, there are a few safety issues generally flouted by small breweries. Some I have mentioned in passing, but they occur often enough to hammer on them a bit:

- Eye and ear protection often sits in its dispensers and packages, or atop heads and around necks. Wearing it this way may look snappy and tribally work-mannish, but in order to be effective it needs to be worn properly. Enforcement of use should be sufficiently serious to get your folks to comply. If firing someone keeps something from happening to them and perhaps somebody else, it's an action worth taking.

- Imagine what would happen to a steel or aluminum gas cylinder should its valve snap: it would rocket around the room. Now install even a lightweight chain loop on the wall in order to keep such a thing from happening.

- While the sturdiness of most chemical containers might minimize the chance of rupture or leakage, these too should be set into safety trays large enough to contain a possible spill. Chemicals should be transported in closed containers, and should never be put into any vessel ordinarily used for drinking. Conversely, no container used for chemicals should ever be drunk out of, no matter how clean and safe. Other people, after all, can't be expected to know what

you're up to when you cross these lines. Gloves and eye protection should also always be worn when working with chemicals. Eyewash stations and showers should be located where easily reached, and fresh solutions regularly stocked.

- Any vessel large enough for a person to fit inside, be it mash tun, fermentor, liquor tank, silo or waste receptacle, needs to be labeled with a warning of the dangers of entry along with protocol reminders for such eventuality. These may involve supervision and/or the wearing of harnesses and breathing equipment, depending on the vessel and specific risk of entry.

- CO_2 accumulates surprisingly quickly in isolated cellars and walk-in coolers. Happily it is considerate enough to sink to the floor, but bend over to retrieve a clamp or turn a valve and you'll note its presence. Exhaust fans will no doubt increase utility bills and perhaps compromise somewhat the refrigeration systems of cold rooms, but activated by a switch or perhaps triggered by an electronic sniffer, the problem is dealt with more moderately. As it comprises most of the air we breathe and just mixes in, nitrogen is a less courteous gas. Beware the areas around its generators and the blow-down of mixed-gas tanks.

- An electrician with whom we've worked for years once ruefully observed that plumbers love to install hose bibs directly above electrical outlets. Be on hand and aware as such things are being installed to make sure this doesn't happen. Obvious? Absolutely.

- We're all familiar with the percussive clang (and clang again) of kegs falling to the floor. When pallets of kegs are stacked two and three high, they should be wrapped or strapped to keep things where they need to be, even when nudged or jostled.

- A little communication is a wonderful thing in the brewery; intentional miscommunication is less wonderful. For example, walking behind someone who might otherwise be unaware of your presence might qualify more as imprudent horseplay. But we once had a delivery driver who thought it hilarious to stand silently behind people and terrify them when they finally got around to noticing him. He pulled this on me one time on the brew deck as I was opening the kettle manway for a hop addition. I jumped, the manway popped open, and I lost the skin on about a foot of my forearm when hot protein gushed out. We found a new delivery driver.

- Along these lines, protocols should be established for dealing with situations of emergency, whether it's something that's happened to a tank or to a person. Such plans of action should be communicated, posted and ingrained.

- Lockouts of electrical panels and equipment control switches should be employed and observed every time someone needs to work remotely and in the guts of a situation. It's best as well to always be aware of the locations of co-workers. Don't be ashamed to check on what they are up to.

- Dust masks and even respirators should be worn when working with grain, and especially diatomaceous earth. DE is comprised of the tiny skeletons of miniscule sea creatures, and if inhaled it will coat your lungs and remain there. The smell of milling malted grain is one of the joys of brewing. But now you're a professional, doing it even more often than you used to when you were a maniacal homebrewer. Too much grain dust inhaled in a single milling can bring on a remarkably uncomfortable histamine reaction. Too much over time can actually result in brown lung disease. You don't want to be that much of a pro.

- Hot water is an ever-present danger, and is not always evaluated as such by OSHA or other safety agencies. It can also injure by secondary action, such as when it soaks clothing and is allowed to be in contact with skin for even the length of time it takes to strip something off. Be aware as well of tight spaces that could turn into traps should a hose end pop off its barb, a valve fail or a tank suddenly overflow.

- This impromptu list could eventually devolve to include silly things like learning to pick up your feet when walking in order to avoid tripping over hoses and other things often found on the floor. Additionally, the baseball-type and trucker's caps that nearly everyone seems to wear on the job can hamper one's vision. They do mildly protect the head from bumping into things, but they bring about as many such incidents as they remedy.

Take inspiration from this ramshackle checklist of pet peeves and institutionalize an awareness of safety procedures in your workplace. The easiest things to fix can serve as a springboard to more minute attentions, and the satisfaction that comes with making life and work generally less dangerous. Leave the thrill of risk to mountain climbers, and perhaps skateboarders.

Your Friend the Insurance Agent

A friend of mine, at the waggish age of seventeen or so, once feigned sincerity and asked his father if it was possible to have too much insurance. You can imagine how humorless the response was. Insurance in general is not something that inspires laughter, passion, or for most people, much interest at all. As the grown-up owner of a small brewery, however, it's in your interest to at least give it sufficient attention to adequately protect yourself and your business against both mischance and misdeed. What can you say? Things sometimes happen.

I've waited until now to mention it, but the insurance you carry for your business can be both a vitally important way to protect against the consequences of accident and an interactive way to prevent many accidents from happening altogether. We all know insurance companies aren't fond of paying claims, but rather than view this as pernicious and difficult, let's think of them as providers of an alternate reality of safety plans and workplace analysis, keeping things preemptively safe by helping you eliminate and mitigate risks to your customers and co-workers. They are generally happy to do this; it's one of the services they provide for the money you pay them.

Some insurance providers specialize in plans for small breweries, such as the Whalen Insurance Agency of Northampton, Massachusetts. Peter Whalen, in fact, wrote a short chapter for a previous edition of this book. This isn't intended as an advertisement for their services, but a visit to their website will provide checklists of common safety issues and ways to remedy them. It also lists types of insurance commonly carried by brewers in particular as well as more general business-related insurance products. And best of all, it includes a six-chapter manual on different bodies of potential safety risk and ways to address each of them.

While it isn't necessarily a workplace-related safety concern, alcohol liability poses great potential risk to any production or retail site. Any place where alcohol is either produced or consumed, after all, presents the possibility of situations where workers and customers alike can come to grief as a result of consumption. This can be as innocent seeming as a shift beer (or two) enjoyed after work or as grave as a motor vehicle accident due to customer inebriation. Like many other hierarchical assignments of responsibility, insurance liability has a pecking order, beginning with the most obvious and trickling down to absolutely anything against which a claim can be filed and payment exacted. This can even apply to beer festivals; brewers guilds and individual breweries should make sure that whatever organization is putting on their event is properly insured, for if the dams before you are not adequately shored, the waters of liability will surely lap at your banks. Another caution to liability pertains to the commercial space used in your brewery; it may not be on quite the right side of the line where licensing and legitimacy is concerned. A couple of pints proffered in the storage bay, for example, or the domestic garage open limited hours for growler or bottle sales may leave the small brewer vulnerable to litigation should some alcohol-related mishap occur.

Everything's cool, one could argue, as long as nothing untoward happens, but it's all on the DIY proprietor as soon as a DUI veers over the center line.

As a legitimate businessperson-to-be, you presumably would not undertake such risk. It's therefore worth mentioning a few other insurance-related ways to protect the safety of your co-workers and customers and the solvency and continuity of your business. Property insurance is something everyone should have, simply to protect what they have. Basic liability insurance covers anything unexpected that might occur: so-called slip-and-falls and the vagaries of day-to-day happenstance. Workers' Compensation in some form is required by law, in order to protect those in the workplace exposed to dangers associated with making beer and performing other functions connected with selling and serving it. Bonding is covered more thoroughly in the chapter dealing with taxes and other compliance, as it has to do with the interface between you and government risk-takers, namely those waiting breathlessly to collect your taxes and the safeguards they feel necessary for you to have in place to ensure this. It is also possible to insure against the misfortune of product loss due to equipment failure. Read that sentence again. If you brew a batch of just plain bad beer and expect someone to offer you financial recompense, you're out of luck; if you leave a valve open, or forget to chill a fermentor adequately but consider it unfair to have to dump that batch of sherry-and-fusel tainted beer, get over it. But if something truly goes wrong—a seal, a filter pump, a power failure—it may be possible to file a claim. Keep in mind, however, the relative worthiness of the claim, and the stakes to be recouped against the potential red flag of being identified as a boy who cries wolf, actuarially speaking. Consider this your get-out-of-jail-free card under conditions of extreme duress—a good thing to have in reserve, but definitely not a thing to overplay. A word to the wise: insure for retail value, if such a thing is possible.

Safety, it turns out, is another one of those words. It can keep you and your co-workers in one piece and working uninterrupted shifts. It can also establish a reflexive awareness. Insurance plans and structures can protect your person by their very formulation, and the policies you undertake with entities whose business it is to play the percentages can actually help keep you in business.

Chapter Highlights

- Breweries are dangerous places.
- A safety team or officer will invariably find things needing improvement.
- No brewery is too small to need safety protocols.
- Keep equipment well maintained and safe.
- Have an accident plan.
- Eliminate accident-proneness.
- Safety issues can extend beyond your own premises.
- Your insurance agent can help identify and rectify safety issues.

EPILOGUE
You Can Do This

The impulse to start a brewery, or any new project, can start any number of ways. Drunken revelation is a popular course. So is musing from the safety of a perfectly good job and a reasonably sound financial situation. The latter, come to think of it, can be undertaken from within the brewing industry itself—e.g. working even contentedly for someone else—contentedly with a kicker, that is. Then there's the outwardly-seeming irresponsible fever of the not-so-sure thing. Because once you start telling people about it, that once taut and inevitable gasbag revealed one drunken evening becomes difficult to keep inflated. My own father, when I told him what I was hoping to do, said something along the lines of "what, so you're a businessman?" He and my mother eventually invested in my brewery, but they are my parents. And, to be perfectly fair, when he said that I hadn't even made homebrew yet without opening a can. It was eight years and a month or so from my first kitchen boilover to the day of pouring Elysian's (somewhat fusel-laden) first beer for a public finally able to legally creep within our licensed premises. That sounds like a short time, but it felt like a long road, settling in as I did to the necessary rhythms of experience on the job, to say nothing of the life that happens when you're making other plans.

Many would say that I did it the safe way, and compared to the all-or-nothing commitments undertaken by our movement's actual pioneers,

they'd be right. I may have been of the next wave, the demi-generation who worked for the actual pioneers. I always had a job, and I always got paid. Was I safe? Or just lucky? It's nice to be both. In those days I didn't get paid all that much, and partly because of that I didn't feel all that safe. I did consistently feel, however, that starting my own brewery was something I was going to do. I know I always felt lucky just to be making beer for a living, such as it may have been.

So yeah, you can do this. Some ways of preparing for it are better than others, but whether you've gone through a comprehensive academic course in brewing or business administration, or both, or simply figured out a way to parlay a rampant hobby into a legally sanctioned entity of even uneasy profitability, you can get there, step by revelatory step. Given overwhelming precedent, the time has never been more ripe, but for that very same reason, nor has it ever been more forbidding. All the more reason to get started now, before anyone can irrevocably talk you out of it, to start learning what it is you have to do before you realize how woefully little you know and how vulnerable that little entrepreneurial acrospire is.

Is this book all you need to know? Certainly not. No single chapter provides a comprehensive look at the subject it pretends, based on my own limited experience, to outline. But it should get you thinking, both about the things you thought you knew and the things you know you need to learn. Nor does it address every possibility and scenario. That's your job: to come up with an idea, a concept, a plan, a portfolio and a way of pulling it all off that none of the rest of us has thought of before. In fact what are you waiting for? Twelve new breweries have opened since you even opened this book, maybe just in your own town, your own neighborhood. It's time for you to get started.

APPENDIX A
Pro-Forma Worksheet

Breakeven sales total	$	Food COG %		%		Beer COG%	%
Expected Annual Sales Total	$	Liquor COG %		%			
Net Income (Annual)	$	Wine COG %		%			
		Payroll Rate %		%			

		Jan	Feb	Mar	Apr	May	June	July	Aug	Sept	Oct	Nov	Dec	Total
		%	%	%	%	%	%	%	%	%	%	%	%	%
Retail Income														
%	Food	$	$	$	$	$	$	$	$	$	$	$	$	$
%	Liquor	$	$	$	$	$	$	$	$	$	$	$	$	$
%	Wine	$	$	$	$	$	$	$	$	$	$	$	$	$
%	Beer	$	$	$	$	$	$	$	$	$	$	$	$	$
%	Other	$	$	$	$	$	$	$	$	$	$	$	$	$
Total Retail Income		$	$	$	$	$	$	$	$	$	$	$	$	$
Total · Retail COG														
Food		$	$	$	$	$	$	$	$	$	$	$	$	$
Liquor		$	$	$	$	$	$	$	$	$	$	$	$	$
Wine		$	$	$	$	$	$	$	$	$	$	$	$	$
Beer		$	$	$	$	$	$	$	$	$	$	$	$	$
Bottled		$	$	$	$	$	$	$	$	$	$	$	$	$
Other		$	$	$	$	$	$	$	$	$	$	$	$	$
Total · Retail COG		$	$	$	$	$	$	$	$	$	$	$	$	$
Net Income		**$**	**$**	**$**	**$**	**$**	**$**	**$**	**$**	**$**	**$**	**$**	**$**	**$**

	Jan	Feb	Mar	Apr	May	June	July	Aug	Sept	Oct	Nov	Dec	Total
Expenses													
6342 · Tele-communications	$	$	$	$	$	$	$	$	$	$	$	$	$
6292 · Rent	$	$	$	$	$	$	$	$	$	$	$	$	$
6242 · Miscellaneous	$	$	$	$	$	$	$	$	$	$	$	$	$
5502 · Over & Short %	$	$	$	$	$	$	$	$	$	$	$	$	$
6436 · Linen Service	$	$	$	$	$	$	$	$	$	$	$	$	$
6435 · Janitorial	$	$	$	$	$	$	$	$	$	$	$	$	$
6245 · Payroll													
6248 · FICA & Medicare	$	$	$	$	$	$	$	$	$	$	$	$	$
6247 · Salaries & Wages	$	$	$	$	$	$	$	$	$	$	$	$	$
6246 · Payroll Fees	$	$	$	$	$	$	$	$	$	$	$	$	$
Total 6245 · Payroll	$	$	$	$	$	$	$	$	$	$	$	$	$
6345 · Alarm System	$	$	$	$	$	$	$	$	$	$	$	$	$
6285 · Advertising	$	$	$	$	$	$	$	$	$	$	$	$	$
6120 · Bank Service Charges 2.30%	$	$	$	$	$	$	$	$	$	$	$	$	$
6140 · Contributions	$	$	$	$	$	$	$	$	$	$	$	$	$
6180 · Insurance													
Medical	$	$	$	$	$	$	$	$	$	$	$	$	$
6410 · Liability Insurance	$	$	$	$	$	$	$	$	$	$	$	$	$
Total 6180 · Insurance	$	$	$	$	$	$	$	$	$	$	$	$	$

	Jan	Feb	Mar	Apr	May	June	July	Aug	Sept	Oct	Nov	Dec	Total
6200 · Interest Expense													
6210 · Finance Charge	$	$	$	$	$	$	$	$	$	$	$	$	$
6220 · Loan Interest	$	$	$	$	$	$	$	$	$	$	$	$	$
6375 · Equipment Lease	$	$	$	$	$	$	$	$	$	$	$	$	$
Total 6200 · Interest Expense	$	$	$	$	$	$	$	$	$	$	$	$	$
6230 · Licenses and Permits	$	$	$	$	$	$	$	$	$	$	$	$	$
6250 · Postage and Delivery	$	$	$	$	$	$	$	$	$	$	$	$	$
6261 · Printing and Reproduction	$	$	$	$	$	$	$	$	$	$	$	$	$
6270 · Professional Fees													
6650 · Accounting	$	$	$	$	$	$	$	$	$	$	$	$	$
Total 6270 · Professional Fees	$	$	$	$	$	$	$	$	$	$	$	$	$
6300 · Repairs													
6330 · Equipment Repairs	$	$	$	$	$	$	$	$	$	$	$	$	$
Total 6300 · Repairs	$	$	$	$	$	$	$	$	$	$	$	$	$
6770 · Supplies													
Kitchen	$	$	$	$	$	$	$	$	$	$	$	$	$
Bar	$	$	$	$	$	$	$	$	$	$	$	$	$
Floor	$	$	$	$	$	$	$	$	$	$	$	$	$
Marketing	$	$	$	$	$	$	$	$	$	$	$	$	$
Office	$	$	$	$	$	$	$	$	$	$	$	$	$
Total 6770 · Supplies	$	$	$	$	$	$	$	$	$	$	$	$	$

	Jan	Feb	Mar	Apr	May	June	July	Aug	Sept	Oct	Nov	Dec	Total
6820 · Taxes													
6830 · Federal	$	$	$	$	$	$	$	$	$	$	$	$	$
6840 · Local	$	$	$	$	$	$	$	$	$	$	$	$	$
6860 · State	$	$	$	$	$	$	$	$	$	$	$	$	$
Total 6820 · Taxes	$	$	$	$	$	$	$	$	$	$	$	$	$
6350 · Travel & Entertainment													
6370 · Meals	$	$	$	$	$	$	$	$	$	$	$	$	$
6380 · Travel	$	$	$	$	$	$	$	$	$	$	$	$	$
Total 6350 · Travel & Entertainment	$	$	$	$	$	$	$	$	$	$	$	$	$
6390 · Utilities													
6420 · Garbage/ Recycling	$	$	$	$	$	$	$	$	$	$	$	$	$
6400 · Gas and Electric	$	$	$	$	$	$	$	$	$	$	$	$	$
6410 · Water	$	$	$	$	$	$	$	$	$	$	$	$	$
Total 6390 · Utilities	$	$	$	$	$	$	$	$	$	$	$	$	$
TOTAL EXPENSES	$	$	$	$	$	$	$	$	$	$	$	$	$
NET INCOME	$	$	$	$	$	$	$	$	$	$	$	$	$
	$	$	$	$	$	$	$	$	$	$	$	$	$

APPENDIX B
Brewsheet

	Rack and/or Transfer (Tax Determined)					Allocation (Including cask)		
>Transfer Date		From		To			Transfer Vol	
Finings			Carb Notes				Plus Cask	
							Total	
Date	CO_2 vols						Bbls Out	Sub Total
>Transfer Date		From		To			Transfer Vol	
Finings			Carb Notes					
Date	CO_2 vols						Bbls Out	Sub Total

		Rack Track (In Bond)				Allocation (Including cask)		
Date	CO_2 vols						Bbls Out	Sub Total
							Total Yield	

Date		Beer				Batch		FV	
Brewer							mill gap	silo depl.	
Mash In		Temp	pH	Milled By					
Rest 1		Temp	pH		lbs	Lot #		lbs	Lot #
Step				Pale :	:	:		:	
				C-77 :	:	:		:	
Rest 2		Temp	pH	Mun :	:	:		:	
Knives		@		C-Hell :	:	:		:	
Recirc				RB :	:	:		:	
Run Off		1st R	pH	Choc :	:	:		:	
Start Sparge				:	:	Total lbs			
End Sparge		Last R	pH	:	:				
Kettle Up		Grav	pH						
Kettle Addition			Variety/Qty						
Boil			AAU divided by		AA%				
E-30			AAU divided by		AA%				
E-10			AAU divided by		AA%				
E-2			AAU divided by		AA%				
WP			AAU divided by		AA%				
End Boil									
				Yeast Source					
WP Full						:	:	/	/
KO		Temp		(vessel)	(batch#/flav)	(gen)		(crop date)	
Oxy On		Off							
End KO		FV Temp			pH	cells/ml			
Set Temp		OG		pH		viability			
						pitch rate			
Date	Time	Temp	Grav						
				pH					
Cask Requests			Filled						
				Notes					
		Total bbls Cask							

APPENDIX C
Sample Business Plan

TABLE OF CONTENTS

Text of the Sample Business Plan

EXECUTIVE SUMMARY

Description of the Business: The Craft Brewing Company Inc. is a privately held corporation owned and managed by the president and vice president. The business of the company is the production of high quality, fresh beer for local and regional markets. The Craft Brewing Company will be located at XX, which is less than a five minute's walk from the center of XX. A five-year lease, renewable for an additional five years at the same rate, is being negotiated. The Craft Brewing Company will initially produce three different styles of beer: a dark ale, an amber ale, and a golden ale. These products will be distributed in kegs to licensed retail outlets. The products of the Craft Brewing Company will be wholesaled to premium pubs, taverns and restaurants in the city of XX, throughout XX County, and then to the broader regional market. In addition, the Craft Brewing Company will have its own taproom where retail customers may come to view the operation of the brewery, while purchasing beer by the glass, beer to go, snacks, and retail items such as company logo T-shirts and glassware.

The Craft Brewing Company will produce beer with a 14-barrel, stainless steel brewing plant. Production capacity of our 14-barrel brewing plant with five fermentors is approximately 700 barrels a year (1 barrel equals 31 gallons, which equals two standard 15.5-gallon kegs). The addition of more fermentation tanks at regular intervals will increase capacity to approximately 2,800 barrels annually, which is the estimated limit imposed by the size of the space being leased. The management team intends to produce and sell approximately 670 barrels in the first year and then double production and sales in the second year. Thereafter, the management team will increase production and sales by approximately 500 to 600 barrels annually, until the approximately 2,800-barrel limit imposed by the space we are initially renting has been reached.

Management Responsibility: As president, XX is responsible for the overall implementation of the Plan of Action and the daily operation of the business. The president will oversee the tenant improvements and installation of the brewery. The president will carry out the licensing process, secure financing of operational expenses, acquire and service retail accounts, and direct the daily start-up operations. The president will also be head brewer, and will be responsible for all tasks related to daily beer production.

As vice president and general manager, XX will assist the president in all areas related to the business start-up and the daily operation of the brewery. The vice president/general manager will specifically be responsible for advertising, promotions, purchasing, inventory control, and the management of the taproom and its retail sales.

Marketing and Distribution: The Craft Brewing Company produces beer in kegs for wholesale to the licensed liquor retail market. Kegs will be self distributed by the Craft Brewing Company to its local clients. In the first year, the president will market the company's products and be personally responsible for acquiring local retail accounts and distributing kegs to those accounts. The president is the individual most familiar with the company's products and with the local market for these products. The president is therefore the best-qualified person to represent the company to its customers. The marketing strategy will consist of direct person to person sales calls by the president to local premium retail outlets. Craft Brewing Company products will also be advertised in the local printed media.

The Craft Brewing Company will also have a taproom on the site where customers may come to purchase our products at retail prices. This retail outlet will allow us to receive pint price on the sale of beer, which will make an important contribution to our profit margin. Snacks and promotional merchandise such as glassware and T-shirts will also be sold to increase our public exposure and profit margin.

Professional Support: The following personnel will be used as needed. See Attachments for professional references and resumes.

Brewing Consultant:	XX
Business Consultant:	XX
Master Brewer:	XX
Accountant:	XX

utilized at the brewery and distributed to our licensed liquor retail clients.

Since our product will be sold to licensed retail outlets, promotions will be handled at the point-of-sale using these low cost promotional items, which will be provided free of charge to our accounts. Direct advertising to the general public will be on a regular but limited scale in the local printed media. We will earn the confidence of our retail licensees and their beer drinking customers by providing a consistent quality product and supporting that product with point-of-sale promotional items.

Production Process: The Craft Brewing Company will initially produce three styles of traditional British ale. Brewing begins by cracking the highest quality malted barley with a roller mill. This grist is then mixed with hot water in the mash tun, producing mash. A sweet liquid called wort is filtered out of the mash and transferred to the brew kettle. The wort is then brought to a rolling boil and hops are added to contribute bitterness, flavor, and aroma. After boiling, the wort is transferred through a heat exchanger, cooling the liquid down to fermentation temperature. The wort is then pumped into the primary fermentor where yeast is added. After one week of fermentation the fresh ale is transferred to a cold conditioning tank where it is clarified and carbonated for a second week. Now at the height of freshness, the ale is racked to kegs where it is ready to be distributed to the market and served. (See attached designs for the specifications on the major brewing equipment.)

Management Team: Craft Brewing Company is a privately held corporation managed by the president and vice president. All decisions will be made by the management team, officers, and shareholders, in compliance with the Company's articles of incorporation and bylaws.

President: XX is an accomplished homebrewer with seven years of experience. XX has been researching and preparing for this project for more than six years and has a solid understanding of the brewing process and the market for craft brewed beer.

Vice President: XX is likewise an experienced homebrewer who is capable of managing the brewing plant unassisted. The vice president has ten years of experience in the retail sales and restaurant industries, working as a cashier, hostess, bartender, and waitress in many fine establishments.

Consultant: The management team will be assisted by XX, a highly qualified professional brewing consultant. Mr. XX is the managing consultant on several successful brewing projects.

The management team is committed to the success of this plan. All decisions will be made with the best interest of the business and other investors in mind. Whenever necessary, the management team will rely on the assistance of professionals on a contractual basis.

Plan of Action: Having signed the Letter of Intent on the building lease and opened the corporate general account with an initial capital contribution of $75,000, as discussed in the Executive Summary above, the following tasks in order of priority will be completed. First, the management team will pursue the required equity capital by means of this business proposal and a share offering circular form which will be delivered to prospective investors.

Once the share offering has been delivered to prospective investors, the president and his brewery consultant, XX, will complete the final building utility and brewery layout designs. Once these plans have been finalized, the president and brewery consultant will place an order for the capital brewing equipment. The capital equipment for the brewery will be delivered ten to twelve weeks from time of order. The brewery consultant will personally supervise the installation of the brewery once the equipment has been delivered.

While the capital equipment is being fabricated, the president will complete the process of acquiring all permits necessary to begin capital improvements to the space being leased. Once a building occupancy permit has been issued, and while waiting for the main brewing plant to be fabricated and delivered, the management team will carry out the building improvements which have been designated as their responsibility in the lease Letter of Intent. At this time, the management team will also complete the process of filing for liquor and business license from the relevant federal, state, county, and city authorities.

The management team is seeking financing from

produced in the Pacific Northwest, and many of the noble hop varieties of Europe which are essential for producing original versions of traditional ales. Finally, our yeast will be supplied by XX. They specialize in storing and shipping yeast cultures in such a variety that brewers have the opportunity to craft beers to their own particular flavor profile.

As the growth of the industry indicates, there is an increasing variety of handcrafted beers being made available to the American public. The advantage our beers enjoy in this market will stem from using the finest ingredients provided by the most reliable local suppliers. Our beers will have their own unique flavor profile and be the freshest available to our local customers. Finally, our products will benefit from the additional demand which is generated by the customers knowledge that these beers have been produced within the community with local pride.

Bottling and Export: When starting a craft brewery, it is necessary to consider all available options. This is especially true when it comes to the issue of how the product will be packaged for sale. The issue of packaging is largely dependent on the amount of capital available and the nature of the local market. While there are some benefits to bottling a portion of the brewery's capacity for local retail sales, a top-quality bottling line entails a large initial capital investment and a much larger input of labor.

After having carefully researched the local market, we have determined that our best option is to initially concentrate solely on draft sales. We have concluded that a sufficient demand exists to support our business with draft sales alone. Our strategy is based on the belief that the most important task is to first concentrate on developing a sound local base of satisfied retail accounts and loyal draft beer drinkers, before diversifying our product line.

Despite our decision to initially concentrate on local draft sales, we recognize that a bottled product on local grocers' shelves would help to raise our public profile and increase our profit margin. For this reason, the management team of Craft Brewing Company is carefully examining the option of hiring another brewery to produce for us sometime after the second year of operation. Many small-scale brewing companies

in the United States have enjoyed tremendous success by contracting with a different brewery to produce a bottled product which the contracting company then distributes to its own customers. By contracting a bottled product from another brewery we will be able to service our own draft accounts without reducing our draft capacity. In addition, contracting would allow us to increase both market exposure and profit margins, without the great expense associated with owning and operating a bottling line.

Finally, we would like to raise the issue of exporting a contracted bottled product. We have carefully researched the beer market and developed several important relationships with beer importers and retailers. It is our firm belief that a specially designed product, contracted from a local brewery and then wholesaled by the Craft Brewing Company, would receive shelf space and enjoy steadily growing sales.

THE INDUSTRY

Industry History: Within the brewing industry, the Craft Brewing Company is considered to be a production craft brewery and brewpub combination. A brewpub is a restaurant or tavern which produces its own beer. A production craft brewery is a small brewery that sells beer in bottles or kegs to other retailers. Today these small breweries are proliferating rapidly, but they are a relatively new phenomenon which can be considered revolutionary.

The craft brewing revolution began in 1977 with the birth of the New Albion Brewing company in Sonoma, California. The primary characteristics, which distinguished New Albion and other new craft breweries from the established industrial breweries, were their small size, limited financing, and concentration on producing premium, specialty lagers and ales rather than the standard pale lagers. The most significant difference was the fact that most new craft breweries were built from the grass roots by homebrewers with more enthusiasm than formal training.

Today there are about 2000 craft breweries and brewpubs operating in the United States (2012). Industry statistics demonstrate that while the major brewing companies are flat-to-declining in sales, the market for premium specialty products is expanding. Tastes are changing, and quality, variety, flavor, and freshness are what the beer drinking public is coming to demand. It has become evident that every city, even small communities, have the potential to support at least one local brewery, and larger cities such as Portland and Seattle are already supporting many more.

As the craft brewing industry has grown and prospered, a whole host of associated industries has sprung up to meet the needs of craft brewers. Brewing consultants, equipment fabricators, ingredient suppliers, publicists, distributors, and even educational programs are now catering to the special needs of craft brewers and, as a result, making the business of small-scale craft brewing much easier today than it was just ten years ago. These enterprises are now devoting large sales staffs and significant resources to servicing the craft brewing industry, because they are confident that this is a growth industry for the future.

Institutional Support: As the craft brewing industry has grown and prospered a variety of new professional organizations, trade associations, and educational programs have been established to assist craft brewers and educate the public.

Professional and trade associations include: the Brewers Association, and the Local Brewers Guild.

These professional organizations perform many essential tasks for the craft brewing industry including: publishing industry statistics and information; representing the industry in legislative lobbying efforts; conducting trade shows and conferences; undertaking public relations with the media; and developing programs for brewery insurance, quality control, and continuing education for brewers.

Some important examples of the quality publications provided by these organizations include: *Zymurgy*® (American Homebrewers Association®), *The New Brewer* (Brewers Association), the *Brewers Resource Directory* (Brewers Publications). These and other publications are an invaluable resource for starting and successfully operating a craft brewery.

The ever-increasing number of trade conferences and craft brewing festivals which help to improve the quality of our product and educate the beer drinking public about our products includes: the Brewers Association's annual Craft Brewers Conference, the American Homebrewers Association National Conference, the Great American Beer Festival®, and a rich range of local and regional beer festivals.

Finally, in any discussion of institutional support we can not neglect the educational programs which recently have been designed specifically to further educate craft brewers. These programs include: the Beer Judge Certification Program; courses on quality control and brewing technology at the Siebel Institute of Technology in Chicago; the Cicerone® Certification Program and a variety of programs on sanitation, microbiology, brewing business management, etc., at the University of California at Davis.

The sources above represent only a portion of the proliferating number of institutional resources available to craft brewers today.

Industry Prospects: Well into the third decade of the craft brewing revolution, a variety of statistical evidence clearly demonstrates that this industry is much more than a temporary fad. We are at this time witnessing a proliferation of craft brewing enterprises, trade associations, institutional support, and beer festivals, organized specifically to celebrate craft brewing. Likewise, the great number of associated industries which view the craft brewing industry as an important market for their products and services is a strong indication that the craft brewing phenomenon has matured into a stable industry.

Industry statistics on annual production levels, malt beverage sales, tax assessments, and contemporary trends in the sales and consumption of various alcoholic beverages, indicate a growing consumer preference for craft brewed beers. In both the United States and Canada, beer is the alcoholic beverage of choice. However, while the production of major domestic brewers and the volume of imported beers has declined recently, the specialty beer market shows no signs of losing momentum.

Two potentially negative trends which may affect the industry are neo-Prohibitionism and tax increases. Neo-Prohibitionist legislation which cuts into the profit of brewers or restricts their market (i.e., alcohol warning label requirements and restrictions on the sale and consumption of alcoholic beverages) will always remain a threat in a pluralistic society. However, lately a greater amount of information has become available proving the healthful aspects of moderate drinking. In addition, the craft brewing industry and support institutions such as the Brewers Association are working to protect their interests.

Unfortunately, in times of economic instability many governing bodies may look at the success of today's and tomorrow's brewers as a way to increase revenues by raising taxes on beer. One answer to this threat are the lobbying associations which have been organized to protect the interests of small brewers. One important example of these lobbying efforts is the exemption won by small brewers (less than 60,000 barrels production) from the Federal Excise Tax on beer, imposed in 1991. In our region, the XX Beer and Wine Wholesalers Association is actively lobbying the State government.

Growth in Adversity: Despite the important efforts of these groups, the potential for new taxes will continue to be the greatest threat to the craft brewing industry. Although small brewers have been exempted from the latest Federal Excise Tax increase, this exemption could be lifted, or other state and local taxes could be imposed. It is important for this reason to consider the potential impact of higher taxes on our industry.

Recent statistical analysis of beer sales have reached the conclusion that beer sales are relatively price inelastic and respond more slowly to increases in the price of beer. These studies would seem to indicate that a not unreasonable rise in taxation on beer would only result in a minor drop in beer sales. Although the determination of who bears the cost of a given price increase is complicated, these studies indicate that with a product as price inelastic as beer, the increase will probably be paid by the retail customer.

One additional set of conclusions from these studies concerns price increases and product substitution. The evidence indicates that there is probably little substitutability, among consumers between beer, wine, and distilled spirits. This means that (all other factors remaining constant) an increase in the price of one category, should not result in the substitution of another category of alcoholic beverage. Consequently, we may conclude that the growth in sales of specialty beers, which are priced as a premium product, is the result of changing consumer tastes, not changes in the price structure of beer.

Studies of income elasticity also demonstrate that beer sales are relatively inelastic with respect to the consumer's income. Recent industry reviews, which consider the impact of the recession and the business cycle on beer sales, have reached the conclusion that the business cycle has little discernible influence on the craft brewing industry. Finally, industry statistics clearly show that throughout the last recession, the craft brewing industry continued to grow at an impressive rate.

Clearly there are threats to our industry, but statistics demonstrate that consumer tastes and preferences are changing. In such a market the best strategy is to provide the consumer with the highest quality product. Beer drinkers are also voters who will go to great lengths to reject unreasonable attacks on their favorite beverage.

THE MARKET AND COMPETITION

Potential Customers: The most important customers of the Craft Brewing Company are the owners and managers of local licensed liquor retail outlets. These local outlets consist of pubs, taverns, and restaurants in the cities of XX, XX, and XX. However, since it is our marketing strategy to concentrate on satisfying the demand of a core group of customers in the first year, a select number of retail outlets in these cities will receive priority.

All of the establishments listed above are located in our core local market. Most of these establishments have at least four taps allocated to specialty and craft brewed beers, several have more than six craft beer taps. The president has spoken with the owners of all of these establishments, and they have all expressed strong interest in featuring a quality local product once it is available.

An important part of our marketing strategy is to concentrate on providing our customers with the best possible, most responsive service they have ever received when purchasing beer. Consequently, it will be necessary to take on new accounts carefully, so as to have enough beer in stock to meet the demand of our core accounts. One potential mistake would be to try to provide beer for more customers than our initial capacity allows. For this reason we will prioritize our accounts according to certain criteria which we would like to see our retail customers meet. The fact is that we do not want to sell our product to simply any retailer that expresses an interest. We want our products in the right places, along side of other quality beers, and receiving the proper attention necessary for serving craft brewed beer at its peak of quality. For this reason we will initially concentrate our sales efforts on establishments which are already serving craft brewed beers, before offering our products to bars which are not yet carrying craft brewed beers.

There are additional licensed retail outlets in XX, which would be satisfactory retailers of our products. The fact is that there has been a very positive response from licensed retailers in our local market. Our only problem will be to decide which outlets may carry our products in the early months when production is still limited, and which will have to wait. We will make this decision carefully so as to develop a core group of satisfied, loyal clients, while planning for a much broader distribution in the future. Eventually we intend to introduce our products in local restaurants and taverns which have not yet begun to offer their customers craft brewed beer.

Competition: Our competitors in the local market are primarily those craft breweries in XX and XX who distribute their products to this region, in addition to the super-premium draft imports being offered. The local breweries include: XX

All of these breweries distribute their products to licensed retail outlets in our local market, through licensed liquor distributors. These local distributors include: XX

First let us begin this evaluation of our competition with a brief discussion of the super-premium imported draft beers which we consider to be our competitors because many of them are similar in style and price to domestic craft brewed beers. Although these beers are by and large excellent products, the fact remains that they find it difficult to compete with domestic craft brewed beers. The imports do have strong name recognition in many cases, but they cannot compete in the areas of freshness, direct and personal service to local retailers, or local brand loyalty. Furthermore, shipping costs and advertising for these products usually place them several dollars above craft brewed beers in price, and these beers are subject to the new, higher Federal Excise Tax rate. Statistics demonstrate that while craft brewed beers are enjoying steady annual growth in sales, the market share of super-premium imports has recently begun to decline.

By and large, the domestic craft breweries listed above all consistently produce quality products. For this reason, it is the responsibility of the individual brewing company to make some effort to help consumers distinguish their beers from those of their competitors. Some brewing companies rely on the excellent quality of their products, social media and word of mouth as their strongest marketing point. This strategy is often used by new brewing companies which in the early years have less capital available for advertising. Other pioneer craft breweries benefit from greater brand recognition, due to their longer operating history and easily recognizable logos.

Another way to win loyal consumer support is to develop a distinctive flavor profile, such as a characteristically assertive hop flavor. In contrast to these methods, some brewers spend thousands of dollars on a strong advertising campaign through the local and national media to increase their market share. Others with smaller advertising budgets may choose to rely on less expensive, but often equally effective, point-of-sale promotional materials.

Finally, the most fundamental marketing strategy which may be employed is through pricing. Some brewers choose to underprice their competition to gain market share. Others, choose to price their products above the market average, in order to capture an image as the brewer with the most premium products. Still others may price their products near the industry average. This strategy helps them to avoid being seen as a discount brewer, while at the same time avoids driving off potential customers who refuse to buy beer which is priced significantly above that of the competition.

All of the brewers competing in our market rely on some mix of the above marketing strategies to acquire a base of loyal local support and then increase their market share. The Craft Brewing Company will likewise pursue a marketing strategy appropriate to its production goals, financial means, and the particular characteristics of our local market. Our marketing strategy will be carefully discussed in the next section of this business plan. However, it should be emphasized here that the demand for craft brewed products is growing and as the statistics demonstrate, the craft brewing industry's share of the beer market is also growing.

Most craft brewers are in agreement that competition is healthy. The great variety of craft brewed products available to consumers has only served to further educate the beer drinking public to the quality of our products, creating ever greater demand. Although we are in competition with other craft brewers, our share of the market will not come so much at their expense, as it will at the expense of imported beers and domestic industrial brewers whose customers are gradually shifting to fresher and more flavorful craft brewed products.

Market Size and Trends: The size of our local craft brewed and specialty ale market in XX is sufficiently large to provide us with a market share which will ensure the initial success of the Craft Brewing Company Likewise, this market has been steadily growing at a rate which is more than adequate to achieve our projected growth in sales. Our market research and conclusions are based on statistical analyses of beer sales volumes by individual breweries, which are reported to the State Liquor Control Board each month. These sales reports have also been analyzed and reprinted in a more comparative form published monthly by the State Wholesalers Association. In addition to these reports, we have carefully questioned brewers, local licensed retailers, and local licensed beer distributors to determine the average monthly level of craft brewed beer sales and the growth in sales which have occurred over the last several years.

Using the above sources, we have determined that for last year, average sales of craft brewed beers in our local market, was approximately XX kegs each month. In addition, approximately another XX kegs of imported ales and other specialty beers were sold in this market each month. We consider specialty imported beers such as Guinness Stout, Bass Ale, Heineken, etc., to be our competitors because these are also considered to be super-premium, specialty products which are priced in a similar range as craft brewed beers. It is these imports, as well as other craft brewed beers, which we will be competing with for tap-handle space at the businesses of local licensed retailers. Consequently, a careful analysis of our local market leads us to the conservative estimate that the size of the local market for our products last year was approximately XX kegs of specialty beers each month, on average. At the average super-premium keg price of $XX, the total dollar-unit market for our products last year was approximately $XX each month on average, or $XX for the year.

The same sources, which we relied on to determine the size of our local market, have also helped us to determine that for the last several years this market has been growing by approximately X percent annually. When questioned on their expectations for future growth, local beer distributors expressed the opinion that they anticipate that our local market will continue to grow at or near the present level of X percent annually. If we trust the experts who are most familiar with our market, we can anticipate that with X percent growth this year, sales of beers in our market should reach approximately XX kegs of specialty beers each month on average. Given the demographic and economic growth trends of our local region, we believe this estimate to be on the conservative side.

Regional Demographic Growth: In a national study of population changes, XX County was projected to be the fifth fastest growing county in the United States between now and the end of the century. In XX County, employment has increased XX percent since 2010, which compares favorably with the State's employment growth rate of XX percent during the same period. During the recession years, although the unemployment rate in XX County rose, it remained below the state and national averages. XX County may not be impervious to recession, but the large number of government officials who are employed and live in this area make our local market less vulnerable to business fluctuations.

One consequence of having government as the largest employer in our local market is reflected in the volume of retail sales. When we examine retail sales levels, it becomes apparent that XX County has developed into a regional consumer market. While retail sales have increased by XX percent since 1990, the population has increased by XX percent. These two figures indicate that a large nonresident population is making purchases in XX County. XX County's retail sales are clearly being augmented by the large number of persons who daily visit the State's center of government. Regardless of who these persons may be, many of them stop to do a little shopping, have some lunch, and even drink a beer, while they are in XX. Of the $XX billion in retail sales that occurred in XX County last year, XX percent occurred in XX, and XX percent occurred in the city of XX.

We are still a relatively small urban area, but it is our smallness and the quality of our environment and living which continue to attract new residents. Retail sales can be expected to grow along with XX County's population. More and more restaurants and pubs will be opened to serve the needs of our growing community. Consequently, local restaurant and bar sales of specialty beers can also be expected to grow with the State, its government, and the city.

Regional Market Growth: XX and XX States are considered to be our broader regional market, which is an important sales region once our local market demand has been satisfied. The following are sales reports posted with the Liquor Control Board and XX Beer and Wine Wholesalers Association for last year that provide the following annual percentage growth rates in beer sales.

Brewery % Change During a One-Year Period

(List primary craft brewing competitors in your market.)

This annual growth in sales figures is a good indication of the overall health of the industry that we propose to enter and compete in. Clearly, the XX craft beer market and our local market have sufficient growth potential to accommodate many new craft breweries.

Estimated Local Market Share and Sales: Sales, distribution, and tax records can help us to determine the relative market share and popularity of our competitors and their products. Our research, counting taps and questioning licensed retailers as to their levels of sales, also gives us a good picture of which craft breweries have the largest shares of our local market. For example, the craft breweries with the most popular products and largest market shares in our local market are the XX, XX, and XX.

XX is perhaps the most successful craft brewer in our local market, selling approximately XX kegs a month on average. As a percentage of the approximately XX kegs of super-premium, specialty beers sold each month in this market last year, XX currently controls a little more than XX percent of the local market we intend to compete in. The other market leaders each control from XX percent to XX percent of the specialty beer market.

The management team of the Craft Brewing Company is determined to produce approximately XX kegs (XX barrels), during the first twelve months of production. Of these XX kegs, approximately XX kegs of beer will be marketed and sold in our local market in this first year of production. These approximately XX kegs will be sold in our local market through the following three marketing channels:

1. Wholesale distribution to local licensed retailers: $XX per keg
2. Retail keg sales to the public from our warehouse: $XX per keg
3. Retail pint sales to the public in our taproom: $XX per pint

The following is the estimated breakdown of sales in our local market through these three channels in the first year of production:

1. Wholesale distribution to local licensed retailers: XX kegs

2. Retail keg sales to the public from our facility: XX kegs

3. Retail pint sales to the public in our taproom: XX kegs

If we include the XX kegs being sold through our own taproom, this means we will be marketing approximately XX kegs or approximately XX kegs each month on average during the first year. If we assume a total local market of approximately XX kegs each month on average for this year and next year, then the Craft Brewing Company intends to capture from 12 to 14 percent of the local market during this time.

Clearly we intend to be a very competitive market-share leader in our local market. Therefore, let us examine what we believe to be the important advantages which we have over our competitors in the local market which will help us to win a 12 to 14 percent market share.

First, the Craft Brewing Company intends to price its products slightly below the level of our strongest competitors. Specialty draft imports and other craft breweries must absorb the additional costs associated with delivering their products to the XX area, often over great distances. The Craft Brewing Company, on the other hand, will handle its own distribution and save on delivery and storage costs in its local market. In addition, it is simply part of our strategy to always price our products slightly below those of other market leaders, since this is what our local licensed retailers have told us would be of particular importance when they are making decisions on trying a new beer on their taps.

Second, the Craft Brewing Company will be a local entity in which the community can take special pride. Our brewery and taproom will create jobs and enhance the atmosphere of the downtown area. It is common sense to assume that given everything is nearly equal in the areas of price, style, and quality, people will choose to patronize local producers rooted in their community.

Third, the Craft Brewing Company will be able to provide the very freshest beers to our local market. Other craft breweries must rely on beer distributors to deliver their products to the XX market, and these beers may spend some time sitting in local warehouses before being distributed to licensed retailers. Our products, on the other hand, will be distributed directly from our own cold room in our own delivery van. Consequently, kegs of our ales will never reach the market beyond their peak level of maturity, nor before they are perfectly matured either.

Fourth, we are committed to making the best beers possible, using the highest quality ingredients available. We are serious when we make this commitment. We would not be entering this market if we were not certain that we could make excellent ales which will be highly competitive. Brewing beer is what we do and we believe that a commitment to quality will go a long way toward assuring our long-term success. Consistently high quality beer can sell itself without much promotion, but a poor quality beer will not succeed for long, no matter how actively it is promoted.

Fifth, the Craft Brewing Company will be able to serve its products on its own taps in a taproom which will be named XX. Our own retail outlet will permit us to try new products before offering them for distribution to the wholesale market. In addition, a taproom will allow us to receive the full retail pint price on a significant percentage of our barrel production. Every keg sold at retail pint price rather than wholesale keg price, will significantly increase our profit margin, while at the same time helping us to reach our 12 to 14 percent market-share target. XX will be a casual drinking room separated from the brewery by a large glass window which will allow customers to view the activities on the production floor while enjoying their favorite beverage. XX will also be the display and sales center for retail promotional items which will bear our corporate and product logos. Although the cash profit on these items is only 50 percent, they represent a much greater value as free advertising by increasing our exposure in the community.

By bringing the management team into direct contact with the customers in our local community, our own retail outlet will help us to increase our market share as well as compete more effectively with outside craft brewers. Two-way communication between the management team and our customers will provide us with invaluable feedback on our products. Furthermore, as beer drinkers make themselves comfortable at our establishment, the Craft Brewing Company's image as a local community enterprise will be enhanced.

Finally, and most importantly, we believe that our commitment to service will assure that we earn a leading share of our local market and increase that share into the future. No other brewer has the potential to provide the level of prompt service to the licensed retailers in our local market that the Craft Brewing Company has. We have already begun to develop close relationships with the licensed retailers in our local market. We know them by name, we have visited them and purchased beers in their establishments, we have questioned them as to their priorities when deciding which beers to put on their taps, and we have carefully observed the preferences of their customers. We at the Craft Brewing Company are committed to the relationships we have begun to develop with our future customers and their customers. By using consumer surveys, delivering our own beer, serving our beer in their establishments, working closely with their employees, and carefully listening to licensed retailers and beer drinkers in XX, we are sure to earn a leading share in our local market and keep it.

As the local market and demand for draft specialty beers continues to grow, the Craft Brewing Company will expand its production to satisfy that demand and increase our market share. The following is a graphic representation of our market-share projections based on the previously stated assumptions concerning our industry's prospects for growth, our estimated monthly sales, and the marketing strategy which we will discuss in the next section.

Assumptions
*   Total local market for craft brewed and specialty draft beer last year equaled XX kegs a month per XX kegs a year.
*   Annual growth rate in local market of X percent for next three years.
*   Total local market for specialty draft beer from summer of last year through summer this year equals XX kegs a month per XX kegs a year.

*   Craft Brewing Company's market share of XX to XX percent.
*   Average wholesale keg price of $XX a unit.
*   Average retail keg price of $XX a unit.
*   Average retail pint price of $XX a unit, at 120 pints per keg.

Local Market-Share Projections

	Production Year		
	Year 1	Year 2	Year 3
Estimated Total Annual Sales in Local Market (Kegs)	XX	XX	XX
Craft Brewing Company Estimated Share of and Annual Sales	13.5%	13.5%	12%
in Local Market (Kegs)	XX	XX	XX

The following is the dollar value breakdown in local beer sales through our three marketing channels for the first three years:

Local Sales Projections by Dollar Value

	Production Year		
	Year 1	Year 2	Year 3
Local Sales Wholesale Kegs	756	926	1,108
Dollars ($85)	$64,260	$78,710	$94,180
Local Sales Retail Kegs	40	140	160
Dollars ($110)	$4,400	$15,400	$17,600
Local Sales Retail Kegs by the Pint	294	336	336
Dollars ($300 per keg)	$88,200	$100,800	$100,800

Estimated Regional Sales: Thus far, this discussion of market share has only concerned the local market for which the management team will be personally responsible for promotions, sales, distribution, and service. In the fifth month of operation, the demand from our local market will no longer be sufficient to absorb all of the barrels being produced by the Craft Brewing Company. At that point, we will begin to market our products through a distributor to the broader regional market. For this purpose we will rely on XX to distribute our beer in the XX market. In the seventh, eighth, and twelfth months of operation we will purchase additional fermentation tanks and kegs in order to increase our production capacity to approximately 1,200 barrels a year. Further equipment purchases will be made in the second and third years of operation in order to increase our production capacity to approximately 1,800 barrels a year as the demand for our products in the local and regional markets continues to expand. All barrels produced above the level which our local market can absorb will be sold in the regional market through licensed wholesale distributors at an average price of $XX a keg.

The following chart indicates the estimated number of kegs which will be sold in the regional market after satisfying the local demand.

REGIONAL SALES PROJECTIONS

	Production Year		
	Year 1	Year 2	Year 3
Estimated Total Regional Sales			
Kegs	252	752	1,512
Dollars ($68)	$17,136	$51,136	$102,816

Total Sales Projections: The following chart indicates the estimated combined total of local and regional sales for the first three years of operation.

TOTAL SALES PROJECTIONS

	Production Year		
	Year 1	Year 2	Year 3
Local Sales Wholesale Kegs	756	926	1,108
Dollars ($85)	$64,260	$78,710	$94,180
Local Sales Retail Kegs	40	140	160
Dollars ($110)	$4,400	$15,400	$17,600
Local Sales Retail Kegs by the Pint	294	336	336
Dollars ($300 per keg)	$88,200	$100,800	$100,800
Regional Sales Wholesale Kegs	252	752	1,512
Dollars ($68)	$17,136	$51,136	$102,816
Total Sales Kegs	1,342	2,154	3,116
Gross Beer Revenue	$173,996	$246,046	$315,396

These figures are based on the previously stated assumptions and represent our projections of sales targets to be achieved by the management team of Craft Brewing Company In the fourth and fifth years we will continue to expand production by the amount of 500 to 600 barrels a year. By the fifth year of operation the Craft Brewing Company will be producing at near the 2,800-barrels-a-year capacity which the space in our brewing facility can accommodate.

MARKETING PLAN

The Fundamentals: It is the intention of the management team to establish the long-term profitability and success of the Craft Brewing Company by carefully concentrating on building a core group of satisfied local customers. This core group consists of the licensed liquor retailers operating pubs, taverns, and restaurants in the cities of XX, XX, and XX. While it is these licensed retailers who are our direct customers, we recognize that ultimately our customers are the beer drinkers within our local market who patronize the establishments of our licensed retail customers and our own taproom. Consequently, the key to our marketing strategy is to make the highest possible quality beers which will satisfy the tastes and demands of beer drinkers in our market, while providing our licensed retail customers with the best service possible.

Our effort to make the best beer possible will be achieved by the following means. First, all beer profiles and recipes have been selected after careful market research to determine exactly what is popular among beer and ale drinkers in our market. The most important part of our research consisted of many long conversations with local licensed retailers, who were eager to tell us what their customers preferred when ordering a craft brewed beer and what they were looking for when buying beer to stock their bar taps. In addition, interviews with local beer distributors have been particularly helpful in pointing out which beers sell well in our local market, why they sell well, and what styles will compete well in this market. Having made the decision as to what flavor profiles we would like to reproduce in our beers, the president as head brewer will rely on his brewing consultant, XX, to determine the exact balance of ingredients and specific brewing techniques necessary to achieve those flavor profiles.

Our three initial products have been designed specifically to satisfy local tastes and demands, as they have been identified by our market research. However, we believe that ale drinkers in our local market have similar preferences to ale drinkers throughout the XX beer market, and we expect our products to be competitive throughout that broader market. As a final note regarding the design of our recipes, we intend to carefully monitor the responses of beer drinkers to our products when they first reach the local market and long after. Consumer feedback will be the means be which we gauge the reactions of beer drinkers to our products, so that we may make any necessary adjustments.

Another key aspect of our marketing strategy, which is intended to ensure we make the best beer possible and then sell that beer, is our determination to use the finest brewing ingredients available. Only premium ingredients will be used, without exception. We have made certain that our suppliers all have excellent reputations among the craft brewing community in our region. Nevertheless, as our operations progress, XX as head brewer, and XX as general manager, will continue to demand the highest quality from our suppliers and will be prepared to find new sources of brewing materials whenever our current suppliers fail to meet the exacting standards of the Craft Brewing Company.

Brewing the best beer possible is our motto, and we will not cut corners to save a few dollars at the expense of beer quality. We will use the finest ingredients, top quality brewing equipment, and well-proven brewing methods to establish our market share. Only a quality product will create consumer loyalty in our core local market and ensure regular growth in sales as that market expands.

Distribution: In the first year of operation, it is our strategy to concentrate on winning the loyalty of licensed retailers in our local market. In this effort the president as head brewer, will have primary responsibility for local sales and for distributing beer from our cold room by delivery van when our customers place an order. We believe that only through close personal contact with our local customers can lines of communication and a long-term business relationship be established. Once this relationship has been firmly established, a properly trained employee of the company will assist in making daily deliveries so that the president can concentrate on acquiring new accounts and increasing sales in the local market.

In the fifth month of operation, while the president maintains the accounts in our local market, the Craft Brewing Company will seek the help of a professional beer distributor to reach out beyond the local XX market. Of the three major liquor distribution companies operating in our region, XX carries XX percent of the craft brewed beers being distributed to licensed retailers in the city of XX. In XX County, XX is represented by import and craft breweries manager, XX. Mr. XX and the company he represents are spoken of highly by local licensed retailers and by the local brewers whose products they distribute. In a meeting with Mr. XX, the president and XX reached a verbal understanding that XX would represent and distribute Craft Brewing Company products at selected retail outlets in XX County and the city of XX. XX is clearly the distributor of choice in our region and will be relied on to distribute our products outside of the city of XX when capacity is being expanded in the second year.

Once full capacity with our five initial fermentors has been achieved, additional fermentors will be added to increase capacity. At this time, with increased capacity, we will more intensively promote sales of specialty and contract beers in our local market while arranging for XX to begin to distribute our flagship products to the XX, XX, market.

Once we are satisfied that we have achieved a competitive market share in XX and that our accounts in that market are being serviced properly by XX, we will then consider a further stage of expansion. While adding additional fermentors and kegs to our production line, we will begin to offer our products to the broader regional market, including the XX area. At this stage we will carefully consider which distributor we want to represent us and which accounts we would like to see our products in.

On-Premise Retail Sales: The taproom is another important distribution and sales outlet for our products. Our taproom has been designed to accommodate a maximum occupancy of fifty persons. The space will contain a serving bar, a display cabinet for retail promotional items, and seating for approximately thirty to forty persons, with some additional standing room available. The XX is designed to be an extension of the brewery where patrons can witness the brewing operation first hand and talk to the brewery staff, while enjoying some of our quality ales.

Our taproom is intended to enhance the experience of drinking a quality ale, when all of one's senses are brought into play. There will be no smoking in the XX because tobacco smoke would interfere with the beer drinkers ability to fully appreciate the flavor and aroma of the beers being served. Furthermore, we believe that a no smoking environment will be greatly appreciated since there are no other nonsmoking drinking establishments in town. The dimensions of our taproom are not large, so we have chosen to light the space well and to paint the walls in light colors in order to avoid the impression of being closed in, and so that customers may appreciate the clarity and rich colors of our products. Decorations will be limited to a few plants, one large fish tank behind the serving bar, wall displays of our corporate and product logos, and a few tasteful posters with aquatic themes. A variety of comfortable chairs and tables will be provided for casual seating. In addition, game boards will be available for those who wish to play a little chess, backgammon, etc., while they visit with friends. A small sound system will provide music whenever appropriate.

In our taproom customers will be able to make a variety of retail purchases. Initially we will have a small selection of T-shirts for sale. But as cash flow permits, we will include other promotional items to increase our merchandise sales. A small selection of snacks, such as nuts, chips, and locally baked pretzels, will also be available to our customers. In regard to beer sales, customers will be able to purchase beer in a variety of volumes. Besides pints and 10-ounce schooners, a sampler of beer which includes a small glass of each of our products will be offered for sale. In addition, customers will also be able to have the take-out vessel of their choice filled for off-premise consumption. Finally, customers in the XX may also purchase a keg of beer at retail price from our cooler, for off-premise consumption.

Pricing: As mentioned previously, our pricing strategy is designed to make our beers competitive and to achieve a profit, while at the same time positioning our products amongst the best beers being produced by our competitors. A keg price of approximately $XX is the median price now being asked by competitors in our local market. Consequently, we intend to ask $XX for our kegs, in order to make our products just slightly less expensive than those of our competitors. When questioned as to their views on pricing, local licensed retailers indicated that this price for a quality product would be one incentive for carrying Craft Brewing Company products.

A further aspect of our pricing strategy is our determination to maintain stable prices over a substantial period of time. Although we can not be certain that significant changes to our cost structure will not occur, it is our plan to maintain prices at the $XX a keg level for at least two years. In this way we will provide our customers with a degree of predictability when purchasing our products. Changes in price will only take place when our own costs rise appreciably and thereby threaten the minimum profit margin we require to meet our operating costs and achieve our projected growth targets. Price changes will also be considered whenever our products fall significantly out of alignment with the median price being asked by our major competitors.

Our discussions with local licensed retailers and with other brewers have also made us aware that when a new brewery is starting up, it is necessary to offer the kegs from the first production runs at a price which is just below the standard price for those products. The first several production runs of any new brewery can be expected to produce excellent beers, but not necessarily the exact style of beer which is being aimed at. It may take two or three adjustments to the start-up recipe before the desired flavor profile is achieved. It may also take several production runs before consistency of flavor for a particular recipe is achieved.

Local retailers have told us that they would be willing to try these early beers, understanding that the recipe may still need some adjustment before we are all satisfied with the finished product. However, they have also expressed the opinion that these early beers should be offered at a discount, below the level that they will be priced at when the desired flavor profile is achieved. This pricing practice is typical of start-up breweries in our market, and we can not ignore the expressed views of our customers. Consequently, our first kegs to be produced in the recipe adjustment phase will be offered to our customers at a price of $XX a keg, which is near the bottom of the price range which our products will compete in. In the effort to achieve the desired flavor profiles with the smallest number of test production runs necessary, the president will be assisted by brewing consultant, XX, and former head brewer of the XX Brewery, XX. Between these three experienced brewers, it is expected that it will require two test runs for each recipe, before the desired flavor profile is achieved with the third production run. At that time we will be justified in pricing our kegs at their full market rate of $XX.

The following is the projected price breakdown of the wholesale and retail items to be sold by the Craft Brewing Company.

Item Price

Beer:	
Wholesale Kegs (1/2 bbl.)	
Self Distributed	$85.00
Wholesale Kegs (1/4 bbl.)	
Self Distributed	$50.00
Wholesale Kegs (1/2 bbl.)	
Distributor	$68.00
Wholesale Kegs (1/4 bbl.)	
Distributor	$38.00
Retail Kegs (1/2 bbl.)	$110.00
Retail Kegs (1/4 bbl.)	$60.00
Pint	$2.50
Schooner	$1.50
Sampler	$2.50

Pint and schooner glasses will be of the standard size prevailing in our industry. The "Sampler" will consist of several small glasses, each containing one of the various products available on our taps.

Promotional Merchandise and Snacks: Promotional merchandise, such as T-shirts, glassware, lapel pins, etc., and snacks, such as fresh baked goods, nuts, chips, etc., will be priced at twice our cost in order to realize a consistent and reasonable profit.

Advertising and Promotions: As general manager, XX is responsible for point-of-sale promotions and advertising. Initially, point-of-sale promotions will consist of table tents, coasters, and tap handles, provided free of charge to our customers. When cash flow permits, other items such as neon signs, bar towels, and mirrors, all displaying our logo will be given to local retailers who have demonstrated a strong sales record with our products. All promotional items are considered to be an advertising tool since they will display the corporate logo and logos of individual products.

The vice president's experience working in the restaurant and bar industry has taught her that the owners of these establishments and their service employees are especially grateful when promotional materials are maintained by the company distributing them. Consequently, we will take full responsibility for the display of our point-of-sale promotional items, placing them on tables, and replacing the supply at regular intervals.

Our research of the food and beverage service industry has also led us to conclude that only a knowledgeable bar and wait staff can properly represent our products to the consumer. Consequently, both the president and vice president will provide brief, yet informative, introductions to our products for the wait staff of our licensed retail customers. These product introductions are intended to familiarize these important representatives of our products with the brewing methods used by Craft Brewing Company. In addition, our licensed retail customers and their wait staffs will be invited to visit the brewery and witness first hand the production of the beer they will later be selling. These brewery tours are intended to help develop a special relationship between the Craft Brewing Company and those who serve our products to beer drinkers in our core market.

The vice president is also responsible for carrying out all direct advertising of Craft Brewing Company products, to the consumers in our local market. Advertising will be conducted through the local printed media. Throughout the year we will run weekly, Friday and Saturday ads in XX newspaper, the paper with the largest circulation in our local market. When XX College is in session, we will also run weekly adds in the college's XX Journal. We believe that this advertising strategy will provide the greatest exposure for our products, in the most cost effective manner. However, we will regularly survey our customers to determine whether or not they learned of our products through these printed ads. Depending on the results of these surveys, certain changes in our advertising strategy may be considered.

In regard to surveying our customers and the general beer drinking public, the following method will be employed. The president and vice president will design a survey sheet to determine the public's response to our products and our advertising campaign. These survey sheets will be distributed and collected by president and vice president in the establishments of our licensed retail customers. In addition, both president and vice president will conduct regular visits to these establishments to maintain contact with our licensed retail customers, their employees, and their customers. These fact-finding visits will be most frequent in the first year of operation, particularly in the first months when product evaluation and recipe adjustments will take place. It is our determination to never lose touch with the needs of our customers and the tastes of the beer drinking public.

Finally, in regard to the issue of public relations, we at the Craft Brewing Company believe that an ounce of prevention is worth a pound of cure. What this means in a practical sense, is that the vice president will actively pursue a strategy of meeting with local groups which are concerned about issues related to excessive drinking. It is our intention to develop an open dialogue and positive relationship with local citizen groups which advocate responsible drinking. Likewise, we will take the initiative to foster a cooperative relationship with local law-enforcement agencies, to show them that we are as concerned about alcohol misuse as they are. At the Craft Brewing Company we advocate the enjoyment of quality beer in moderation, not the consumption of alcohol in large quantities. In order to avoid any potentially harmful publicity in the future, which may stem from the misuse of our products, we will make certain that the relevant interest groups understand that we take the issue of alcohol misuse as seriously as they do.

COMPANY STRUCTURE

Management Team: The following is a list of the key management roles and the individuals who will be responsible for them.

President. XX has overall responsibility for the start-up and daily operation of the Craft Brewing Company. In the start-up phase, the president will choose and supervise all utility subcontractors; the president will approve, supervise, and assist in all construction; the president will approve the design and purchase of all brewing equipment; and the president will supervise and assist the installation of all brewing equipment.

Head brewer. In the daily operations phase of the project, XX will be responsible for all tasks related to the production of beer. The president will supervise the design of all product recipes and any necessary adjustments to those recipes. The head brewer will perform the regular brewing routine and all tasks associated with preparing Craft Brewing Company products for the market.

Sales and distribution manager. As previously indicated, the president will be responsible for acquiring and servicing accounts in our local market. Likewise, the president will be responsible for distributing full kegs and picking up empty kegs from clients. The president will be assisted in sales calls by the vice president and in distribution by corporate employees.

Vice president. XX will act as vice president, which involves providing assistance to the president at every level of the brewery start-up and daily operations. Should the president be temporarily unable to perform his roles as president and head brewer, the vice president will be sufficiently familiar with all aspects of the business that the vice president will be able to train and supervise any employees needed to assist her in the full operation of the business.

General manager. XX will be responsible for all tasks associated with purchasing, inventory control, accounts receivable, accounts payable, record keeping, and the preparation of all production and sales reports required by the relevant licensing agencies. In these tasks, the general manager will be assisted by the president who will provide information on sales, beer inventory, and the status of raw materials' stocks. In addition, XX of XX will review our books regularly in preparation for the quarterly tax filing which is required. As general manager, XX will also be responsible for managing the operations of our retail outlet, XX. The general manager will be responsible for maintaining the retail inventory and tracking sales. The general manager will also be responsible for overseeing the employee hired to run the bar. When time permits, the general manager and president will take over at the bar, and the employee can be assigned to other tasks, such as brew-house sanitation and deliveries.

XX's final area of responsibility as general manager is that of promotions, advertising, and public relations for Craft Brewing Company. The general manager will supervise the design and creation of all corporate and product logos. The general manager will manage the advertising account and evaluate the influence of our advertising strategy on sales. The general manager will act as public relations officer to the community in order to enhance our image as a community entity concerned with the welfare of our community. The general manger will also assist the president in working with our customers to promote sales and maintain open lines of communication.

The president and vice president believe it is important to be personally involved with every facet of the company's operation. No task will be assigned to an employee before we have repeatedly performed that task ourselves and can then instruct and oversee the employee properly. This same philosophy extends to the management of our corporate accounting, which we intend to be directly involved in.

The president and vice president feel confident that with the assistance of the employees discussed below, they can perform the tasks outlined above. They have a long-standing relation of eleven years and a well-demonstrated record of working together to solve problems. In addition, the management team will be assisted in many areas by the specially contracted professionals discussed below. For further information on the credentials and experience of the management team, see their attached resumes.

Management Compensation: For his responsibilities as head brewer, XX will draw an initial monthly salary of $XX. For her responsibilities as general manager, XX will draw an initial monthly salary of $XX. These salaries are the minimum income which XX and XX require to pay for their living expenses. At this time the management team is receiving no compensation or payments from the company. Wage payments will begin at the end of the first month of production and sales of 28 barrels or more, which is projected to be July 20XX. All future wage increases or bonuses will be granted to the president and general manager/vice president as a reward for significant production and sales increases, but only after due consideration by the Board of Directors.

Board of Directors: The Craft Brewing Company has been established by its founders and management team, XX and XX, as a corporation under the laws of XX State. The Board of Directors meets monthly to conduct any such business as may come before it. The activities and affairs of the corporation are managed by the Board of Directors. The Board of Directors has delegated responsibility for management of the day to day operation of the business to the management team, XX and XX. Members of the Board of Directors receive no compensation for their services and all directors hold office until the next annual meeting of the shareholders or until their successors have been elected and qualified. Executive officers are appointed by the Board of Directors and serve at the pleasure of the Board of Directors.

The management team has decided to provide themselves with the most reliable professional support and counseling available, in order to acquire the breadth of experience which is necessary to ensure the success of the Craft Brewing Company. Toward this end, the following individual has accepted our invitation to join the Board of Directors so that she can lend her experience to and question the decisions of the management team.

XX has accepted the management team's invitation to join the Board of Directors as a financial advisor, director, and executive secretary. Among her many responsibilities at this position, XX, has been involved in working with small businesses in the areas of finance and the preparation of commercial loan packages. XX is also currently a board member of the XX, a nonprofit corporation of XX State. XX is a community development loan fund, which pools investment dollars from individuals and organizations in order to provide loans for small businesses and nonprofit organizations that benefit the region.

XX's primary responsibilities involve providing the management team with financial advice and recommendations during Board meetings. In addition, XX will perform the role of executive secretary, preparing the company's annual reports and maintaining regular communications with shareholders. XX will not receive a salary for her efforts, but the Board of Directors may vote her a bonus for exceptional performance.

XX has demonstrated her commitment o the Craft Brewing Company by purchasing 5,000 shares of Company's stock for $XX. As an incentive to join our board and perform the responsibilities of executive secretary, XX has been awarded 5,000 matching shares in addition to the 5,000 shares the executive secretary purchased.

Executive Officers: The directors, executive officers, and significant personnel of the Company are as follows:

XX   Chairman of the Board
President
Brewery Manager
Director

XX   Executive Treasurer
Vice President
General Manager
Director

XX   Executive Secretary
Director

Employees: The Craft Brewing Company is scheduled and budgeted to hire employees at regular intervals. The first full-time employee will be hired in July so as to have sufficient time to properly train that employee before full brewing and sales operations commence.

The first employee will be hired primarily as a beverage server and retail sales person in the taproom. However, this individual must be flexible and prepared to perform a variety of additional tasks, including cleaning, brewing assistance, and deliveries. The management is already talking with individuals they believe can be trusted to fill this position and who would be an asset to the Company as well.

In the twelfth month of operations an additional employee will be hired. Once again this person must be flexible and prepared to perform a variety of assignments on the production floor and in the taproom. However, it is anticipated that the primary responsibility of this second employee will be as a brewing and delivery assistant.

At the beginning of the nineteenth month of operation and again in the twenty-eighth month, additional employees will be hired and trained to perform a variety of tasks associated with beer production and deliveries. The need to hire these additional employees at regular intervals is anticipated because of the workload associated with projected increases in brewing capacity and sales in our local market. This brings our total number of full-time employees to help with retail sales and beer production at near full-production capacity to a total of four employees by the end of year three of operations. It is not anticipated that any additional employees will be required beyond this number.

It is the management teams philosophy that employees are an asset to the company, not a drain on resources. We intend to train our employees thoroughly, treat them well, and provide them with responsibility when they earn it. All full-time employees will be given a starting salary of $XX a month or approximately $XX per hour. Employees who perform well and demonstrate an interest in long-term employment with Craft Brewing Company will be compensated for their efforts in year-end bonuses to be decided by the management team and Board of Directors. Eventually we hope to develop a profit-sharing program to properly reward all those employees of the Craft Brewing Company who make a significant contribution toward the Company's success.

Supporting Professional Services: The following individuals will be contracted by the Craft Brewing Company to provide services during the start-up and operational phases of this project. See Attachments for their resumes and references.

Technical advisor. XX will draw up the plans for formal approval by the city and will assist the president in directing the building improvements to be carried out by the Craft Brewing Company. The technical advisor will also help to choose utility subcontractors and coordinate their activities with the overall construction project.

Accounting. XX has assisted the Craft Brewing Company in identifying our tax responsibilities. During the operational phase, the accountant will also help the management team to implement their own accounting software program and periodically review tax reports.

Legal representation. XX will act as attorney for the Craft Brewing Company. XX will review our lease; prepare the initial articles of incorporation, bylaws, and subscription agreement; and provide legal council whenever necessary.

Business consultant. XX, director and business development specialist with the Small Business Development Center in XX, XX, has worked closely with the management team since the initiation of this project. XX has personally reviewed and critiqued our business plan and pro formas. XX is personally as well as professionally interested in this project, and the business consultant has offered to continue to provide business and financial counseling at no cost, whenever requested.

Master brewer. XX will act as a local resource to the president in the early stages of brewery operation. The master brewer has worked closely with our brewing consultant at XX as head brewer and manager. XX will be involved in the initial recipe formulation, and since the master brewer lives in XX, the master brewer will be available to troubleshoot any problems or assist the president whenever his services may be required.

Brewing consultant. XX will act as consultant in all matters related to designing, purchasing, and installing the brewing plant. The brewery consultant will assist the president in designing the brewery layout, choosing equipment, ordering equipment, and arranging for its delivery. The brewery consultant will supervise the installation of the brewing plant and work with utility subcontractors to connect equipment to all necessary utilities. The brewery consultant will also help design the product recipes and supervise the initial production runs.

Banker. XX is a vice president and commercial loan officer for XX, XX, XX. Primary area of expertise is small-business loans and SBA guarantees.

The management team comes to this project with a variety of important skills and experiences which will benefit the Company. In those areas where they lack experience, the management team has wisely decided to contract on a temporary or part-time basis with qualified professionals. In this way the Craft Brewing Company will be provided with all the necessary professional support, and costly mistakes will be avoided.

BUILDING AND CONSTRUCTION PLAN

Leased Facilities: The facilities being leased by the Craft Brewing Company are comprised of the following three distinct sections: (refer to the attached building and site drawings)

1. The Production Floor, 1,800 square feet (60 by 30) of open-floor warehouse, with a 19-foot high ceiling, containing the brewing plant, a cool room for fermentation and keg storage, and a loading dock for shipping and receiving
2. XX, 570 square feet (19 by 30) of ground floor retail sales space, adjacent to the Production Floor
3. The Corporate Office, 285 square feet (19 by 15) of second story loft above the retail sales space, including a space for grain storage and milling

These spaces have been acquired in accordance with the conditions specified in the enclosed lease.

Building Improvements: In accordance with the attached lease agreement, the following building improvements will be carried out in order to prepare the leased space for brewery operations. Likewise, the cost of these building improvements will be born in accordance with the terms of the attached Letter of Intent to Lease:

1. Removal of all extraneous hardware from the leased space
2. Power washing the interior of the leased space
3. Painting the interior of the leased space
4. Building of a demising wall between the leased space and the remainder of the building
5. Framing and finishing the loft and ground-floor retail space
6. Installing two handicap accessible bathrooms
7. Moving the stairs from the northwest to northeast loft
8. Cutting an access door in the northeast wall of the warehouse
9. Improving the sliding doors on the north end of the building
10. Installing drains at certain points on the production floor
11. Installing an insulated cool fermentation room
12. Painting the exterior of the warehouse
13. Preparing the public alley on the north end of the building to be paved by the city

The above list represents the primary building improvements which must be completed to prepare the leased space for operation. These improvements must be completed before the brewing plant can be installed and connected to the necessary utilities. The president will be assisted by the technical adviser in the planning, coordination, and execution of these building improvements. The estimated costs of these improvements are included in the financial plan cost schedule.

Subcontracting: In addition to the building improvements listed above, the following utility upgrades will be carried out by licensed professionals:

1. Plumbing. Installation of drainage system, connecting of all sinks and bathroom facilities to the drainage system, all welding necessary to prepare the brewing plant for operation, installation of separate utility meter.
2. Electrical. All wiring necessary to install appropriate lighting, all wiring necessary to prepare the brewing plant for operation, all wiring necessary to bring newly constructed walls and rooms up to code, installation of separate utility meter.
3. Gas. Installation of forced air gas heater, connecting of burners to the brewing kettle and hot liquor tank, installation of separate utility meter.
4. Refrigeration. Installation of cool room refrigeration unit and primary fermentor glycol system.
5. Telephone. Installation of business phone lines.

The subcontractors listed above will be chosen by the president through a competitive bidding process. The president will be assisted in this choice and in the overseeing of the work of these professionals by the technical adviser.

The Lease Agreement

The management team has negotiated and executed a Letter of Intent to lease a piece of commercial real estate at XX. The Letter of Intent was signed by all parties in March 20XX. This letter is the foundation from which the final lease will be drafted, and therefore, it represents the main points of agreement between the landlords and the tenants. See the attached Letter of Intent for full details of the lease agreement.

The total area being leased is 2,365 square feet of floor space and 285 square feet of loft space. In addition, the Letter of Intent guarantees the Craft Brewing Company "first right of refusal" on any additional space which may become available in the future.

The lease is to commence on May 1, 20XX, with the rent commencement date set for July 1, 20XX. A provision delaying our full responsibility for the lease has been included, which states that should financing not be acquired by the Craft Brewing Company by December 31, 20XX, then the lease will be invalid. This clause is intended to protect the Company should the necessary start-up capital not be raised.

The lease is for five years, with a one-time option to renew the lease at the same terms and conditions for an additional five years. Rent is $XX a month, plus the triple nets (NNN) which represent our pro-rata share of the landlords taxes, insurance, and maintenance costs on the building.

OVERALL SCHEDULE

The following is an outline of the specific tasks which must be performed or milestones which must be achieved during the start-up phase of operation. This outline represents our projections of the time required to perform these tasks. These tasks have been ordered both chronologically and by priority.

Milestones

Period — March 15 to 31:
    Mail Out Business Proposal and Share Offering
    Begin to Raise Investor Equity Capital
    Prepare for Building Permit Plan Review
    Seek Bids on Fabricating Brewing Vessels
    Complete Bidding Process on Building
       Improvements

    Complete Final Licensing Applications
    Clean and Prepare Building Interior
    Approve Graphic Designs for Logos
    Finalize and Sign Lease Agreement

Period — April 1 to 15:
    Raise Investor Equity Capital
    Meet with Potential Investors to
    Promote Share Sales
    Choose Fabricator for Brewing Vessels
    Receive Building Permit
    Seek Bids on Utility Subcontracting

Period — April 16 to 30:
    Raise Investor Equity Capital
    Achieve Minimum Investment Level
    Notify Investors of Minimum Level
    Transfer Investor Capital to General Funds
       Account
    Begin Building Improvements
    Have Interior Washed and Painted
    Cut Cement Floors for Drains and Plumbing
    Disassemble Existing Stairs and Loft
    Begin to Design the Interior of the Taproom

Period — May 1 to 15:
    Order and Make Down Payment
       on Brewing Vessels
    Continue to Raise Investor Equity Capital
    Building Improvements
    Rough in Plumbing
    Inspect Hook-up to Sewer System
    Grade and Pave Alley
    Pour New Cement Floor Slab
    Cut Exterior Door Openings
    Begin to Frame in Demising Wall Exterior Doors

Period — May 16 to 31:
    Continue to Raise Investor Equity Capital
    Building Improvements
    Continue Framing in New Walls
    Frame In Bathrooms
    Build New Loft Floor and Ceiling
    Schedule Framing and Wiring Inspections

Period — June 1 to 15:
   Continue to Raise Investor Equity Capital
   Purchase Miscellaneous Brewing Equipment
   Continue Building Improvements
   Complete Framing of New Walls, Doors, Etc.
   Install Heating Systems
   Framing and Wiring Inspections

Period — June, 16 to 30:
   Continue to Raise Investor Equity Capital
   Continue to Purchase Miscellaneous
      Brewing Equipment
   Install Cold Room and Refrigeration
   Receive Delivery of Brewing Plant
   Install and Hook-up Brewing Plant
   Complete Building Improvements
   Have Exterior of Building Painted

Period — July 1 to 15:
   Sell Final Shares for Equity Capital
   Final Occupancy and Health Inspection
   Receive Final Permits and Licenses to Operate
   Complete Brewery Installation and Hook-up
   Make Final Equipment Purchases
   Begin Installing Fixtures and
      Furnishings for Taproom
   Install Taproom Bar and Sink
   Final Utility Inspections
   Purchase Brewing Ingredients
   Begin Test Recipe Brewing
   Begin Advertising in Local Printed Media
   Meet with Local Licensed Retailers to Discuss
      First Sales

Period — July 16 to 31:
   Complete Taproom Preparations
   Paint Corporate Logo on North Frontage
   Plant Sidewalk Trees
   Keg First Brew Runs
   Begin to Market Products

We believe these tasks can be completed within the scheduled time periods above. However, one serious potential delay would be in achieving the minimum level of investors equity capital which is necessary for us to begin ordering brewing equipment and scheduling building improvements. Further delays might arise in acquiring a building permit and in coordinating the work of the subcontractor with the overall project and with city inspectors which review many stages of the building improvement process. Any such delays would influence the timing of the entire project and could potentially delay start-up by as much as several months. A delay in our start-up of beer production would entail certain additional expenses until sales of beer began. Nevertheless, we are confident that even should certain reasonable delays occur, the overall success of this project would not be jeopardized.

THE FINANCIAL PLAN

Assumptions: The following information has been provided in order to fully identify the assumptions which the management team has made in projecting the growth in sales, expenses, revenue, and profit of the Craft Brewing Company for the first three years of operation.

Revenue: The Revenue section is broken down into several categories: wholesale through distributor, wholesale self-distributed, retail keg sales, and retail pint sales. All beer sales are based on barrel volumes where one barrel equals 31 gallons or two 15.5-gallon kegs. There is also a separate revenue line for food and merchandise sales. First year production and sales levels are based on our research of the local market and are considered to be relatively conservative projections of local demand. In following years, wholesale self-distributed sales are projected to increase by 1.5 percent each month, wholesale through a distributor sales are projected to increase by 6 percent each month, and retail keg sales are projected to flatten out at approximately 14 kegs each month on average. Retail pint sales are projected to flatten out at 28 kegs each month since they will be limited by the size of our taproom. See the sections on projected local, regional, and total beer sales in the business proposal.

Cost of Goods Sold: This figure includes the ingredients, energy, water, excise and business taxes required to produce beer. The numbers for brewing ingredients are based on actual costs from suppliers and correspond with the given production levels and historical production cost averages. Utility costs are based on estimates of local energy and water rates for a given level of production. Tax rates are based on current rates of $XX per barrel federal excise tax, approximately $XX per barrel state excise tax, and a nominal local business and occupation tax. These excise taxes could be subject to increases in the near future. Costs of food and merchandise sold in our retail outlet are taken to be 50 percent of the retail sales price. Costs of brewing ingredients, water, energy, and supplies are projected to remain relatively constant over time as a proportion of the costs of producing a given volume of beer (approximately $17.50 per barrel). We anticipate that rising prices for these ingredients will be offset by the savings realized through larger volume purchases.

Gross Profit: When the Total Cost of Goods Sold is subtracted from Gross Sales, the resulting figure represents our Gross Profit. Our Gross Profit percentage from year to year will decrease slightly as the ratio of beer sales through a distributor (which have the smallest profit margin) increase, while our ratio of retail beer sales (which have the largest profit margin) remain relatively stable.

Operating Expenses—General and Administrative Expenses: Refer to the Pro Forma General and Administrative Expense Schedule-First Year Supplement. These numbers are based on cost estimates from suppliers and service providers. In some cases, irregularly billed payments are spread out over the twelve months of the year as average monthly payments. The different expenses on the General and Administrative Schedule are projected to increase by 1 percent each month. The exceptions are rent and parking which remain constant, and salaries and payroll taxes which will be increased in accordance with the discussions in the sections of this proposal on employees and management compensation. The costs of all employees hired after the first year and their corresponding payroll taxes appear on separate lines in the Second and Third Years Income Statement.

The final expense which is factored into the Company's Operating Expenses is the depreciation rate on certain assets. The assets being depreciated include: start-up leasehold improvements (building construction costs), brewery equipment, handling equipment (the delivery van, keg dolly, etc.), cooperage (kegs), fixtures and furnishings (taproom furnishings, office equipment, lighting, etc.), and other capital assets purchased during the operational phase to expand production capacity. Depreciation is based on a straight line method over a period of seven years.

EBIT (Earnings Before Income Taxes): When Operating Expenses are subtracted from the Gross Profit, the resulting figure represents the Company's Earnings before corporate income taxes. Interest Income from cash in the Company's general account at XX Bank is then added to the EBIT line, with the resulting sum being the Company's Profit before corporate income taxes. Corporate Income Taxes are calculated at current rates and when subtracted from the Profit before taxes, result in the Company's Net Income or Loss.

Net Earnings: This line represents the Company's earnings once paid out dividends, any loan principle, and any new equipment purchases have been subtracted from the Company's Net Income/Loss.

INDEX